Authenticity and Authentication of Heritage

Authenticity and Authentication of Heritage presents an assimilation of chapters that critically address some of the key emerging areas associated with authenticity. It presents a variety of inspiring pieces of work that range from host-guest authentication and intangible heritage to knowledge transfer processes, authenticating heritage in fairy-tale settings, authenticity and anxiety in the smell of death and life, understanding the boundaries of authenticity, nostalgia, sustainability, marketing, destination competitiveness, examining affective connotations of authenticity, and their contribution towards optimising hedonic and eudaimonic well-being during times of disruption.

The contentious concept of authenticity continues to be valorised in heritage tourism. This scholarly initiative seeks to broaden the discursive parameters of authenticity and identify power mechanisms that shape the way authenticity is produced, marketed and consumed. This is an attempt to share contemporary views on how the contemporary notions of authenticity are derived, interpreted, applied, processed and legitimised in local and global contexts. Furthermore, the significant relationship between health and authenticity is explored. To put it simply, this pandemic has significantly halted the way people connect with their cultural resources and seek authenticity within their inner selves and the outside realms in the heritage tourism system. Heightened sense of global consciousness is a call to polish our authentic selves and elevate above inauthenticity or moral hypocrisy. So, is authenticity an evolving story or is it a story of floating immobility? Who can tell the story and who decides what elements to fossilise? How can existentialist authenticity and self authentication promote moral selving and well-being of the self and the society? Many questions like these have emerged in recent literature, and this book uses conceptual, empirical and theoretical explorations to identify and engage with such inquiries.

The chapters in this book, except for the concluding chapter, were originally published as a special issue of the *Journal of Heritage Tourism.*

Deepak Chhabra is Associate Professor in the School of Community Resources and Development at Arizona State University, Phoenix, USA. Her research interests include authenticity and authentication of heritage; social and economic viability of different forms of tourism; and wellness and well-being through alternate healing/preventive therapeutic settings and programs.

Authenticity and Authentication of Heritage

Edited by
Deepak Chhabra

Routledge
Taylor & Francis Group
LONDON AND NEW YORK

First published 2021
by Routledge
2 Park Square, Milton Park, Abingdon, Oxon OX14 4RN

and by Routledge
605 Third Avenue, New York, NY 10158

Routledge is an imprint of the Taylor & Francis Group, an informa business

British Library Cataloguing in Publication Data
A catalogue record for this book is available from the British Library

ISBN: 978-0-367-67206-5 (hbk)
ISBN: 978-0-367-67208-9 (pbk)
ISBN: 978-1-003-13025-3 (ebk)

Typeset in Minion Pro
by Newgen Publishing UK

Publisher's Note
The publisher accepts responsibility for any inconsistencies that may have arisen during the conversion of this book from journal articles to book chapters, namely the inclusion of journal terminology.

Contents

Citation Information

The chapters in this book were originally published in *Journal of Heritage Tourism*, volume 14, issue 5–6 (2019). When citing this material, please use the original page numbering for each article, as follows:

Introduction

Authenticity and the authentication of heritage: dialogical perceptiveness
Deepak Chhabra
Journal of Heritage Tourism, volume 14, issue 5–6 (2019), pp. 389–395

Chapter 1

Host–guest authentication of intangible cultural heritage: a literature review and conceptual model
Shahida Khanom, Brent Moyle, Noel Scott and Millicent Kennelly
Journal of Heritage Tourism, volume 14, issue 5–6 (2019), pp. 396–408

Chapter 2

Knowledge transfer processes in the authenticity of the intangible cultural heritage in tourism destination competitiveness
Desiderio Juan García-Almeida
Journal of Heritage Tourism, volume 14, issue 5–6 (2019), pp. 409–421

Chapter 3

Development of intangible cultural heritage as a sustainable tourism resource: the intangible cultural heritage practitioners' perspectives
Soojung Kim, Michelle Whitford and Charles Arcodia
Journal of Heritage Tourism, volume 14, issue 5–6 (2019), pp. 422–435

Chapter 4

Time, authenticity and photographic storytelling in The Museum of Innocence
Kevin Hannam and Edward Ryan
Journal of Heritage Tourism, volume 14, issue 5–6 (2019), pp. 436–447

Chapter 5

Fairytale authenticity: historic city tourism, Harry Potter, medievalism and the magical gaze
Jane Lovell
Journal of Heritage Tourism, volume 14, issue 5–6 (2019), pp. 448–465

Chapter 6

'The smell of death and the smell of life': authenticity, anxiety and perceptions of death at Varanasi's cremation grounds
Nitasha Sharma and Jillian Rickly
Journal of Heritage Tourism, volume 14, issue 5–6 (2019), pp. 466–477

Chapter 7

Using geographical and semiotic means to establish fixed points of a never-ending story: searching for parameters of authenticity in a case study of Australian history
Michael Fagence
Journal of Heritage Tourism, volume 14, issue 5–6 (2019), pp. 478–490

Chapter 8

The role of authenticity, experience quality, emotions, and satisfaction in a cultural heritage destination
Ana M. Domínguez-Quintero, M. Rosario González-Rodríguez and José Luis Roldán
Journal of Heritage Tourism, volume 14, issue 5–6 (2019), pp. 491–505

Chapter 9

Authenticity and nostalgia – subjective well-being of Chinese rural-urban migrants
Zhenhao (Mark) Meng, Liping A. Cai, Jonathan Day, Chun-Hung (Hugo) Tang, Ying (Tracy) Lu and Hongmei Zhang
Journal of Heritage Tourism, volume 14, issue 5–6 (2019), pp. 506–524

Notes on Contributors

Charles Arcodia, Department of Tourism, Sport and Hotel Management, Griffith University, Brisbane, Australia.

Liping A. Cai, School of Hospitality and Tourism Management, Purdue University, West Lafayette, IN, USA.

Deepak Chhabra, School of Community Resources & Development, Arizona State University, Phoenix, AZ, USA.

Jonathan Day, School of Hospitality and Tourism Management, Purdue University, West Lafayette, IN, USA.

Ana M. Domínguez-Quintero, Faculty of Economics and Business Sciences, Department of Applied Economics I, University of Seville Seville, Spain.

Michael Fagence, School of Earth and Environmental Sciences, The University of Queensland, St Lucia, Australia.

Desiderio Juan García-Almeida, School of Economics, Business Administration and Tourism, University of Las Palmas de Gran Canaria, Las Palmas de Gran Canaria, Spain.

M. Rosario González-Rodríguez, Faculty of Economics and Business Sciences, Department of Applied Economics I, University of Seville Seville, Spain.

Kevin Hannam, Faculty of International Tourism and Management, City University of Macau, Macau SAR, China; School of Tourism and Hospitality, University of Johannesburg, Johannesburg, South Africa.

Millicent Kennelly, Department of Tourism, Sport and Hotel Management, Griffith University, Southport, Australia.

Shahida Khanom, Griffith Institute of Tourism, Griffith University, Southport, Australia.

Soojung Kim, Department of Tourism, Sport and Hotel Management, Griffith University, Brisbane, Australia.

Jane Lovell, Section of Geography, Events, Leisure and Tourism, Canterbury Christ Church University, Canterbury, UK.

Ying (Tracy) Lu, School of Human and Environmental Sciences, University of Kentucky, Lexington, KY, USA.

Zhenhao (Mark) Meng, School of Business, Indiana University Kokomo, Kokomo, IN, USA.

Brent Moyle, USC Business, Faculty of Arts, Business and Law, University of the Sunshine Coast, Queensland, Australia.

Jillian Rickly, Nottingham University Business School, University of Nottingham, Nottingham, UK.

José Luis Roldán, Faculty of Economics and Business Sciences, Department of Business Administration and Marketing, University of Seville Seville, Spain.

Edward Ryan, School of Art and Design, Middlesex University Dubai, Dubai, UAE.

Noel Scott, USC Business, Faculty of Arts, Business and Law, University of the Sunshine Coast, Queensland, Australia.

Nitasha Sharma, Faculty of Spatial Sciences, University of Groningen, Groningen, Netherlands.

Chun-Hung (Hugo) Tang, School of Hospitality and Tourism Management, Purdue University, West Lafayette, IN, USA.

Michelle Whitford, Department of Tourism, Sport and Hotel Management, Griffith University, Brisbane, Australia.

Hongmei Zhang, School of Geography and Tourism, Anhui Normal University, Anhui, China.

Preface

This book is a rich collection of work by scholars of heritage tourism from across the globe. As the different chapters in this book illustrate, authenticity and authentication of heritage tourism span a broad spectrum of discourses. Through this book, stimulating and creative routes are suggested to further the dialectic on authenticity and authentication. Since the time, the chapters in this book were penned to the current moment, the world has been under the shadow of the corona virus outbreak. All forms of tourism, including heritage tourism are under the microscope for amplifying the spread, particularly through long distance travel. Tourism hordes and their noise have vanished and overtourism and despoiling scenarios in popular destinations, resulting from time-space compression, are now witnessing deafening silence (Niewiadomski 2020). How far the novel corona virus will continue to compel the heritage tourism industry, to reset itself into more cognizant modes of planetary limitations and gravitate meaningfully towards degrowth and deglobalization, will unfold in the coming years. The distance between home and away has exponentially grown and resort bubble and air bubble are becoming the new norm to counter the spread of corona virus. The regenerative tourism options on the table are gravitating towards proximate travel. Staying close to home is awakening consciousness of "staying local and slowing down" (Everingham & Chassagne 2020, p. 6). Slow heritage tourism, balancing existentialist and transcendental experiences in indigenous/cultural and therapeutic settings, is emerging as the new transformative antidote (Galvani, Lew & Perez et al. 2020; Shang, Qiao & Chen 2020). Slow tourism involves unhurried pace of travel for visitors seeking essentialist and/or existentially authentic experiences based on immersive engagements, deep and meaningful connections, and moral selving by being mindful of the human footprint on the host environment (Dickinson, Lumsdom & Robbins 2011; Meng & Choi 2016).

The significant relationship between health, economics and sustainability is becoming unquestionable. Galvani et al. write that; "COVID-19 is making us re-think how we conceive of ourselves as human beings, realizing that being human means caring… and seeking harmony between the physical–emotional–mental–spiritual worlds. There are indications that a sustainable development empathy is emerging that will enhance our emotional and subconscious connections with peoples and environments" (2020, p. 573). To put it simply, this pandemic although an uncommon occurrence, has significantly interrupted the way people connect with their cultural resources and seek authenticity within their inner selves and outside realms in the heritage tourism system. Heightened sense of global consciousness is a call to polish our authentic selves and elevate above inauthenticity or moral hypocrisy, that is, pretending to be sustainable. We have reached an introspective juncture facing a period of uncertainty as covid-19 continues to unfold or return and we await a cure from the medical community; at the current time of reckoning, all reorganization strategies are pivoted around social distancing, face coverings, and safe hygiene. The reset point of this year is self-inquiry and awareness of dissonance within ourselves, which has opened the path for moralized/virtuous self- authentication to build roots.

While the introductory chapter places the contributions of various authors in a dialogical context, the concluding chapter furthers the dialogical perceptiveness of authenticity and authentication of heritage, particularly from the standpoint of transcendence, ethical behavior, and hedonic and eudaimonic well-being. It discusses transformative solutions and calls for further deliberations to address the challenges posed by intra- and post- pandemic times. It is stressed that the pandemic crisis is a time of reckoning to transcend the self and transform the finite spectrum of cultural/heritage resources by aspiring for healthy choices that can promote moral-selving while enriching our inner beings to harmonize ourselves, our finite cultural/heritage inheritances and the society at large. Unforeseen factors will continue to shape the manner in which we live, authenticate, and transcend our intrinsic (self) and extrinsic (natural/cultural/heritage) authenticities. Undeniably, the human civilization is resilient and will continue to make new meanings from chaos and disequilibrium situations and innovate/contextualize its connections with the self and the existing social and materialistic structures. As Judith aptly says: *if the outer world is to be transformed, the process must begin within. If the inner world is to be transformed, it must be understood in light of the outer forces that shape it* (2004, p. ix).

References

Dickinson, J., Lumsdon L., & Robbins, D. (2011). Slow travel: Issues for tourism and climate change. *Journal of Sustainable Tourism, 19*(3), 281–300.

Everingham, P., & Chassagne, N. (2020). Post COVID-19 ecological and social reset: moving away from capitalist growth models towards tourism as Buen Vivir. *Tourism Geographies, 22*(3), 555–566.

Galvani, A., Lew, A. A., & Perez, M. S. (2020). COVID-19 is expanding global consciousness and the sustainability of travel and tourism. *Tourism Geographies, 22*(3), 567–576.

Judith, A. (2004). *Eastern Body, Western Mind.* Second edition, Celestial Arts: Berkeley.

Meng, B. & Choi, K. (2016). The role of authenticity in forming slow tourists' intentions: developing an extended model of goal-directed behavior. *Tourism Management, 57*, 397–410.

Niewiadomski, P. (2020). From temporary de-globalisation to a re-discovery of tourism? *Tourism Geographies, 22*(3), 651–656.

Shang, W., Qiao, G., & Chen, N. (2020). Tourist experience of slow tourism: from authenticity to place attachment–a mixed-method study based on the case of slow city in China. *Asia Pacific Journal of Tourism Research, 25*(2), 170–188.

Introduction

Authenticity and the authentication of heritage: dialogical perceptiveness

Deepak Chhabra

ABSTRACT

The dialogue on authenticity continues to evolve across different temporalities and disciplines. This editorial for the special issue summarizes contemporary progress made by scholars of heritage tourism and shares innovative corridors for deep deliberations. A broad spectrum of provocative ideas are touched upon, ranging from host–guest authentication and intangible heritage to knowledge transfer processes, authenticating heritage in fairytale settings, authenticity and anxiety in the smell of death and life, understanding the boundaries of authenticity, nostalgia, sustainability, marketing, destination competitiveness, and examining affective connotations of authenticity. Discursive insights are offered on how different authenticities are legitimized and critically deconstructed and re-constructed again in the authentication process, to underline the existence of power and authority interventions. Inspiring/innovative pathways, for future research, are also recommended.

The dialogical concept of authenticity continues to be valorized in heritage tourism (Bryce, Murdy, & Alexander, 2017; Cohen, 2007; Timothy, 2011). As documented extensively in the literature, most authenticity discussions have anchored on three dominant ideologies (objective, existentialist and constructivist) with mixed efforts to bridge them in a meaningful manner (Dueholm & Smed, 2014; Rickly-Boyd 2012; Wang, 1999). Proponents of the objective dimension continue to fossilize/legitimize tangible and intangible heritage and offer a moral map. For many scholars, objective authenticity remains a common reference point, especially in the context of heritage tourism (Chhabra, 2010, 2012; Peterson, 2005). Worthy of note is also the constructivist (commodified) notion popularly embraced by marketing agents. Brand authenticity has emerged as a new technique to attract seekers of 'alternative hedonism.' Others focus on the over-arching existentialist dimension, which is anchored in the self, such as association with the social, self-identity, and self-actualization (Wang, 1999). Furthermore, recent studies have moved beyond the conceptual dissection of authenticity to examine the dynamic process of authentication. Cohen and Cohen (2012) refer to authentication as a social process through which authenticity is confirmed. Zhu (2015, p. 12) contends that 'authentication has become a governance strategy to legitimize inclusion and exclusion and to allocate economic, moral and aesthetics values'. Aligned to this, Xie (2011) examines authentication in the context of power relations and actors involved in legitimizing authenticity.

This special issue presents an assimilation of papers that critically address some of the key emerging areas associated with authenticity. It presents a variety of inspiring pieces of work that range from host–guest authentication and intangible heritage to knowledge transfer processes, authenticating heritage in fairytale settings, authenticity and anxiety in the smell of death and life, understanding the boundaries of authenticity, nostalgia, sustainability, marketing, destination competitiveness, and examining affective connotations of authenticity. Multiple insights are needed to critically deconstruct and construct these areas of exploration to enrich understanding of authenticity and its authentication in heritage tourism. The discursive parameters of authenticity are broadened using a variety of unique settings and perspectives in this issue. Overall, what unfolds here is how contemporary notions of authenticity are derived, interpreted, applied, processed and legitimized in local and global contexts.

Of late, intangible cultural heritage (ICH) has taken a central position of heritage tourism. It is a distinct selling asset for host communities and a key generator of satisfactory heritage tourism experiences for tourists. It is argued that ICH is deeply guided by the objective version of cultural authenticity and can play a key role in making a heritage destination competitive (Chhabra, Healy, & Sills, 2003; Mody, Hanks, & Dogru, 2019; Timothy, 2011) besides generating socio-economic benefits for its stakeholders (Esfehani & Albrecht, 2018). However, it needs to be regarded and developed as a sustainable tourism commodity, as it runs the risk of commodification, and ongoing initiatives are needed to protect the 'cultural continuity of communities' (World Tourism Organisation 2012). Hence, the paper on ICH authentication, by Khanum, Moyle, Scott and Kennelly is timely and shares a unique perspective centered on the mutual authentication process orchestrating collaboration and interaction between hosts and guests. The authors propose a mutual host–guest authentication model unifying the perspectives of host and guest interactions and paving the ground for community empowerment, in the context of ICH. The conceptual model highlights power dynamics between hosts and guests in the authentication process in addition to sharing the manner in which community empowerment is impacted across the political, social, psychological and economic environments. The authors make an important contribution by showing how extended benefits of mutual authentication are associated with more interactive and immersive experiences and community empowerment. Another notable article on ICH centers on knowledge transfer processes. Garcia-Almeida argues that as the knowledge transmission process occurs, in ICH settings, the authenticity of something (or its perception) is likely to change. Different settings of these transfers include tour guiding, destination, etc. Transfer later happens when the heritage knowledge is codified in museums, training programs for tour guides are set up, or when the younger generation is receiving the transmission. Several challenges are highlighted by offering scenarios, where authenticity vanishes or undergoes modification. An analysis is shared on how knowledge transmissions take place and highlighted are different kinds of authentic mechanisms that are required to retain the uniqueness of a destination. Garcia-Almeida stresses that different types of transmissions are capable of endorsing the objective authenticity of intangible heritage, although 'intergenerational knowledge transfer' is most prominent.

Kim, Whitford and Arcodia also focus on intangible cultural heritage and offer a discussion of how it is tapped as a novel selling tool; they discuss sustainable strategies that are required to ensure strategic commodification happens so that the authenticity of ICH is not compromised. The authors share practitioner views and accentuate the holistic nature of authenticity as it integrates traditional meanings transmitted through inheritance and the social-constructivist identities of practitioners. Kim et al place emphasis on public sector support to inform different types of audiences of ICH, particularly aiming to augment the awareness of youth populations by featuring ICH as a mandatory element of the educational system. This paper contributes to the debate about the authenticity of cultural heritage by exploring ICH practitioners' perceptions in safeguarding ICH authenticity. The study results offer a discourse on how heritage tourism can be sustainably developed by using ICH as an authentic cultural resource. The authors commendably note that 'the development of ICH as a sustainable tourism resource requires a positive and constructive symbiotic relationship between safeguarding ICH authenticity and increasing the socioeconomic value of ICH.' The aim is to make a community self-reliant. An important step in this direction is to be alert to the potential externalities associated with the commodification of ICH. Local interests and awareness are stressed in addition to empowerment of the local industry so that parallel development can happen between tourism development and the sustainable transmission of ICH.

One article in this issue is devoted to the notion of authenticity and temporality in a unique museum setting. Hannam and Ryan look at how selected material and intangible affordances are used to revive memories of a relived event/experience associated with a museum constructed solely to showcase different characters of a famous novel. The authors use visual ethnography to demonstrate that the art of storytelling through photographic intervention and onsite visit shape the experience and performance of authenticity through an interplay of temporalities. They offer insights on the association between storytelling, authenticity and time; that is, they argue that progression of time and visual storytelling can influence the approach in which visitors experience and perform authenticity. The performative nature of authenticity here implies that spaces are authenticated by the manner visitors emotionally relate to them. Through a museum setting, Hannam and Ryan refer to the notion of authenticity as a string of stories narrated in a graded style to smooth temporalities distinguished by the interplay of past, present and future. The authors illustrate that this process makes authenticity significant not only from a materialistic and experiential perspective but also makes it an evolving story mirroring the influence of time. It can be deduced that both place and time matter in negotiating existentialist authenticity. The existentialist perspective is championed in a unique manner.

Almost three decades ago, Shackley (1994) brought to light some of the issues associated with the sustainability of the authenticity of intangible cultural heritage. She lamented that economic forces are driving away old and traditional jobs. The generation most impacted is Generation Y, which seems to question the authenticity of knowledge as they see it. It can be argued that contrary to the argument presented by Cohen and Cohen (2012), cool authentication fossilizes and compromises value, knowledge transmission can reverse the process and case feelings of pride, thereby increasing motivation levels of both suppliers and receivers and lead to a sense of pride. The concept of mutual authentication is reiterated here in this special issue. Promotional activities and materials, travel agents and previous visitors convey the authenticity of a destination, which is relevant for attracting tourists. Higher tourist perceptions of authenticity tend to result when they interact with local residents, experts of local heritage, to be informed. In most cases, such interactions generate a higher degree of satisfaction.

The article by Lovell makes an original contribution to the authenticity debate by examining how tourists' experiences of medieval historic environments are linked to fairytales, providing a new way for tourists to imaginatively authenticate heritage. The architecture of some historic cities is preponderantly medieval, representing an era that is strongly associated with fairytales, magic and myths. Magical-historical double affectiveness has been compounded in the collective imagination through modern fairytales, such as the fantasy stories of Harry Potter and Game of Thrones, both of which employ historic city locationsand faux-medieval settings, establishing a fluid magi-heritage simulacrum. This is concretised by the appearance in many historic cities of evidence of magical placemaking and staged magical authenticity, such as wizarding shops. Lovell's research findings indicate that the magical gaze offers an imaginative way of authenticating heritage environments with fairytale schemata, much the same way that fiction-based literary tourism has in the past 'authenticated' the make-believe locations of Robin Hood and Peter Rabbit in the minds of would-be visitors, creating 'authentic' spaces from places than never truly existed (Shackley, 2001; Squire, 1993).

Existentialist authenticity remains an important topic of discourse as visitors desire a release from day-to-day routines, and heritage tourism offers a window to connect with their true selves and others in a genuine way (Brown 2013). Existentialist authenticity is an important experiential consumption tool and is sought for optimizing tourism experiences. It is relational and closely connected with 'a sense of self and identity' and has become a leading motivation factor and generator of satisfactory consumer experiences (Fu, Liu, Wang and Chao 2018, p. 10). Today, it is mostly about establishing emotional bonds with the physical settings and objects and seeking optimized experience; heritage tourists especially appear to seek experiences that help them to get in touch with their true selves (Breathnach, 2006; Poria, Biran, & Reichel, 2006). Existentialist authenticity can be experienced in different kinds of objectively authentic settings. A mix of existentialist and objective authenticity experiences has been popularly termed theoplacity (Chhabra, 2010). Trilling (1972) refers to authenticity as a polemical notion. The paper by Sharma and Rickly in this collection focuses on a unique dark tourism setting and the negative authentic experience in India: Hindu cremation grounds. It examines tourists' views of death, self and the 'other' at the dark tourism site and offers insights on existential anxiety in such authentic experiences. Sharma and Rickly report that confrontations with mortality at dark sites reminds people of their own vulnerability, influences perceptions of the self and sometimes results in the questioning of one's own values. The authors point out that anxiety is also a state of existential authenticity and warn that not all existentially authentic types of experiences are gratifying. Tourists have an opportunity to show alertness to the fragility of life; they get a chance to interact with the setting and develop feelings of anxiety in an embodied way, which can inspire them to make lifestyle changes.

A dark tour site can be the actual place of death, or it can refer to a setting where deaths are commemorated although they may have occurred elsewhere (Wight, 2006). That is, a dark locality can incorporate actual artifacts of the dead or merely present markers that symbolize death or human suffering. Some studies have examined dark tourism from an ethical perspective, especially in the context of sites that have zero to short chronological distance from a dark event (Heuermann & Chhabra, 2014). The study by Sharma and Rickly opens a path for examining the voyeuristic nature of this dark experience and investigates whether any intrusion-related issues exist (Buda & McIntosh, 2013). As an example, souvenirs are sold at the 9/11 Memorial in New York (USA), thereby commodifying its history and boosting voyeuristic behavior at a site that has a short chronological distance and is likely to generate trauma for those with living memory of a lost one (Potts, 2012). Heuermann and Chhabra (2014) argue that experiences offered or desired by tourists at each type of dark site relate to different types of authenticity. Furthermore, some studies have indicated that an existentialist authentic disposition held by heritage tourists holds potential to support ethical consumption behavior (Guignon, 1986; Wang, 1999). That said, it is also postulated that the existentialist ideology can encourage indulgence in hedonistic pleasures or deviant leisure pursuits, especially in objectively authentic dark tourism settings, such as India's cremation grounds. It is noteworthy to mention Stone's (2006) dark tourism framework conceptualized around shades of darkness. Heurermann and Chhabra write that a degree of authenticity can be accorded to each shade of darkness. They examined signature websites of popular dark tourism sites in the US and reported that approximately one third of dark tourism websites mirror the negotiation category that refers to a compromise between objectively authentic and constructivist ideologies. Closely following are dark sites that support the theoplacity perspective, thereby implying that many dark tourism localities are taking initiatives to connect with the visitors' state of mind by 'offering a slightly commodified experience relating to their emotional and spiritual needs.'

Fagence offers a thought-provoking discourse on the manner in which heritage tourism engages with never-ending process of telling stories. In a unique manner, the authors point to the negotiation between past and present in that stories are juxtaposed in historical sites and historical objects. The author makes use of geography and semiotics to examine static points in the narratives marked by tangible and visual markers. Noteworthy is the discourse on the manner in which stories are operationalized. The process of authenticating a never-ending story by making fixed points as objectively authentic for some time and then changing their position as space and time evolve. Fagence illustrates the power of authentic story telling in a negotiated manner by establishing a connection between past and present. The essential challenge for tourism is to tell the story by using history-linked sites and objects as cultural 'texts' and as conduits between the past and the present – for providing the experience of 'being there' without 'being there'. Using a story about an episode of Australian history, this paper experiments with perspectives of geography and semiotics to probe fixed points in the story; it looks at points that are marked by tangible and visual characteristics and which are at least indicative of important elements that create identity and significance of the storyscape. It is posited that a story told through tourism will seldom be permanently fixed, which can have a knock-on-effect on some of the ideological interpretations of 'authenticity.' Moreover, although the fundamental shape of the story might not be compromised, it can affect the quality of tourism experience. Fagence points out some noteworthy implications of this challenge.

In regard to marketing, it cannot be denied that heritage tourism is an important component of a destination's marketing portfolio and gives it a competitive advantage. For instance, UNESCO's World Heritage Site (WHS) status is often used by countries as a branding tool to showcase their unique heritage and expand their tourist base. Likewise, authenticity has emerged as a strategic branding tool, and its significance is recognized across multiple disciplines. Extant contemporary research is concerned with how consumers perceive and consume authenticity (Dueholm & Smed, 2014). Because of the accentuated focus on experiential consumption, emotive implications of authentic experiences constitute an important topic of study. Also, crucial for the protection/conservation of authenticity and its authentication is sustainable marketing (Chhabra, 2010). Sustainable marketing of heritage involves 'place and product promotion in such a way that it does not diminish their historical or physical integrity' (Timothy, 2011, p. 290). Two insightful papers highlighting the emotive aspects of authenticity and offering important implications for sustainable marketing strategies are devoted to this topic. The paper by Domínguez-Quintero, González-Rodríguez and Roldán examines the significance of different dimensions of authenticity in combination with experience quality, and emotions in generating satisfaction at a heritage destination. They report that objective and existentialist versions of authenticity have positive and significant effects on quality of experience and emotions. In other words, both cognitive and affective aspects of authenticity are crucial areas of study. The paper by Meng, Cai, Day, Tang, Lu and Zhang focuses on the motivational aspects of marketing. They examine the personal well-being of rural-to-urban migrants in China to understand the impact of nostalgia and perceived authenticity and report that 'old home' memories generate nostalgic motivations that inspire urban migrants to visit rural places. Meng et al.'s study employs nostalgia as an important emotional push factor and investigates the manner in which it affects the migrants in terms of their perceptions and evaluation of other pull factors including the authenticity of culture, food and architecture.

Conclusion

Disguised experts (such as art historians, heritage managers and conservationists) wearing different hats 'actively produce and negotiate regimes of value thus mediating the authenticity of specific objects' (Jones 2010, p. 182). Almost three decades ago, while summarizing concepts at an annual meeting of the American Society for Applied Anthropologists, titled 'Social Science for the Next Generation', Shackley (1994, p. 396) posed the following question: 'are we, in heritage tourism, displaying a frozen ethnographic moment or a process that is undergoing continual cultural evolution?'. So, two natural follow-up questions can be: *Is authenticity a never-ending story (*McAuley & Pervan, 2014*) or is it a story of floating fixity (*Latham, 2016*)? Who can tell the story and who decides what elements to fossilize?* Devoted efforts are made to address these questions in this issue.

Furthermore, conservation, excess commodification and the floating nature of authenticity are ongoing debates in heritage tourism, and there is no single or 'correct' path, for each setting has its own peculiarities. Recently, scholars have argued that authenticity is a culturally constructed quality and differs with the type of audience and context. It is continually subjected to tremors and revisions because fluidity is inherent in the phenomenon as culture continues to evolve in the face of changing micro and macro environmental forces. Most articles in this theme issue underline the significance of negotiated authenticity and stress the sustainable use/marketing of objective authenticity. Although only one paper directly pursues the authentication phenomenon, other articles indirectly point to the power dynamics of authenticating agents and the pseudo, as well as genuine, nature of different authenticating markers.

Beyond the unique contribution of this issue and the suggestions offered by several authors on how to advance the authenticity and authentication discourse, I call for research scholars to critically engage in ontological alienation and e-lineation (Rickly-Boyd 2013; Tribe & Mkono, 2017) perspectives to further advance the complex notion of authenticity and its authentication in the knowledge era. Given the immense scholarly progress in this field, the academic dialogue on the authentication of heritage and the impact of digital toxicity on different dimensions/experiences of authenticity is still meager. Going forward, the next issue should also focus on the role of tourists as authenticating agents of heritage, especially using digitalization as a backdrop and cases embracing co-created processes of mutual authentication, between the tourists and heritage agencies/host communities.

Disclosure statement

No potential conflict of interest was reported by the author.

References

Breathnach, T. (2006). Looking for the real me: Locating the self in heritage tourism. *Journal of Heritage Tourism, 1*(2), 100–120.

Bryce, D., Murdy, S., & Alexander, M. (2017). Diaspora, authenticity and the imagined past. *Annals of Tourism Research, 66*, 49–60.

Brown, L. (2013). Tourism: A catalyst for existential authenticity. *Annals of Tourism Research, 40*(1), 176–190.

Buda, D. M., & McIntosh, A. (2013). Dark tourism and voyeurism: Tourist arrested for 'spying' in Iran. *International Journal of Culture, Tourism and Hospitality Research, 7*(3), 214–226.

Chhabra, D., Healy, B. & Sills, E. (2003). Staged Authenticity and Heritage Tourism. *Annals of Tourism Research, 30* (3), 702–719.

Chhabra, D. (2010). *Sustainable marketing of cultural and heritage tourism*. Abington: Routledge.

Chhabra, D. (2012). Authenticity of the objectively authentic. *Annals of Tourism Research, 39*(1), 499–502.

Cohen, E. (2007). 'Authenticity' in tourism studies: Aprés la Lutte. *Tourism Recreation Research, 32*(2), 75–82.

Cohen, E., & Cohen, S. A. (2012). Authentication: Hot and cool. *Annals of Tourism Research, 39*(3), 1295–1314.

Dueholm, J., & Smed, K. M. (2014). Heritage authenticities–a case study of authenticity perceptions at a Danish heritage site. *Journal of Heritage Tourism, 9*(4), 285–298.

Esfehani, M. H., & Albrecht, J. N. (2018). Roles of intangible cultural heritage in tourism in natural protected areas. *Journal of Heritage Tourism, 13*(1), 15–29.

Fu, Y., Liu, X., Wang, Y., & Chao, R. F. (2018). How experiential consumption moderates the effects of souvenir authenticity on behavioral intention through perceived value. *Tourism Management, 69*, 356–367.

Guignon, C. (1986). Existentialist ethics. In J. De Marco & R. Fox (Eds.), *New directions in ethics* (pp. 73–91). London: Routledge.

Heuermann, K., & Chhabra, D. (2014). The darker side of dark tourism: An authenticity perspective. *Tourism Analysis, 19*(2), 213–225.

Jones, S. (2010). Negotiating authentic objects and authentic selves: Beyond the deconstruction of authenticity. *Journal of Material Culture, 15*(2), 181–203.

Latham, K. F. (2016). The curious case of floating fixity (and its relationship to authenticity). *Proceedings from the Document Academy, 3*(2), 2.

McAuley, A., & Pervan, S. (2014). Celtic marketing: Assessing the authenticity of a never ending story. *Journal of Consumer Behaviour, 13*, 81–87.

Mody, M., Hanks, L., & Dogru, T. (2019). Parallel pathways to brand loyalty: Mapping the consequences of authentic consumption experiences for hotels and Airbnb. *Tourism Management, 74*, 65–80.

Peterson, R. (2005). In search of authenticity. *Journal of Management Studies, 42*(5), 1083–1098.

Poria, Y., Biran, A., & Reichel, A. (2006). Tourist perceptions: Personal vs. non-personal. *Journal of Heritage Tourism*, *1*(2), 121–132.

Potts, T. J. (2012). 'Dark tourism' and the 'kitschification' of 9/11. *Tourist Studies*, *12*, 232–249.

Rickly-Boyd, J. M. (2012). Authenticity & aura: A Benjaminian approach to tourism. *Annals of Tourism research*, *39* (1), 269–289.

Rickly-Boyd, J. M. (2013). Alienation: Authenticity's forgotten cousin. *Annals of Tourism Research*, *40*(1), 412–415.

Shackley, M. (1994). When is the past? Authenticity and the commoditization of heritage. *Tourism Management*, *15* (5), 396–397.

Shackley, M. (2001). The legend of Robin Hood: Myth, inauthenticity, and tourism development in Nottingham, England. In V. L. Smith & M. Brent (Eds.), *Hosts and guests revisited: Tourism issues in the 21st century* (pp. 315–322). New York: Cognizant.

Squire, S. J. (1993). Valuing countryside: Reflections on Beatrix Potter tourism. *Area*, *25*(1), 5–10.

Stone, P. R. (2006). A dark tourism spectrum: Towards a typology of death and macabre related tourist sites, attractions and exhibitions. *Turizam: međunarodni znanstveno-stručni časopis*, *54*(2), 145–160.

Timothy, D. J. (2011). *Cultural heritage and tourism: An introduction*. Bristol: Channel View Publications.

Tribe, J., & Mkono, M. (2017). Not such smart tourism? The concept of e-lienation. *Annals of Tourism Research*, *66*, 105–115.

Trilling, L. (1972). *Sincerity and authenticity*. London: Oxford University Press.

Wang, N. (1999). Rethinking authenticity in tourism experience. *Annals of Tourism Research*, *26*(2), 349–370.

Wight, C. (2006). Philosophical and methodological praxes in dark tourism: Controversy, contention and the evolving paradigm. *Journal of Vacation Marketing*, *12*, 119–129.

World Tourism Organisation. (2012). *Tourism and intangible cultural heritage*. Madrid: UNWTO.

Xie, P. (2011). *Authenticating ethnic tourism*. Bristol: Channel View Publications.

Zhu, Y. (2015). Cultural effects of authenticity: Contested heritage practices in China. *International Journal of Heritage Studies*, *21*(6), 594–608.

Host–guest authentication of intangible cultural heritage: a literature review and conceptual model

Shahida Khanom, Brent Moyle, Noel Scott and Millicent Kennelly

ABSTRACT

Cultural tourism and intangible cultural heritage (ICH) play a key role in tourism worldwide, and are especially important for communities in developing countries, due to the demand for authentic experiences. This article provides a review of existing literature on the authenticity and authentication of ICH. The review reveals scholarly inquiry has evolved from external-expert 'cool' authentication to direct host–guest on-site or 'hot' authentication whereby tourists participate in the process of determining authenticity. Further, existing models for authentication of ICH have focused only on either a guest's or host's perspectives with little attention to the inevitable mutual interaction of the host and guest in the authentication of ICH. Mutual authentication can enhance the tourist experience and improve community empowerment. This paper develops a conceptual model of the mutual (host–guest) authentication of ICH, incorporating both hosts' and tourists' perspectives. The model has application in ICH based tourism and emphasizes power relationships between the host and guest, and community empowerment across political, social, psychological and economic domains. Future research is needed to test and validate this conceptual model.

Introduction

Cultural tourism can provide economic benefits for local communities and is a growing part of the global tourism economy (Moswete & Thapa, 2015; UNESCO, 2011). Cultural tourism is especially important in developing countries where 'exotic' traditional practices, dissimilar to those of tourists' origin countries, remain part of everyday life (Timothy & Nyaupane, 2009). Cultural tourists are interested in experiencing the authentic culture of local communities, particularly the traditional practices, festivals, and rituals which form the intangible cultural heritage (ICH) of those communities. Cultural tourism experiences enable close interaction between tourists and the local people (Cohen, 1988).

There are many examples of destinations where tourists experience historically significant ICH such as the traditional cultural practices or festivals of the local community. Examples of festivals that draw a large number of visitors every year include the Mekong Naga Fireball ceremony in Thailand (Cohen, 2007), Holy Week on the island of Sardinia (Giudici, Melis, Dessì, & Francine Pollnow Galvao Ramos, 2013), and the Rush Mela festival in Bangladesh (Islam, Sunny, Hossain, & Friess, 2018). These festivals are usually associated with the religious beliefs of the local community, practiced over many centuries, and have a significant influence on the local economy. They have become major tourist attractions, providing additional economic benefits to the local community as well as revenue to the government (Moswete & Thapa, 2015; UNESCO, 2011). However, the growth of cultural tourism in developing countries requires the protection and management of communities' ICH.

This is because cultural tourism may also be associated with unsustainable tourism practices that can impact a community's natural environment, and cause modifications to the ICH practices that constituted the inherent tourist attraction itself (Fiorello & Bo, 2012; Zhou, Zhang, Zhang, & Ma, 2015). These impacts include the commercialization of local products (Greenwood, 1977), and the potential threat of exoticizing of local culture by tourists (Boonzaaier & Wels, 2018), thus shifting community values from traditional spiritual beliefs to economic returns, which ultimately may result in the loss of ICH authenticity. An example is the Komodo Dragon festival in Indonesia (Walpole & Goodwin, 2001). The commodification process potentially destroys the essential meaning and significance of the ICH to the local community and reduces the enthusiasm of the locals for their ICH (Zhou et al., 2015).

Impacts on the authenticity of a community's ICH can be addressed through a community-based approach with particular emphasis on clearly defining the 'ownership' of (power over) the ICH attraction. However, this raises issues regarding the related concepts of authenticity and authentication, as well as their links to community empowerment. A host community creates, maintains and transmits ICH over generations (UNESCO, 2011) and is, therefore, the primary stakeholder in its authentication. However, guests' perspectives and institutional role in such authentication are also vital for tourism development and safeguarding ICH (Cohen & Cohen, 2012; Mkono, 2013). The recent literature discusses the authentication of ICH from either the host's or the guest's perspectives (Cho, 2012; Kolar & Zabkar, 2010; Zhou, Zhang, & Edelheim, 2013; Zhou et al., 2015). However, there is little discussion of the mutual (host–guest) authentication of ICH and the related power relation between host and guest, although community empowerment is considered essential for safeguarding ICH (Alexander, 2009; Cole, 2007). A better understanding of the linkage between the mutual authentication of ICH and community empowerment could help to prevent the commodification of ICH as well as strengthening the community's role in ICH based tourism.

This article presents a critical review of the authentication of ICH, either by the host or the guest, contrasting it with a proposed mutual authentication approach, with a special focus on how such forms of authentication variously influence community empowerment. The aims of this narrative review are: to ascertain the disciplinary orientation of previous research; to identify core theories and concepts relevant in existing studies, and to identify gaps in knowledge and avenues for future research. Based on this review, a conceptual model that connects host and guest perspectives on the authenticity of ICH with community empowerment is provided.

Methodology

A narrative literature review (Cronin, Ryan, & Coughlan, 2008; Rumrill & Fitzgerald, 2001) was conducted to analyze extant research on the nexus between authenticity, ICH and community empowerment. A narrative literature review was deemed appropriate because it enabled us to trace the historical development of the ICH literature and examine theoretical development in this space (Cronin et al., 2008; Crouch, 1995; Rumrill & Fitzgerald, 2001). The literature on these topics is broad and diffuse so this review began with an initial Google Scholar search using the terms: authenticity, intangible culture and heritage, and empowerment to yield a pool of potential articles. Google Scholar is considered a viable search engine to support literature reviews across a range of topics and disciplines (Gentles, Charles, Nicholas, Ploeg, & McKibbon, 2016; Harzing & van der Wal, 2008).

This initial search elicited 421 articles from a range of disciplines, including sociology, psychology, anthropology, environmental, cultural, marketing and consumer research. The paper metadata was imported into EndNoteX8 bibliographic management software to enable further analysis. The abstracts of these articles were then examined in order to refine the keywords adopted in the initial Google Scholar search, as not all 421 articles were relevant. The revised keywords were: authenticity, intangible cultural heritage, authentication, host(s) and guest(s), community empowerment, and community-based ecotourism. With the refined keywords, a further keyword-based search was conducted (Loulanski & Loulanski, 2011) using Science Direct, ProQuest, and Sage databases to ensure any additional articles not captured in the Google Scholar search were identified.

The second key-word search identified a total of 150 articles relevant to the topic of this research. Further, an in-depth review of these articles was conducted, focusing on the conceptual development of authenticity, the authenticity of ICH and its relationship to community empowerment, and the existing models of authentication. As part of this review process, the lead researcher focused specifically on identifying gaps in knowledge in authentication of ICH to develop a conceptual model for future testing.

Types of authenticity

The concept of authenticity was initially applied in museums to describe the outcome of the process used by curators and ethnographers to clarify the provenance of artifacts. This was later conceptualized as objective authenticity (Trilling, 1972). Wang (1999, p. 352) defined objective authenticity as the authenticity of originals, that is, from a historical point of view, whether the objects are original items and not copies or fakes. 'Authentic,' in this sense, is equivalent to the term 'genuine,'

Early conceptualizations of authenticity attracted scholarly attention, as issues surrounding the commodification of culture were identified to have the potential to destroy the meaning of the local ICH, and inadvertently detract from the tourist experience (Greenwood, 1977). Specifically, studies during the 1970s found that the propensity of tourism to transform destination communities was critical to tourists' perceptions of the authenticity of the local products. Concerns about the touristic consumption of ICH also became prominent, with the potential commodification of local customs such as rituals and feasts and folk and ethnic arts, beginning to enter the scholarly discourse (Appadurai, 1986). Alternative views then emerged, stating that tourism does not necessarily destroy the meaning of ICH products for the host and the guest, but this depends on the touristic experience. As such, authenticity was identified as undefined, primitive and in need of conceptual clarification and theoretical refinement to provide empirically driven insights into the nature of modern tourism and its impact upon host communities (Cohen, 1988).

During the 1990s, the literature experienced a shift in focus from objective to existential authenticity, with acknowledgment of the need to encompass the living values embedded in the ICH that build host community empowerment, thus reducing the potential negative impacts on destination communities (Casey, 1993). Existential authenticity is defined as

> a potential existential state of Being that is to be activated by tourist activities. Correspondingly, authentic experiences in tourism are to achieve this activated existential state of Being within the liminal process of tourism. (Wang, 1999, p. 352)

Existential authenticity involves personal or intersubjective feelings activated by tourist experiences of ICH, including visiting friends and relatives, beach holidays, nature tourism, ocean cruising, shopping, fishing, hunting or sports (Wang, 1999). However, few studies have focused on how to shift tourist motivations, or on an integration of a community's ICH into community empowerment (Agrawal, 2000; Brohman, 1996).

This ongoing debate attracted the attention of global organizations such as UNESCO (2003), who sought to integrate the values of traditional custodians into policy and planning as exemplified by the UNESCO, 2003 Convention of Safeguarding of Intangible Cultural Heritage. The concept of 'cool authenticity' emerged to describe the ICH based on scientific knowledge by a recognized expert or institution (Cohen & Cohen, 2012; Mkono, 2013). Concurrently, the 'hot authenticity' concept also arose to describe the ICH certified by the local community based on its existential authenticity, using a performative process that allows for public participation (Cohen & Cohen, 2012). Within tourism, 'cool authenticity' is normally implemented by national and international agencies (Cohen & Cohen, 2012). For example, the declaration of the Bregenzerwald region in the Austrian Alps as a World Heritage Area for its cultural significance for agricultural production is an example of cool authenticity, as UNESCO exercised the power to declare the authenticity of ICH. This local level example has since been used to inform global policy intervention with respect to ICH (Daugstad & Kirchengast, 2013).

Authenticity and power

The above discussion is effectively about who has the legitimacy of power to declare an ICH practice as authentic (Cohen & Cohen, 2012). The process through which an ICH practice is deemed authentic is termed authentication. As stated earlier, Cohen and Cohen (2012) argue that cool authenticity is associated with an external expert's (or institution's) power to authenticate an object or event. They also suggest that the necessity for such an authentication process is due to tourists' quest for authenticity. In contrast, hot authenticity relies not on any scientific evidence of authenticity nor on authentication by an expert. Instead, it focuses on the host community's beliefs about the authenticity of a festival or practice in which they engage. Here the community shares the political power that authenticates the attractions. In a festival demonstrating hot authenticity, a community authenticates it by participating in its running and operation. This inevitably leads to interaction between hosts and guests.

Distinguishing between a hot and cool authentication process, however, fails to adequately take into account the interaction between host and guest, which raises the issue of mutual authentication (Cohen & Cohen, 2012). Further, because a community is directly in contact with a guest, host–guest power relations are crucial for the hot authentication of ICH (Gnotha & Wang, 2015). Accordingly, hot authentication allows guests to have an empathic understanding of the rights of hosts during the development of the festival. This understanding is based on the development of trust between the host and guest and such trust also increases the empowerment of the community (Gnotha & Wang, 2015).

Most prior studies focus on tourists from developed countries and their views of the authenticity of local festivals and rituals, leaving the domestic tourist's views concerning authenticity unknown (Cho, 2012; Cohen & Cohen, 2012; Lin, 2017; Medina, 2003; Nguyen & Cheung, 2016). However, Cho (2012) found that domestic tourists were able to evaluate the authenticity of the ICH if they had a strong interest and motivation for cultural experiences and novelty or cultural education. Understanding the views of both international and domestic tourists is crucial for creating destination image and authenticity of toured objects and events. Stone and Nyaupane (2018) urged that the 'tourist gaze' concept could be applied to gather perception of both international and domestic tourists on the tourist destination image.

Hosts also need to understand that tourists from an increasingly urbanized society who may not feel nostalgia towards the past want an authentic experience of traditional objects and culture (Cho, 2012). However, this authentic experience needs to be explained to them. One way the host community can meet the requirements of tourists for authenticity is by providing authentic cuisine (Sims, 2009; Timothy & Ron, 2013), and also by speaking in their own native language when explaining the meaning of cultural practices (Canziani, 2016). Therefore, a significant involvement of the host community is needed to provide an authentic experience of their ICH to tourists. As such, mutual interaction between the host and guest is necessary for the hot authentication of an ICH festival, which can satisfy the tourist as well as empower the community.

Relationship between ICH-based tourism and community empowerment

As discussed above, ICH, particularly traditional cultural festivals of indigenous communities, have gained popularity for both domestic and international tourists. For instance, the Holy Week celebration of Christian communities in Sardinia, that includes events on several days such as Palm Sunday, Holy Thursday, Good Friday and Holy Saturday, in the week leading to Easter Sunday, attract many domestic and international tourists, mainly of Christian backgrounds (Giudici et al., 2013). Another example is the Rush Mela festival in Sundarbans, Bangladesh. Rush Mela is a large folk festival predominantly observed by the Hindu community, which has become a major attraction with both domestic and international visitors in recent years (Islam et al., 2018; Yusuf, 2016). A community's ICH in the form of a cultural festival can be considered to be a good or service from the economic point of view, in addition to its evident status as a major expression of cultural heritage. Festivals are crucial for generating income for the host as they tend to foster interaction at some level between the community (host) and the tourists (guests) (Heuman, 2005).

Much intangible cultural heritage, irrespective of its form of expression, is promoted by the government or local community without understanding the guest's interest in authenticity. While ICH-based tourism brings economic benefits and recognition of traditional cultures, there are claims of the commodification of ICH due to mass tourism. During the early 1980s, the emergence of mass tourism led to an ongoing debate in the literature surrounding the influence of Western culture on the ICH of indigenous, remote and traditional communities across the globe (Wood, 1984). As such, tourism in destinations with limited alternative development options is promoted purely to grow the numbers of Western tourists, rather than with the intention to preserve the community's unique ICH (Van den Berghe & Keyes, 1984). For instance, mass tourism led to the integration of costumes in traditional dance being modified to accommodate Western tourists' notions of exoticism in Tahiti (Dilley, 1986).

The increasing recognition of the importance of ICH resulted in a shift in academic literature, with studies beginning to examine issues surrounding the preservation and protection of oral traditions and expressions, performing arts, social practices, rituals and festive events, and traditional craftsmanship, all with the emphasis on host community empowerment (Boley & Johnson Gaither, 2016; Kirshenblatt-Gimblett, 2004). One such study on the Pataxo Indians of Porto Seguro of Brazil indicated how ICH was transformed with the primary motive of preserving authenticity through the commodification of craftwork and performing arts. Initially, craftwork had been limited to necklaces made from tree seeds. However, this research uncovered that wood items, earrings, necklaces, loincloths, rattles and a variety of additional decorative objects were critical to revising and sustaining this group's cultural heritage (De Azeredo Grünewald, 2002).

In reaction to the commodification of ICH and the inequitable distribution of benefits from tourism in general, ecotourism emerged as an alternative to empower communities at economic, psychological, social and political levels for them to exert control at the top end of the participation ladder in terms of community-based ecotourism (CBET) (Di Castri, 2004; Scheyvens, 1999). However, the business behind ecotourism often modified the value of ICH, thus eliminating the psychological empowerment of destination communities (Entwistle, 2000). For example, the commodification of Komodo dragons in the Komodo National Park, Indonesia changed the host community's attitudes to the conservation of this charismatic vertebrate. This shift was driven by the desire for an economic return from ecotourism, rather than by intangible values, such as relationships to spiritual worship, folklore or art, or their use for food or handicrafts (Walpole & Goodwin, 2001). This is especially common in developing countries, where conservation is dominated by flagship species preferred by international tourists and donor and membership groups, rather than an emphasis on the conservation of local cultural and religious interests (Bowen-Jones & Entwistle, 2002).

In the early 2000s, the literature focused on how to maintain authenticity and reduce commodification, while still providing communities with an opportunity to preserve the unique cultural heritage and generate opportunities for a sustainable livelihood (De Azeredo Grünewald, 2002; Mason,

2004; Medina, 2003; Taylor, 2001). More specifically, it was recognized that the kind of food and drinks offered to tourists can have implications for the economic, cultural and environmental sustainability of tourism destinations. Arguably, a focus on locally sourced products can result in a benefit for both guests and hosts, and empower the local community (Torres, 2002). Medina (2003) conducted an ethnographic study of a Mayan host community, finding that traditional lifestyles had been modified to suit tourists. To overcome this issue, archaeologists worked closely with traditional owners to ensure the unique ideology surrounding ancient Mayan cosmology was portrayed to tourists in an authentic manner, while still delivering a high-quality experience. In this research, the conceptual clarification of objective and existential authenticity from both the hosts' and guests' perspectives was essential to consider the commodification of ICH. As the negative impacts became increasingly evident, it became clear that the power relations to certify the authenticity of ICH from a host's perspective were especially important to add conceptual clarity and refinement, with the potential to enhance host community empowerment and improve destination development (Kato, 2006; Kontogeorgopoulos, 2005).

During the early 2000s, much of the conservation of ICH was not properly integrated, resulting in a political and social disempowerment (Tosun, 2000). For instance, Campbell (2002a) noted the International Union for Conservation of Nature (IUCN) relied heavily on Western scientific criteria to determine appropriate conservation practices. In addition, contemporary examples of bioprospecting in Costa Rica demonstrated that the employment of locals was fairly minimal, especially as external investors acquired the patent for the genetic resources of endemic medicinal plants, clearly showing their political empowerment to the detriment of the local community (Campbell, 2002b). A further example of such disempowerment is an ecotourism project in Xishuangbanna, Yunnan, China, where tour operators influenced the host community to devalue their culture in order to give a highly stereotypical cultural experience to ecotourists. In turn, this marginalized the community's social empowerment, with commodification used to present the local traditions to ecotourists (Walter, 2004).

During the late 2000s, there was a shift away from authenticity to an emphasis on the power relations involved in the process of authentication from a host–guest perspective, specifically to empower host community (Alexander, 2009; Ateljevic & Doorne, 2005; Cole, 2007; Noy, 2009). For example, recent research on performance in tourism studies (Knudsen & Waade, 2010) has documented the constitutive role of the public in the authentication of objects, sites or events as tourist attractions. The findings stressed that performance leads to the permeability of barriers between the 'stage' and the 'audience' to enhance host–guest interaction for the authentication of the ICH. To ensure the sustainability of the authenticity of the ICH, host community empowerment was noted in studies to consider both the antecedents and consequences of host authentic experiences (Xie, 2011). Moreover, Fiorello and Bo (2012), in a study of CBET in the indigenous reserve of Malekus, Costa Rica, mentioned that the commodification of the ICH based on the touristic experience of authenticity empowered the host community at the physiological, social and political levels. This research found an equitable distribution of benefits among the host community stimulated cultural pride, generated social capital and contributed to positive governance practices. However, findings did not clarify how the authenticity of the ICH was negotiated between the hosts and guests without commodifying unique cultural traditions, which is critical for ensuring community empowerment.

Now let us turn to the various models of how authentication and empowerment are negotiated between hosts and guests.

Evaluation of existing models of authentication and empowerment

The above-discussed debates are embodied in several authentication models developed based on hosts' and guests' perceptions of authenticity (Cho, 2012; Kolar & Zabkar, 2010; Zhou et al., 2013). The consumer-based model of authentication was developed by Kolar and Zabkar (2010), in order to demonstrate the relationship among tourists' cultural motivation, authentic experience and tourist loyalty towards the tour attraction (Figure 1). An empirical examination of the model suggested that tourists' cultural motivation was an important precursor of both object-based and existential authenticity, which influenced tourist loyalty. Zhou et al. (2013) have further updated Kolar and Zabkar's (2010) consumer-based model by adding 'attitude' as another variable and amended the relationships between the variables in the structural model (Figure 2). Attitude was defined by Zhou et al. (2013) as the tourists' level of understanding of the traditional culture and the extent of their preference for it. The study found that ignorance of traditional culture by the public affected the perceptions of authenticity, which led the tourist to give importance to the aesthetics and form of the objects or materials, rather than focusing on the experience of traditional culture.

Cho (2012) built an alternative conceptual model to explore the relationship between tourists' motivation, authenticity and tourists' satisfaction (Figure 3). Motivation affects both objective and existential authenticity, which influence tourist satisfaction through both expense and experience (Cho, 2012). Satisfaction is found to encompass cognitive and affective components, yet is considered to be the key driver of consumer loyalty (Fornell, Johnson, Anderson, Cha, & Bryant, 1996; Oliver, 1997). However, Zhou et al. (2013) argued that motivation has no effect on existential authenticity, which opposes Kolar and Zabkar's (2010) and Cho's (2012) findings that both forms of authenticity are related to motivation. Zhou et al. (2013) found that attitude, including individual beliefs, interests, and understanding of tourism activities, has no effect on the motivation for visiting the ICH attractions and does not influence loyalty directly.

Subsequent studies have tended to focus on the process of host authentication. For instance, Zhou et al. (2015) revealed that the hosts' attitude towards traditional culture plays a role in the process of host authentication since it affects both objective and existential authenticity (Figure 4). Host attitude is directly influenced by personal emotional benefit, whereas personal economic benefits are indirect and hidden from any obvious position in the hosts' support of tourism. Therefore, personal emotional benefits potentially emanate from the mutual exchange of culture between host and guest, thus enhancing cohesion and identity to ensure psychological empowerment. However, Zhou et al.'s (2015) study did not clarify the social and political dimensions of empowerment in relation to stated economic and psychological advantages. A quantitative study by Boley, McGehee, Perdue, and Long (2014) concluded that psychological empowerment and personal economic benefit have direct and positive effects on the hosts' support for tourism.

Current research on authentication models have focused on consumer behavior and partial empowerment (economic and psychological) to verify the authenticity of experiences from the guests' and hosts' perspective (Cho, 2012; Kolar & Zabkar, 2010; Zhou et al., 2013, 2015). However, this research is limited by the use of highly quantitative approaches with structural equation modeling used as the form of analysis to assess authentication. This approach is useful for exploring relationships among variables but, arguably, each concept embedded within these models requires deeper investigation through inductive qualitative methods (Kolar & Zabkar, 2010; Zhou et al., 2013, 2015).

Further, an authentic experience depends on subjective negotiation between tourism entrepreneurs and government and other key stakeholders who act as an intermediary between hosts and guests (Chhabra, 2010). In such a context, the lack of interaction between a host and tourists can

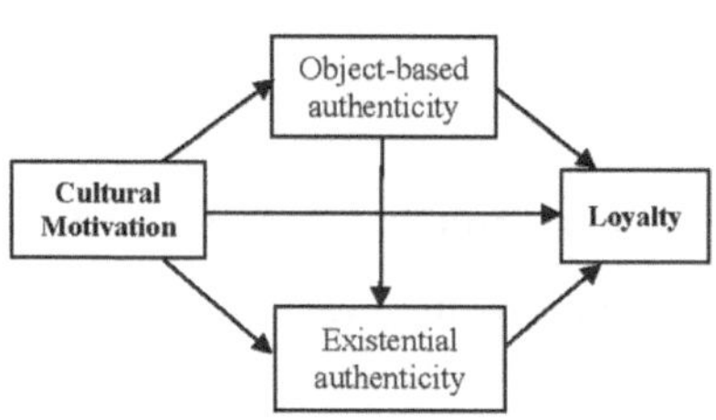

Figure 1. Consumer-based model of the authenticity of cultural heritage (Kolar & Zabkar, 2010).

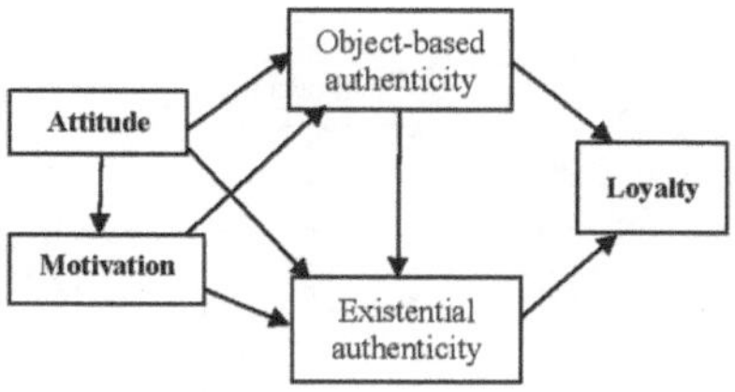

Figure 2. Modified consumer-based model of the authenticity of cultural heritage (Zhou et al., 2013).

devalue the authentic experience for the tourist as well as curtail benefits to the host community and affect host empowerment (Cho, 2012; Zhou et al., 2015). As such, direct interaction can enhance the mutual authentication of tourist attractions and build trust between hosts and guests to amplify host community empowerment (Moyle, Glen Croy, & Weiler, 2010; Zhu, 2012). Since the current models of authentication of the ICH consider the guest (tourist) and host (community) perspective separately, they can provide only a partial understanding of the common grounds and interaction or linkages between host and guest in the authentication process and in community empowerment. A mutual authentication model (host–guest) would be necessary to reveal the relationships between host and guest for authenticating tourist attractions like ICH and their impact on community empowerment.

A model of host- guest authentication of ICH addressing issues above

Considering the above discussion, a conceptual model is proposed for the mutual host–guest authentication of ICH (Figure 5) which incorporates both hosts' and guests' perspectives. This model supports tourism development and enhanced community empowerment. In this model, the authenticity of ICH is considered to be established by the authentication of the objects of cultural significance (e.g. structures, artifacts or similar architectural physical elements) as well as by the existence of cultural traditional practices (e.g. rituals, festivals) by both the hosts (i.e. the local community) and guests (i.e. tourists). Physical objects used in performing the cultural practices, either in religious and social events or in the daily lifestyle of the community, are the elements which measure the objective authenticity of the community's ICH (Asplet & Cooper, 2000). The traditional cultural practices, customs, and the way the community perform rituals and festivals that define the unique identity of the community all constitute the elements appropriate for measuring the existential authenticity of this ICH (Zhou et al., 2015).

A host community can influence the authenticity of its ICH with their attitude, motivation, economic and psychological relationships, and participation in the cultural practices, individually or through institutions. A host's attitude towards that community's ICH is crucial for determining

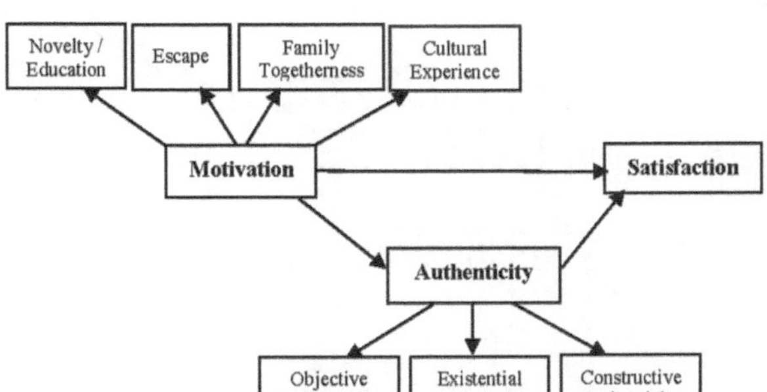

Figure 3. Model for tourists' authentication and satisfaction (Cho, 2012).

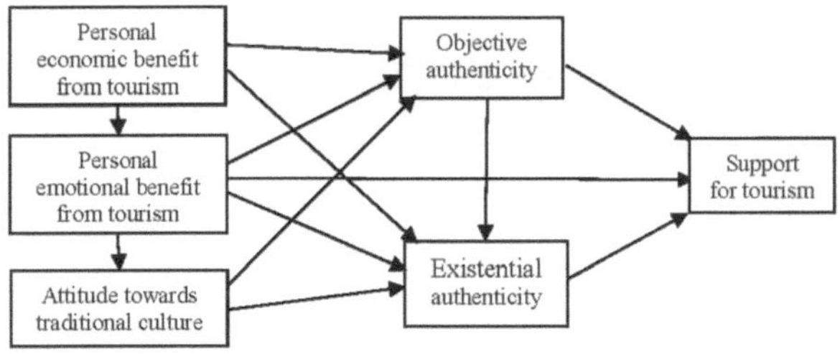

Figure 4. Structural model of host authenticity (Zhou et al., 2015).

the authenticity of this ICH (Zhou et al., 2013), as it shows the feeling of the host community toward traditional ownership of the ICH. A host's attitude can directly or indirectly influence ICH-based tourism as well. Also, the host community's motivation towards the preservation of its own ICH would justify the authenticity of their ICH as well as their support for tourism. Most importantly, the economic benefits from ICH (e.g. festivals) and psychological or emotional benefits from ICH (e.g. religious or social rituals) received by the host, reinforce the host's perception towards the authenticity of their ICH and towards support for ICH-based tourism (Xie, 2011; Zhu, 2012). Further, the host community's active participation in their traditional cultural practices, either individually or institutionally, can reflect the host's perception towards the authenticity of ICH.

The guests' attitude towards the traditional culture, expressed by authentic objects or the existence of genuine cultural events, can also contribute to the authenticity of the ICH. In addition, guest motivation or intention to experience ICH through tourism can reinforce the authenticity of the ICH and guest satisfaction and loyalty towards ICH-based tourism (Kolar & Zabkar, 2010). When guests find authentic objects or experiences of events, this can also influence the ICH's authenticity.

This mutual host–guest authentication of ICH will ultimately impact community empowerment through tourism. Economic benefit from ICH-based tourism (selling traditional crafts, food, and accommodation for tourists) will enhance the economic empowerment of the community. The guests also make a major economic contribution to valuing the traditional authentic objects and events, in compensation for satisfying their touristic consumption of the ICH. Similarly, the psychological empowerment of the community will be enhanced by owning the authentic ICH (objects and

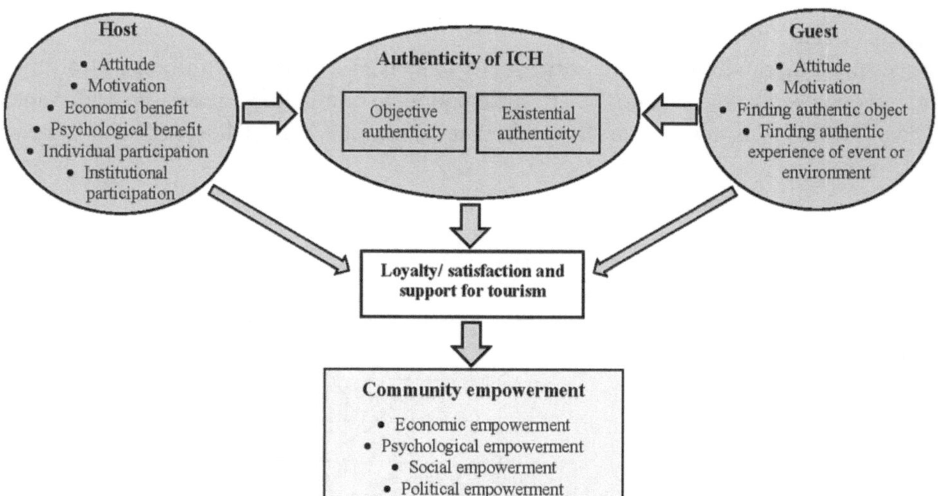

Figure 5. Conceptual model of mutual host-guest authentication of ICH.

traditional practices) and positioning themselves as a unique community in the global society. Participating in the authentic traditional cultural practices individually or as a group can increase social cohesion and shared feelings, enhancing the social empowerment of the community. Everyone in the community can recognize their own identity with respect to their authentic ICH. Further, local institutions and leadership can be developed for managing ICH (e.g. organizing traditional cultural events, managing historical objects), which ensures the political empowerment of the community.

The proposed model includes measuring the authenticity of ICH through both the hosts' and guests' perspectives, and hence can help to determine common grounds on which the authenticity of ICH stands, and how it can link to the perception of hosts and guests. The common issues emphasized by both hosts and guests may comprise the major determinants of ICH's authenticity as well as highlighting the main concerns for enhancing ICH-based tourism and community empowerment.

Conclusion

The authentication of ICH is a crucial issue for managing and preserving ICH in the face of commodification by the influence of modern trends of social change and commercialization. This review article has identified the current issues and knowledge gaps surrounding the topic on authentication of ICH and proposed a conceptual model for mutual authentication. In the quest for authentication concepts and tools, this review of the existing literature has revealed an evolution from an external-expert-based 'cool' authentication process to a direct host -guest influenced 'hot' authentication process, where it is mainly tourists that participate in the decision making about ICH authenticity. Most prior research on authentication has a tendency to focus on well-informed and wealthy international travelers and overlooked the critical role of domestic tourists in host–guest ICH authentication. Recent studies have proposed several authentication models based on host and guest perspectives such as the consumer-based model of authentication (Cho, 2012; Kolar & Zabkar, 2010; Zhou et al., 2013) and the host authentication model (Zhou et al., 2013). These models consider hosts' and guests' perspectives separately without showing the linkage between ICH authenticity and community empowerment. A detailed investigation is required to better understand the direct interaction between the host community and guests for the mutual authentication of tourist attractions, including ICH that can enhance community empowerment (Moyle et al., 2010; Zhu, 2012). Further, the recent authentication models are based on a highly quantitative structural equation modeling approach. Each of the variables and concepts embedded in the models needs further detailed investigation using inductive qualitative approaches (Kolar & Zabkar, 2010; Zhou et al., 2013, 2015).

Considering the significance of improving the authentication process and its implications for sustainable tourism development, a conceptual model of mutual host–guest authentication of the ICH has been proposed, which can integrate both hosts' and guests' perspectives and link to fundamental elements of community empowerment. This model emphasizes host and guest interactions and provides an opportunity for authenticating ICH mutually by the host and guest in ICH tourism context. The conceptual model emphasizes power relationships between host and guest in the authentication process as well as the influence on community empowerment across the political, social, psychological and economic domains. Further detailed research is required to test and validate the conceptual model in various contexts of ICH-based tourism and other tourist attractions using a quantitative approach. An elaborated framework incorporating the host, guest, government and tour operator can be developed to enhance the sustainable management of ICH, tourism and community empowerment in the long term.

Disclosure statement

No potential conflict of interest was reported by the authors.

ORCID

Millicent Kennelly http://orcid.org/0000-0001-8890-9849

References

Agrawal, A. (2000). Adaptive management in transboundary protected areas: The Bialowieza National Park and Biosphere reserve as a case study. *Environmental Conservation*, *27*(4), 326–333.

Alexander, N. (2009). Brand authentication: Creating and maintaining brand auras. *European Journal of Marketing*, *43* (3/4), 551–562.

Appadurai, A. (1986). Introduction: Commodities and the Politics of value. In A. Appadurai (Ed.), *The social life of things- Commodities in cultural perspective* (pp. 3–63). Cambridge: Cambridge University Press.

Asplet, M., & Cooper, M. (2000). Cultural designs in New Zealand souvenir clothing: The question of authenticity. *Tourism Management*, *21*(3), 307–312.

Ateljevic, I., & Doorne, S. (2005). Dialectics of authentication: Performing 'exotic otherness' in a backpacker enclave of Dali, China. *Journal of Tourism and Cultural Change*, *3*(1), 1–17.

Boley, B. B., & Johnson Gaither, C. (2016). Exploring empowerment within the Gullah Geechee cultural heritage corridor: Implications for heritage tourism development in the Lowcountry. *Journal of Heritage Tourism*, *11*(2), 155–176.

Boley, B. B., McGehee, N. G., Perdue, R. R., & Long, P. (2014). Empowerment and resident attitudes toward tourism: Strengthening the theoretical foundation through a Weberian lens. *Annals of Tourism Research*, *49*, 33–50.

Boonzaaier, C., & Wels, H. (2018). Authenticity lost? The significance of cultural villages in the conservation of heritage in South Africa. *Journal of Heritage Tourism*, *13*(2), 181–193.

Bowen-Jones, E., & Entwistle, A. (2002). Identifying appropriate flagship species: The importance of culture and local contexts. *Oryx*, *36*(2), 189–195.

Brohman, J. (1996). New directions in tourism for third world development. *Annals of Tourism Research*, *23*(1), 48–70.

Campbell, L. M. (2002a). Science and sustainable use: Views of marine turtle conservation experts. *Ecological Applications*, *12*(4), 1229–1246.

Campbell, L. M. (2002b). Conservation narratives in Costa Rica: Conflict and co-existence. *Development and Change*, *33*(1), 29–56.

Canziani, B. F. (2016). Cultural resource valuation in tourist destinations. *Annals of Tourism Research*, *61*, 22–24.

Casey, E. S. (1993). *Getting back into place: Toward a renewed understanding of the place-world*. Bloomington: Indiana University Press.

Chhabra, D. (2010). How they see us: Perceived effects of tourist gaze on the Old Order Amish. *Journal of Travel Research*, *49*(1), 93–105.

Cho, M. H. (2012). A study of authenticity in traditional Korean folk villages. *International Journal of Hospitality & Tourism Administration*, *13*(2), 145–171.
Cohen, E. (1988). Authenticity and commoditization in tourism. *Annals of Tourism Research*, *15*(3), 371–386.
Cohen, E. (2007). 'Authenticity' in tourism studies: Aprés la lutte. *Tourism Recreation Research*, *32*(2), 75–82.
Cohen, E., & Cohen, S. A. (2012). Authentication: Hot and cool. *Annals of Tourism Research*, *39*(3), 1295–1314.
Cole, S. (2007). Beyond authenticity and commodification. *Annals of Tourism Research*, *34*(4), 943–960.
Cronin, P., Ryan, F., & Coughlan, M. (2008). Undertaking a literature review: A step-by-step approach. *British Journal of Nursing*, *17*(1), 38–43.
Crouch, G. I. (1995). A meta-analysis of tourism demand. *Annals of Tourism Research*, *22*(1), 103–118.
Daugstad, K., & Kirchengast, C. (2013). Authenticity and the pseudo-backstage of agri-tourism. *Annals of Tourism Research*, *43*, 170–191.
De Azeredo Grünewald, R. (2002). Tourism and cultural revival. *Annals of Tourism Research*, *29*(4), 1004–1021.
Di Castri, F. (2004). Sustainable tourism in small islands: Local empowerment as the key factor. *Insula-Paris*, *13*(1/2), 49.
Dilley, R. S. (1986). Tourist brochures and tourist images. *The Canadian Geographer/Le Géographe Canadien*, *30*(1), 59–65.
Entwistle, A. (2000). Flagships for the future? *Oryx*, *34*(4), 239–240.
Fiorello, A., & Bo, D. (2012). Community-based ecotourism to meet the new tourist's expectations: An exploratory study. *Journal of Hospitality Marketing & Management*, *21*(7), 758–778.
Fornell, C., Johnson, M. D., Anderson, E. W., Cha, J., & Bryant, B. E. (1996). The American customer satisfaction index: Nature, purpose, and findings. *The Journal of Marketing*, *60*(4), 7–18.
Gentles, S., Charles, C., Nicholas, D., Ploeg, J., & McKibbon, A. (2016). Reviewing the research methods literature: Principles and strategies illustrated by a systematic overview of sampling in qualitative research. *Systematic Reviews*, *5*(172), 1–11.
Giudici, E., Melis, C., Dessì, S., & Francine Pollnow Galvao Ramos, B. (2013). Is intangible cultural heritage able to promote sustainability in tourism? *International Journal of Quality and Service Sciences*, *5*(1), 101–114.
Gnotha, J., & Wang, N. (2015). Authentic knowledge and empathy in tourism. *Annals of Tourism Research*, *50*, 170–172.
Greenwood, D. J. (1977). Culture by the pound: An anthropological perspective on tourism as cultural commoditization. In V. L. Smith (Ed.), *Hosts and guests* (pp. 129–139). Philadelphia: University of Pennsylvania Press.
Harzing, A., & van der Wal, R. (2008). Google Scholar as a new source for citation analysis. *Ethics in Science and Environmental Politics*, *8*, 61–73.
Heuman, D. (2005). Hospitality and reciprocity: Working tourists in Dominica. *Annals of Tourism Research*, *32*(2), 407–418.
Islam, M. M., Sunny, A. R., Hossain, M. M., & Friess, D. A. (2018). Drivers of mangrove ecosystem service change in the Sundarbans of Bangladesh. *Singapore Journal of Tropical Geography*, *39*(2), 244–265.
Kato, K. (2006). Community, connection and conservation: Intangible cultural values in natural heritage—the case of Shirakami-sanchi World Heritage Area. *International Journal of Heritage Studies*, *12*(5), 458–473.
Kirshenblatt-Gimblett, B. (2004). Intangible heritage as metacultural production. *Museum International*, *56*(1-2), 52–65.
Knudsen, B. T., & Waade, A. M. (2010). *Re-investing authenticity: Tourism, place and emotions.* Bristol: Channel View Publications.
Kolar, T., & Zabkar, V. (2010). A consumer-based model of authenticity: An oxymoron or the foundation of cultural heritage marketing? *Tourism Management*, *31*(5), 652–664.
Kontogeorgopoulos, N. (2005). Community-based ecotourism in Phuket and Ao Phangnga, Thailand: Partial victories and bittersweet remedies. *Journal of Sustainable Tourism*, *13*(1), 4–23.
Lin, Y. C. (2017). The willingness of heritage tourists to pay for perceived authenticity in Pingxi, Taiwan. *Current Issues in Tourism*, *20*(10), 1044–1069.
Loulanski, T., & Loulanski, V. (2011). The sustainable integration of cultural heritage and tourism: A meta-study. *Journal of Sustainable Tourism*, *19*(7), 837–862.
Mason, K. (2004). Sound and meaning in Aboriginal tourism. *Annals of Tourism Research*, *31*(4), 837–854.
Medina, L. K. (2003). Commoditizing culture: Tourism and Maya identity. *Annals of Tourism Research*, *30*(2), 353–368.
Mkono, M. (2013). Hot and cool authentication: A netnographic illustration. *Annals of Tourism Research*, *41*, 215–218.
Moswete, N., & Thapa, B. (2015). Factors that influence support for community-based ecotourism in the rural communities adjacent to the Kgalagadi Transfrontier Park, Botswana. *Journal of Ecotourism*, *14*(2-3), 243–263.
Moyle, B., Glen Croy, W., & Weiler, B. (2010). Community perceptions of tourism: Bruny and Magnetic islands, Australia. *Asia Pacific Journal of Tourism Research*, *15*(3), 353–366.
Nguyen, T. H. H., & Cheung, C. (2016). Chinese heritage tourists to heritage sites: What are the effects of heritage motivation and perceived authenticity on satisfaction? *Asia Pacific Journal of Tourism Research*, *21*(11), 1155–1168.

Noy, C. (2009). Authenticating tourists: The politics of authenticity in a national heritage site in Israel. *Qualitative Sociology Review*, *5*(1), 112–129.

Oliver, R. L. (1997). *Satisfaction: A behavioral perspective on the consumer*. New York: McGraw-Hill.

Rumrill, J. P. D., & Fitzgerald, S. M. (2001). Using narrative literature reviews to build a scientific knowledge base. *Work*, *16*(2), 165–170.

Scheyvens, R. (1999). Ecotourism and the empowerment of local communities. *Tourism Management*, *20*(2), 245–249.

Sims, R. (2009). Food, place and authenticity: Local food and the sustainable tourism experience. *Journal of Sustainable Tourism*, *17*(3), 321–336.

Stone, L. S., & Nyaupane, G. P. (2018). The tourist gaze: Domestic versus international tourists. *Journal of Travel Research*, doi:10.1177/0047287518781890.

Taylor, J. P. (2001). Authenticity and sincerity in tourism. *Annals of Tourism Research*, *28*(1), 7–26.

Timothy, D. J., & Nyaupane, G. P. (2009). *Cultural heritage and tourism in the developing world: A regional perspective*. London: Routledge.

Timothy, D. J., & Ron, A. S. (2013). Understanding heritage cuisines and tourism: Identity, image, authenticity, and change. *Journal of Heritage Tourism*, *8*(2-3), 99–104.

Torres, R. (2002). Toward a better understanding of tourism and agriculture linkages in the Yucatan: Tourist food consumption and preferences. *Tourism Geographies*, *4*(3), 282–306.

Tosun, C. (2000). Limits to community participation in the tourism development process in developing countries. *Tourism Management*, *21*(6), 613–633.

Trilling, L. (1972). *Sincerity and authenticity*. London: Oxford University Press.

UNESCO. (2003). Safeguarding of the Intangible Cultural Heritage. Retrieved from http://www.unesco.org/culture/ich/en/convention

UNESCO. (2011). What is intangible cultural heritage? *UNESCO*. Retrieved from https://ich.unesco.org/doc/src/01851-EN.pdf

Van den Berghe, P. L., & Keyes, C. F. (1984). Introduction tourism and re-created ethnicity. *Annals of Tourism Research*, *11*(3), 343–352.

Walpole, M. J., & Goodwin, H. J. (2001). Local attitudes towards conservation and tourism around Komodo National Park, Indonesia. *Environmental Conservation*, *28*(2), 160–166.

Walter, P. (2004). Tourism and forest management among the Hani in Xishuangbanna, China. In D. Nathan, G. Kelkar, & P. Walter (Eds.), *Globalization and indigenous peoples in Asia: Changing the local-global interface* (pp. 207–224). Thousand Oaks: Sage.

Wang, N. (1999). Rethinking authenticity in tourism experience. *Annals of Tourism Research*, *26*(2), 349–370.

Wood, R. E. (1984). Ethnic tourism, the state, and cultural change in Southeast Asia. *Annals of Tourism Research*, *11* (3), 353–374.

Xie, P. F. (2011). *Authenticating ethnic tourism*. Bristol: Channel View Publications.

Yusuf, A. (2016, December 7). Rashmela: Largest folk festival deep inside Sundarbans. *The Daily Star*. Retrieved from http://showtodaytv.com/play-clip-rashmela-largest-folk-festival-deep-inside-sundarbans_tvyMwEjO20P6s

Zhou, Q. B., Zhang, J., & Edelheim, J. R. (2013). Rethinking traditional Chinese culture: A consumer-based model regarding the authenticity of Chinese calligraphic landscape. *Tourism Management*, *36*, 99–112.

Zhou, Q. B., Zhang, J., Zhang, H., & Ma, J. (2015). A structural model of host authenticity. *Annals of Tourism Research*, *55*, 28–45.

Zhu, Y. (2012). Performing heritage: Rethinking authenticity in tourism. *Annals of Tourism Research*, *39*(3), 1495–1513.

Knowledge transfer processes in the authenticity of the intangible cultural heritage in tourism destination competitiveness

Desiderio Juan García-Almeida

ABSTRACT

As tourism based on intangible cultural heritage usually encompasses a knowledge transfer process, the authenticity of the heritage (or its perception) can be affected by knowledge transfer. These knowledge transfers occur to present the heritage to the tourists (courses, tour guiding, etc.), but also in the destination itself when the heritage knowledge is codified in museums, tour guides are trained, or the heritage is transferred to newer generations. These situations present potential challenges where authenticity is distorted or even lost, and it affects the competitiveness of the destination. The work attempts to analyse those knowledge transfers and their challenges regarding authenticity to sustain the competitiveness of the destination.

Introduction

As competition in the tourism sector increases, destinations strive to attract and retain tourists (García-Almeida & Hormiga, 2017). Due to the impact of globalization, the analysis of competitiveness in the tourism industry has increasingly focused not only on the business world but also on the destination arena (Kozac, Baloglu, & Bahar, 2009). In their quest for attracting, satisfying, and retaining tourists, destinations should provide relevant attractions and offer products which can target one or several segments of tourists.

Heritage tourism has experienced a dramatic growth in recent decades (Chhabra, 2010). For Prentice (1993), cultural and historical attractions are very relevant factors to motivate travel and this has generated the growth of a large heritage tourism industry. The tourism economies of some destinations are based completely on cultural heritage, and for some others, it is a relevant attraction (Timothy, 2011). Heritage can become a relevant resource to become and stay competitive in the long run, since it can be the basis of the destination's sustainable competitive advantage. In recent years, intangible heritage has become an interesting field of research (Pfeilstetter, 2015), though research on the relationship between intangible cultural heritage and tourism is scarce (López-Guzmán & Santa-Cruz, 2017).

Enjoying intangible heritage assets by travellers is generally part of the cultural tourism experience (WTO, 2012). For Datta, Bigham, Zou, and Hill (2015), intangible heritage site ecologies are intangible manifestations of history and culture via dance, song, art style, audio-visual presentations, among others. It is constantly recreated by groups providing them with a sense of identity and continuity (WTO, 2012). In the tourism field, authenticity is also a concern in the analysis of intangible heritage (e.g. Gonzalez, 2008).

The concept of authenticity has played a prominent role in tourism research (Olsen, 2002), and discussions of this issue are a core aspect of heritage tourism (Walter, 2017). Searching for authentic experiences is one of the key trends in tourism, especially in heritage tourism, and consequently, it is a relevant aspect in the development and marketing of this kind of tourism (Chhabra, 2012; Kolar & Zabkar, 2010). Authenticity has been examined and discussed from several perspectives, notably objectivism, constructivism, postmodernism, and existentialism (Rickly-Boyd, 2012a; Wang, 1999). Thus, the analysis of this concept and its implications have been enriched from the lenses which several scientific frameworks adopt to explain it. However, the processes by which authenticity is constructed remain understudied (Cohen & Cohen, 2012). The knowledge-based view has not been used to understand the concept of authenticity, its sustainability in the long term, and the process of authentication. But authenticity regarding tourism and intangible heritage is only revealed, perceived, and experienced if the underlying knowledge is transferred to the tourist. Moreover, the sustainable exploitation, and even existence, of the intangible heritage depends on several transfer processes in the destination.

This work attempts to analyse the implications of knowledge transfer in the authenticity and authentication of intangible heritage tourism by studying its role from the supply and demand perspectives. This broad goal of the work can be achieved by addressing and meeting three objectives. The first objective of this study is to explore the relevance of authenticity in the competitiveness of a destination regarding the underlying knowledge of its intangible heritage attractions, and how knowledge transfer can affect it. As authenticity could be enhanced or destroyed with knowledge transfer processes, the second objective is to identify the challenges of authenticity with regard to intangible heritage attractions when heritage knowledge is transferred in the destination. But key knowledge transfer processes regarding intangible heritage occur where tourists are the knowledge recipients, and it affects their perception of authenticity. Consequently, the third objective of the work is to analyse the knowledge transfer processes that involve the tourists' participation and how they influence heritage authenticity.

Authenticity of intangible cultural heritage in tourism competitiveness from a knowledge transfer view

According to Buhalis (2000), a tourism destination is a defined geographical region which is perceived by its visitors as a unique entity, with a political and legislative framework for tourism management. Thus, a destination could refer to a country or several countries, a region, a province, an island, a city, a national park, a natural area with outstanding beauty, or a coastal area (Fyall & Wanhill, 2008).

Destinations have resources or attractions that act as magnets and/or become motivations for visitors. Leiper (1979) defines tourist attractions as sights, events and facilities oriented to experiential opportunities for tourists. In their competitive race for tourism markets, destinations have to face the challenge of managing and organizing their scarce resources efficiently in order to supply a holiday experience that must outperform alternative destination experiences on the tourist market (Cracolici & Nijkamp, 2009). A salient concept to understand these tourism dynamics is competitiveness. Destination competitiveness can be defined as the degree to which a destination can attract and satisfy potential tourists (Enright & Newton, 2004). Destinations are seen as amalgams of tourism products, offering an integrated experience to consumers (Buhalis, 2000). The key to compete on tourism markets is the experience offered to the tourist, and several agents interact to offer that experience: firms that offer tourism services or supporting activities, destination management organizations, public administrations, local residents and other publics (Crouch, 2011). In an era of globalization with strong homogenizing forces, the distinctive social and cultural characteristics of places are obscured (Peterson, 2005). But precisely due to that, many tourism destinations analyse and reflect on which resources they have in order to explore differentiation advantages and compete in the tourism sector.

Heritage tourism can be defined as the activities of travellers seeing or experiencing built heritage, living culture or contemporary arts (Timothy, 2011). Intangible heritage tourism directly refers to the element in that definition related to the sight and experience of the living culture in a destination. The concept of intangible heritage includes practices, representations, expressions, knowledge, skills of communities and groups, and sometimes individuals, as well as the instruments, objects, artefacts and cultural spaces linked to them (Pereira Roders & van Oers, 2011; UNESCO, 2003). Intangible cultural heritage is an attraction included in many tourism products. Thus, Wang (1999) include festivals, rituals, cuisine, dress, and housing as products of tourism which can be described as authentic or inauthentic. Moreover, Esfehani and Albrecht (2018) indicate that by merely staying in the local communities and being exposed to the local lifestyle, traditional practices, or customs in person, intangible heritage becomes an element of the overall visitor experience, sometimes even in an unintended way.

As authenticity is a positive characteristic of the tourism experience related to the perceived value of heritage attractions, it becomes a relevant aspect of destination competitiveness. As Timothy and Ron (2013, p. 102) indicate, authenticity 'is a current buzzword that sells very well in the tourism marketplace.' By integrating the objective and constructive perspectives, Yang and Wall (2016, p. 26) state that authenticity 'involves a negotiated and creative process with stereotypes, judgments, and local values imposed on the setting or products by a variety of stakeholders, including tourists, hosts and suppliers.' The tourism literature often displays assertions that authenticity (along with uniqueness) is a core value of many tourism markets (Carson & Harwood, 2007). Custódio Santos, Ferreira, and Costa (2014) empirically find that authenticity is more important than traditional variables such as prices, quality of the gastronomy or health and leisure facilities for the competitiveness of a destination. Carson and Harwood (2007) state that authenticity is differently evaluated by different markets and even segments in those markets, and it could be the source of competitive advantages for some destinations. Authenticity can be seen as fantasy that has considerable implications for the impetus and motivation to travel (Knudsen, Rickly, & Vidon, 2016).

Intangible heritage has a strong knowledge element. The concept of knowledge is complex and widely discussed in the academic literature, since it can be approached and understood from several perspectives. Alavi and Leidner (2001) observe several views to address the concept: a state of mind, an object, a process, a condition of having access to information, or a capability. Learning theories outline the importance of the active construction of knowledge and that this develops over time and with experience (Koohang & Paliszkiewicz, 2013; Lee, Lajoie, Poitras, Nkangu, & Doleck, 2017). Leonard and Sensiper (1998) view knowledge as information that is relevant, applicable and at least partly based on experience, emphasizing the time dimension. Knowledge is held by individuals, but is also possible to refer to group, organizational and community knowledge. Nosek (2004, p. 54) outlines that 'group cognition means moving away from idiosyncratic, subjective mental models of the world to the notion that agents with similar capacities to act can potentially discern similar action possibilities in the world.' This is the conceptual framework to include intangible heritage as knowledge developed by a group or community and transmitted to newer generations along time.

Authenticity has been often regarded as the most important criterion for the development of cultural tourism (Xie & Wall, 2002) and the literature confirms that the objective manifestations of authenticity motivate heritage tourists to travel to distant places and times (Chhabra, 2012). In addition, discourses on authenticity influence the approach to heritage and its conservation (Boonzaaier & Wels, 2018), which are also relevant aspects for sustainable competitiveness in destinations with cultural attractions. The authenticity of the underlying knowledge in the intangible heritage is then an aspect of interest in heritage tourism. If the community's knowledge is the central element to define the authenticity of intangible heritage, an objective view is adopted.

The assessment of authenticity of intangible cultural knowledge is conducted from several perspectives. In the tourism context, intangible heritage products/elements are usually described as authentic or not depending on whether they are made or performed by locals according to their traditions (Reisinger & Steiner, 2006a). The most recognized means to assess the singularity of intangible heritage worldwide is its inclusion on the Representative List of the Intangible Cultural Heritage of Humanity by UNESCO, which inscribes those intangible heritage elements that help demonstrate the diversity of this heritage and raise awareness about its importance (UNESCO, 2003). One of the criteria for the inscription is to reflect cultural diversity and to testify to human creativity. The reference to creativity of the knowledge present in the intangible heritage calls for the recognition of its authenticity, based on the ideas of originality and genuineness underlying the objective perspective of heritage. However, it is also important to note that this indirect relevance of authenticity in the UNESCO's Representative List is directly downplayed on the Yamato Declaration on Integrated Approaches for Safeguarding Tangible and Intangible Cultural Heritage (UNESCO, 2006), since it states that 'the term "authenticity" as applied to tangible cultural heritage is not relevant when identifying and safeguarding intangible cultural heritage' (UNESCO, 2006, p. 18). This idea is based on the fact that intangible cultural heritage is constantly recreated and contradicts the view of the 1994 Nara Document on Authenticity, which indicates that 'the understanding of authenticity plays a fundamental role in all scientific studies of the cultural heritage, in conservation and restoration planning, as well as within the inscription procedures used for the World Heritage Convention and other cultural heritage inventories' (UNESCO, 2018, p. 3). Moreover, the relevance of the quest for authenticity in many tourist segments makes the analysis of authenticity appropriate and pertinent in a competitiveness context.

The objective authenticity discourse is based on the genuine, original, made by locals versions of heritage (Chhabra, 2012), and this kind of authenticity is related to pure authenticity in the literature (Chhabra, Lee, Zhao, & Scott, 2013). Though the community's knowledge is subject to evolution, the core aspects are sought to be retained along time in a frozen way. This objective discourse of authenticity remains the dominant vision in heritage tourism (Chhabra, 2012). The literature outlines the relevance of the creation of authenticity in tourism since tourists' decision of the destination to visit and ex ante and ex post evaluation is, in many cases, strongly influenced by the desire to witness and participate in authentic experiences (e.g. Xie, 2003). Nevertheless, authenticity must be perceived by the tourist, as well as underpinned in the destination. For that to happen, knowledge transfer processes are necessary.

Knowledge transfer is conceived as an event through which one entity learns from the experience of another (Darr & Kurtzberg, 2000; Kumar & Ganesh, 2009). The participating entities in this event or process can be individuals, groups, organizations or even communities. Many authors have used a communication-based model to describe the transfer process, from a source or sender to a recipient agent through a channel. However, the process of knowledge transfer is not, per se, a mere transfer of knowledge (Liyanage, Elhag, Ballal, & Li, 2009), since receivers construct their knowledge by integrating the knowledge inputs with their prior knowledge. Knowledge construction in the heritage setting is not new. For example, Falk and Dierking (2000) use the term knowledge construction when referring to the experience enjoyed by two visitors in a museum.

By utilizing the knowledge transfer view of authenticity, some processes and dynamics regarding the concept can be better understood as they deeply affect tourists, hosts, local governments, and tourism firms. Due to its immaterial nature, one of the key challenges of intangible cultural heritage in tourism destination competitiveness is how its authenticity develops as its underlying knowledge is transmitted. This can be paramount because if the destination's intangible heritage is characterized by authenticity, then transferability and replicability by competitors are highly hindered. But some transfer processes are required and need to be fostered. Assuming the importance of the knowledge component in the underlying pillars of the intangible cultural heritage, the relationship between authenticity of the intangible heritage and the transfer of the underlying knowledge of that heritage becomes a strategic aspect for the destination. That relationship can be analysed from two different perspectives: a demand-based view and a supply-based one.

Authenticity and knowledge transfer in intangible heritage contexts

Cultural heritage is an element of the tourism resource base for most countries in the world (Timothy, 2011). Timothy and Boyd (2003) observe heritage supply as a mix of elements that encompasses the heritage attractions offered to visitors, the setting and context in which the heritage exists, and the support services which have developed in the tourism activities and flows. In that sense, heritage tourism is a unique sector since supply usually precedes demand (Timothy, 2011).

The core of heritage tourism lies on heritage attractions (Timothy & Boyd, 2003). In the case of intangible heritage, the living culture inherited from the past is obviously the main attraction. In the long-term perspective and tourism development, the protection, safeguarding and even exploitation of the intangible cultural heritage require that certain knowledge transfer processes are implemented. But in these processes authenticity can be damaged or even lost.

The most obvious transfer process is the intergenerational transfer of the underlying knowledge of intangible cultural heritage. Intangible heritage is constantly recreated by groups in response to their environment, their interactions with nature and their history, providing them with a sense of identity and continuity, and it is transmitted from generation to generation (WTO, 2012). For Rickly-Boyd (2012b), authenticity is connected to aura, since they result from and are embedded in ritual and tradition. However, that tradition can be altered after transmitting it to the younger generation. Social and economic factors can distort the authentic nature of the reconstruction of knowledge that the recipients (that is, the younger generation) conduct.

Zhu (2012) documents how intangible heritage knowledge is transferred to a dongba. Witnessing rituals in the family, having mentors, and even attending formal training activities were relevant to 'inherit' the knowledge (Zhu, 2012). The formal training activities lack the necessary social context to fully acquire the knowledge, so social embeddedness is also required (Zhu, 2012). These knowledge transfers assume that source and recipient do want to teach/receive the knowledge, but it cannot be taken for granted.

According to Reisinger and Steiner (2006a), one of the two meanings contained in the term 'authenticity' is related to a human attribute (the other one refers to genuineness of artefacts and events). Authenticity as a human characteristic refers to 'being one's true self or being true to one's essential nature' (Reisinger & Steiner, 2006a, p. 299). Wang (1999) and Cohen (2007) have classified this interpretation of authenticity in the light of the existentialist discourse of the concept. However, from the knowledge perspective, this human-attribute view of authenticity can be observed in a more complex way, since younger individuals in a knowledge transfer setting of intangible cultural heritage can feel two opposing forces. The first one would be viewing authenticity as following one's aspirations and desire to evolve after being exposed to new cultural environments, and the second one would be observing authenticity as keeping values and cultural elements that the society and relevant groups have embedded in earlier stages of life and consequently in 'one's essential nature.' The former one reflects a 'future orientation' associated with the idea of 'being true to oneself' and the latter could be defined in terms of a 'past orientation' which decisively impose the tradition and cultural elements from the past as a major force in determining one's life path. This tension could result in a smooth transfer process, or in adaptation or even rejection of key intangible heritage knowledge which permeates modern cultural elements and alters the 'objective' authenticity. Wesener's findings (2017) in his empirical analysis in an intangible heritage context can relate to this, since there are people only welcoming 'new experiences' closely related to traditional processes, and others embracing new processes and structures as authentic.

Zhu (2012) describes the evolution/clash of a local culture that suddenly becomes an attraction after the inscription of Lijian (China) in the UNESCO World Heritage List. The residents who live in the destination have elements of judgment to evaluate whether their culture and heritage remains authentic when their distinctive traditional culture is being eroded by commodification (Zhou, Zhang, Zhang, & Ma, 2015). In intangible heritage destinations, locals with traditional knowledge are exposed and confronted to socio-economic transitions which can alter the authenticity of the knowledge (Zhu, 2012). Zhou et al. (2015) outline that authenticity is a concept that derives its meaning only when comparing to its opposite, since people is aware of authenticity when the environment is gradually becoming inauthentic Thus, authenticity can be deemed altered or lost, causing social tension and family frictions, even before the tourist arrives.

Another relevant strategy to protect, safeguard and exploit the intangible cultural heritage is the creation of museums or other cultural institutions and even to disseminate digital content. These knowledge repositories should carefully integrate the knowledge and its context to keep the elements underpinning its authenticity. Regarding intangible heritage and its preservation, the classical museums have evolved to new formats such as open-air museums which are also concerned with the broader cultural and social environment in which they exist, including a sense of place and locality (Alivizatou, 2016).

Cultural institutions worldwide face many challenges in understanding and presenting intangible heritage (Alivizatou, 2016). Dalkir (2005) defines tacit knowledge management as the process of capturing the experience and expertise of the individual in an organization or community and making it available to anyone who needs it. Museums play a relevant role in this collective codification process that entails a transfer of knowledge. Knowledge has to be analysed and codified in such a way that it can become a part of the existing knowledge base (Dalkir, 2005) of the community. But this codification process can have negative similarities with commodification, since it is also producing a substitute of the reality where many nuances and details are lost in the translation and adaptation to tourism needs. Like cultural commodification, the knowledge codification in the knowledge transfer processes can destroy local authenticity.

The implication and participation of the community with the cultural institutions to transfer their knowledge provide authenticity. This is so because the knowledge stems from the source and it is not the result of outsiders' descriptions and interpretation that do not reflect the cultural framework, values and identity that sustain the intangible heritage. Oral histories and traditional knowledge and beliefs are increasingly incorporated in official museum narratives (Alivizatou, 2016). According to Halewood & Hannam (2001), the lack of authenticity often stems from the commodification processes, since they provide an alienating and explicit exchange value. Thus, Cohen and Cohen (2012) mention stagnation occurs when local residents have to dress and behave in petrified traditional ways in 'living museums.' These isolated representations are somehow separated from the original reality and prevent any experience of authenticity (MacCannell, 1992).

However, hyperreality is an element in modern tourism (Yang & Wall, 2016) and the digital approach to many cultural sites and events complement the tourism experience. In that sense, staged authenticity can be preferred to the real or original manifestation of the cultural elements due to sustainability and fragility concerns about the heritage (Cohen, 1995; Yang & Wall, 2016).

Special attention should be also paid to tour guides who often become intermediaries of the experience related to intangible cultural heritage, as they become first recipients but also sources of the intangible heritage knowledge. The analysis of the knowledge authenticity with regard to tour guides require to review the conditions to avoid the superficial approach it can take. Training activities and embeddedness in the practice are paramount to construct the knowledge they will have to share with tourists in a later stage. Their role as translators and boundary spanning with tourists who possess another cultural framework than the one the intangible heritage has is very relevant to effectively transfer knowledge. If tour guides are locals, the training process is more effective and efficient, but the subsequent knowledge transfer to tourists will be more problematic (language and cultural barriers). If tour guides are not so familiar with the heritage culture, as it is frequent with foreign tour guides with similar nationalities than the tourists, their absorptive capacity can be a problem to learn the heritage knowledge since they lack prior knowledge to be able to understand it (Szulanski, 1996).

Knowledge transfer to the tourist and authenticity

Regarding the demand perspective, the encounter between tourists and individuals who possess knowledge about the intangible cultural heritage and/or knowledge repositories on the topic is often evaluated by the former in terms of the level of authenticity that the experience provides. Thus, attraction and satisfaction as key competitive variables regarding destinations are affected by knowledge transfers happening prior and during the visit.

MacCannell (1973) indicated that tourists are motivated by a desire to see life as it is really lived, even to get in with the natives. Though this can be questioned in light of the tourist who just seeks fun and excitement (e.g. Boorstin, 1992), the recognition of different needs for tourism and expectations, and the postmodernity view of authenticity still holds for several tourism products. Tourists seem to seek authenticity in varying degrees of intensity (Cohen, 1988). In the case of intangible heritage, the addition of the time dimension increases the value of the potential experience, since the tourist does not only anticipate the exoticism of the spatial difference but also the ancient origin of the underlying knowledge. But the mere observation can be extended to a deeper need for involvement, and there are places where people seek out to satisfy their learning needs, like museums (Falk & Dierking, 2000). The classical economic framework distinguishing between search and experience goods (Klein, 1998) can provide interesting insights for this discussion. The 'intangible' nature of heritage knowledge causes tourists to be uncertain about the potential satisfaction of their tourism needs in a higher degree than tangible heritage. Though tourism is widely considered a service, the tangible nature of the attractions reveals some product attributes for which much information can be obtained before the purchase; in contrast, intangible heritage, though repetitive and recreated along time, is more limited in providing that kind of information and the uncertainty about the tourism experience could be higher. Authenticity could help to make informed travel decisions for those segments.

Lord (1999) addresses the demand of cultural tourism by presenting four categories of tourists: the greatly motivated ones, the motivated in part ones, the adjunct ones, and the accidental ones. For the two first groups, the experience provided by the intangible heritage is central on their trip, and it suggests their willingness in knowing more about the intangible cultural setting and heritage. For the other two groups, though their participation in knowledge transfer activities cannot be dismissed, the ex ante perception of authenticity can be a major driver to engage in the visit to the intangible cultural setting due to their initial lack of motivation and interest in the cultural product.

The first knowledge transfer process occurs when the individual (or leading person in a joint decision-making) obtains data, information and insights about the intangible heritage destination, often in a competitive format. Systematic patterns of tourist behaviour are attributable to the information available to them (Fodness & Murray, 1999). Brochures, guidebooks, digital content, articles in specialized publications or magazines/newspapers, and other written promotional material issued by tour operators and travel agents are codified knowledge. Much of this knowledge usually implies a transfer of the introduction to the intangible heritage knowledge in a cool format. UNESCO's listings and other certification methods such as studies by historians are ways to coolly authenticate intangible heritage (Cohen & Cohen, 2012). Nevertheless, this cool authentication is not effective if that knowledge is not successfully transferred to the tourist who must assimilate that knowledge and integrate it in his/her prior experiences. Heritage attractions reveal as a means for the discovery and articulation of identity, with public administrations often selecting particular versions to communicate and acting as a mediator (Henderson, 2002). Once the relevance of authenticity has been outlined by segments (Cohen, 1988; Xie, 2003), the knowledge transferred in these formats can attract tourists in search of authenticity, probably including those who value external status or recognition of the experience.

Other tourists who have experienced the intangible heritage in the destination (i.e. relatives, friends, co-workers, etc.) and travel agents with direct experience on the specific destination will also transfer knowledge and will include in their message their perception or even feelings about its authenticity. This hot authentication (Cohen & Cohen, 2012) is based on tacit knowledge and tends to be customized as a result of the interaction with the potential tourist. The knowledge and hints that a potential tourist got from these sources reveal elements of authenticity that can appeal the tourist in a different register than the one provided by cool formats.

The message of authenticity can be reinforced in 'at destination' referrals (Wang, Severt, & Rompf, 2006), which become knowledge transfers with recommendations and comments by locals. These referrals by individuals who are in direct contact with and even live the intangible heritage on a daily basis transmit a higher degree of authenticity based on the source credibility. In fact, hosts make their own interpretation of authenticity (Zhou et al., 2015). The relevance of locals' referrals and recommendations are two-fold: on the one hand, it attracts tourists whose main motivations for the visit are not the intangible heritage; on the other hand, it contributes to appreciate the authenticity of the experience based on the insiders'/locals' comments. This last aspect connects with the satisfaction of the experience as one of the pillars of destination competitiveness.

Tourist's satisfaction is another relevant aspect of tourism competitiveness, and the perception of authenticity through knowledge transfer about the intangible heritage can increase it. In that sense, destinations with intangible heritage provide the tourist with a formative experience where learning usually occurs. There are several sources at the destination which provide knowledge to tourists about the intangible heritage's history and its cultural meaning. Not only tourists interact with locals in different degrees, but they also visit museums, participate in local tours, access digital and written sources about the heritage, etc.

Van Winkle and Lagay (2012) empirically find that tourists increase their perception of authenticity when learning in their travels. The knowledge transfers at the destination in which the tourists participate are endowed with a higher degree of authenticity. As in museums, people engage in some learning characterized by its free-choice nature (Falk & Dierking, 2000). Most visitors learn something important during their visit to heritage sites (Prentice, Witt, & Hamer, 1998). The intangible heritage setting is one of those contexts where tourists decide to experience and learn about past culture. Rickly-Boyd (2012a) observes that the experience in a heritage site includes the past as a function of the present through symbolic cues and narrative communication. Free-choice learning tends to be non-linear, personally motivated and characterized by a high degree of discretionary behaviour in the selection of the elements, places and times to learn (Falk & Dierking, 2000). Tourism presents a unique learning environment enabling both unplanned and planned opportunities (Van Winkle & Lagay, 2012).

Timothy (2011) states that several characteristics affect the heritage tourist's understanding and evaluation of experiences and behaviours, such as demographic and psychographic variables and places of origin. Falk and Dierking (2000) analyse learning in museums in a model of overlapping personal, sociocultural and physical contexts along time. This model has become very influential in the heritage field (King, 2015) and it shows how the personal context encompasses the preferred modes of learning and a variety of experiences and knowledge (Falk & Dierking, 2016). The learning styles, and the preferences for activities to learn in tourism experiences, also vary across different groups of tourists.

In the objective view of authenticity, the authentic experience is generated by the recognition of the toured objects as authentic (Wang, 1999). Hence, the validity of the knowledge source in the transfer is paramount. In the constructive perspective, events appear authentic not due to an inherent authenticity but because they are constructed as such from the perspective of beliefs and points of view (Wang, 1999). Under this theoretical orientation, the role of knowledge transfer is different since the emotional element and the transfer of stereotypes that fit the tourist's expectations occupy a central position in the mobilization of knowledge. Existential authenticity is based on the idea that people feel more freely self-expressed and authentic than in everyday life because they engage in non-ordinary activities (Wang, 1999). Though this shows an individual-centred process, knowledge transfers that would show a different reality away of daily routines and situations that the tourist experiences at home tend to foster that existential authenticity.

As for the specific sources with provide the knowledge, they have the power to transmit varying degrees of authenticity. Locals in the events and performances associated with the intangible heritage could leave the strongest impact on the tourist. The tourist learns some basic ideas of the practices, even when s/he does not fully understand the underlying values and meaning. MacCannell (1973) indicated that some tourists make incursions into the life of the society they visit, or are at least actually allowed to observe some aspects of daily life. Though the commodification of culture for tourism purposes could dilute the heritage, witnessing the practices and being able to construct knowledge from it increase the perception of authenticity if the event is 'credible.' Nevertheless, it is not possible to take for granted that locals are going to transmit their knowledge to tourists, because residents at some destinations could see sharing and preserving their culture as conflicting goals (Besculides, Lee, & McCormick, 2002). Furthermore, it also applies the paradox that the knowledge which is characterized or recognized as authentic reduces its degree of authenticity (Cohen, 2007; MacCannell, 1976), in the sense that the feeling of 'knowledge discovery' is somehow lost.

Museums and culture repositories (videos, digital content, books, etc.) on intangible heritage areas are also key elements in demand-oriented knowledge transfer processes, and where tourists can form an opinion/perception about authenticity. In that sense, museums and culture repositories along with tour guides are key elements in the recognition of authenticity, since authentication endow an event with authenticity (Cohen & Cohen, 2012). But the experience in the museum must be carefully designed in order to transfer knowledge and 'defend' authenticity. The mere presentation of expressions and representations de-contextualized from the original places where the knowledge was developed presents limitations to generate rents in the long term from that knowledge for most categories of tourists; staged or constructive authenticity could be hence rejected by many tourists who could only accept it under certain conditions (security problems, extreme rarity or accessibility, secondary or push motivations for the tourism experience, etc.). Old-fashioned museums de-authenticate the heritage (Cohen & Cohen, 2012). In addition, there could be some debate about the intensity of knowledge construction that tourists undertake in their visits to intangible heritage museums, but Falk and Dierking (2000) categorically assert that people do learn in museums. In fact, the learning that takes place in those free-choice learning settings is key for the survival of these institutions (Falk & Dierking, 2000) or for its competitiveness in the tourism industry. As for books and written material about the intangible heritage knowledge, they can complement the authenticity of the experience. The authentic reproduction of a pioneer village described by Rickly-Boyd (2012a) attempts to reinforce authenticity through meaning transfer with the village's guidebook.

Tour guides could be classified as an example of hot authentication, since they tend to preserve and reinforce the authenticity of intangible heritage often without being a well-recognized authenticating agent (Cohen & Cohen, 2012). Rickly-Boyd (2012a) indicates that heritage interpreters are significant to the tourists' narrative engagement with their knowledge transfers, but Reisinger and Steiner (2006b) are more sceptical about the authenticity that tour guide interpretation can provide since tourists adopt a passive role with them. The knowledge tour guides provide can reinforce the perception of authenticity of intangible heritage by explaining its origin and historical connections. However, their knowledge transfer towards the tourist could also jeopardize his/her perception of objective authenticity by influencing the evaluation of its key characteristics due to the partially commercial goals which underlie the transfer. Those characteristics are origins, genuineness, pristinity, creativity/novelty, flow of life, and even sincerity (Cohen, 2007). Guides who have been embedded in the intangible heritage provide a more authentic experience, as Shackley (1994) suggests.

Conclusions

This work has analysed how knowledge transfer processes regarding intangible heritage can have an impact on authenticity, which is a variable with a significant impact on heritage tourism competitiveness. The knowledge nature of the intangible heritage makes it possible to use the framework of the knowledge-based view. Addressing authenticity under this view provides new academic implications in the long debate about the concept in tourism, apart from clarifying its role on destination competitiveness.

Several knowledge transfers occur at the destination that are relevant to offer authenticity in the intangible heritage attractions. The most strategic one is the intergenerational knowledge transfer since it safeguards its existence in the long- term. Shackley (1994) addresses the sustainability of the authenticity of the intangible cultural heritage, as old jobs are not kept and disappear due to modernization and economic forces. The new generations who acquire this knowledge can be confronted with the genuineness of a knowledge that they have not experienced in first person as part of their daily life. Though Cohen and Cohen (2012) contend that cool authentication can lead to fossilization and loss of value, knowledge transfers can invert this process due to the diffusion of the value of the intangible heritage and even the increase in the pride of keeping it. It would result in an increase of motivation for both sources and recipients in the knowledge transfer.

Codification processes in open-air museums, institutions that preserve living culture, and digital repositories, along with training processes for tour guides and heritage interpretation are also relevant knowledge transfers in the supply side of the heritage. Those transfers can entail a loss of authenticity if the cultural framework is not also conveyed. Destination management organizations should know the main elements in the planning and development of those processes to give advice on the retention and enhancement of authenticity, since modern tourism trends underline their role in increasing competitiveness in internal aspects of the destination.

The knowledge transfer perspective also sheds light on how authenticity affects destination competitiveness. Promotional activities and material, travel agents and previous visitors convey the authenticity of the destination, which is relevant for the attraction of tourists. The transfer interaction between locals with heritage knowledge and tourists increase the perception of higher authenticity and influences the latter's attraction to and the satisfaction with intangible heritage products. This interaction can have multiple barriers such as language, culture, space and time limitations, and even source motivation as overtourism is becoming a major problem in certain destinations. The experience provided by museums and tours is also relevant to increase the perception of authenticity and hence the satisfaction with intangible heritage knowledge. Destination management organizations have a clear role in most of the marketing activities that entail a knowledge transfer to the tourists and can facilitate the enhancement of authenticity with them. Their role in those intra-destination barriers of demand-based knowledge transfer with an effect on authenticity is more limited but as leading agents in the tourism industry should also contribute to reduce them. In particular, the learning challenges associated with heritage knowledge and the strengthening of sustainable tourism should be on their agenda.

Disclosure statement

No potential conflict of interest was reported by the author.

References

Alavi, M., & Leidner, D. E. (2001). Knowledge management and knowledge management systems: Conceptual foundations and research issues. *MIS Quarterly*, *25*(1), 107–136.

Alivizatou, M. (2016). *Intangible heritage and the museum: New perspectives on cultural preservation*. New York, NY: Routledge.

Besculides, A., Lee, M. E., & McCormick, P. J. (2002). Residents' perceptions of the cultural benefits of tourism. *Annals of Tourism Research, 29*(2), 303–319.

Boonzaaier, C., & Wels, H. (2018). Authenticity lost? The significance of cultural villages in the conservation of heritage in South Africa. *Journal of Heritage Tourism, 13*(2), 181–193.

Boorstin, D. J. (1992). *The image: A guide to pseudo-events in America*. New York, NY: Vintage Books.

Buhalis, D. (2000). Marketing: The competitive destination of the future. *Tourism Management, 21*(1), 97–116.

Carson, D., & Harwood, S. (2007). *Authenticity as competitive advantage for remote tourism destinations. Proceedings of the 17th annual CAUTHE 2007: Tourism-past achievements, future challenges*. Sydney: University of Technology.

Chhabra, D. (2010). *Sustainable marketing of cultural and heritage tourism*. New York, NY: Routledge.

Chhabra, D. (2012). Authenticity of the objectively authentic. *Annals of Tourism Research, 39*(1), 499–502.

Chhabra, D., Lee, W., Zhao, S., & Scott, K. (2013). Marketing of ethnic food experiences: Authentication analysis of Indian cuisine abroad. *Journal of Heritage Tourism, 8*(2–3), 145–157.

Cohen, E. (1995). Contemporary tourism - trends and challenges: Sustainable authenticity or contrived post-modernity? In R. Butler & D. Pearce (Eds.), *Change in tourism: People, places, processes* (pp. 12–29). London: Routledge.

Cohen, E. (1988). Authenticity and commoditization in tourism. *Annals of tourism research, 15*(3), 371–386.

Cohen, E. (2007). 'Authenticity' in tourism studies: Aprés la Lutte. *Tourism Recreation Research, 32*(2), 75–82.

Cohen, E., & Cohen, S. A. (2012). Authentication: Hot and cool. *Annals of Tourism Research, 39*(3), 1295–1314.

Cracolici, M. F., & Nijkamp, P. (2009). The attractiveness and competitiveness of tourist destinations: A study of Southern Italian regions. *Tourism management, 30*(3), 336–344.

Crouch, G. I. (2011). Destination competitiveness: An analysis of determinant attributes. *Journal of Travel Research, 50* (1), 27–45.

Custódio Santos, M., Ferreira, A. M., & Costa, C. (2014). Influential factors in the competitiveness of mature tourism destinations. *Tourism & Management Studies, 10*(1), 73–81.

Dalkir, K. (2005). *Knowledge management in theory and practice*. Burlington, MA: Elsevier Butterworth–Heinemann.

Darr, E. D., & Kurtzberg, T. R. (2000). An investigation of partner similarity dimensions on knowledge transfer. *Organizational Behavior and Human Decision Processes, 82*(1), 28–44.

Datta, P., Bigham, G., Zou, Z., & Hill, G. (2015). A global study of heritage site ecology, proclivity & loyalty. *Journal of Hospitality and Tourism Management, 25*, 19–29.

Enright, M. J., & Newton, J. (2004). Tourism destination competitiveness: A quantitative approach. *Tourism management, 25*(6), 777–788.

Esfehani, M. H., & Albrecht, J. N. (2018). Roles of intangible cultural heritage in tourism in natural protected areas. *Journal of Heritage Tourism, 13*(1), 15–29.

Falk, J. H., & Dierking, L. D. (2000). *Learning from museums: Visitor experiences and the making of meaning*. Lanham, MD: AltaMira Press.

Falk, J. H., & Dierking, L. D. (2016). *The museum experience revisited*. New York, NY: Routledge.

Fodness, D., & Murray, B. (1999). A model of tourist information search behavior. *Journal of Travel Research, 37*(3), 220–230.

Fyall, A., & Wanhill, S. (2008). Destinations. In C. Cooper, J. Fletcher, A. Fyall, D. Gilbert, & S. Wanhill (Eds.), *Tourism: Principles and practice* (pp. 474–503). Harlow: Pearson Education.

García-Almeida, D. J., & Hormiga, E. (2017). Immigration and the competitiveness of an island tourism destination: A knowledge-based reputation analysis of Lanzarote, Canary Islands. *Island Studies Journal, 12*(1), 207–222.

Gonzalez, M. V. (2008). Intangible heritage tourism and identity. *Tourism Management, 29*(4), 807–810.

Halewood, C., & Hannam, K. (2001). Viking heritage tourism: Authenticity and commodification. *Annals of tourism research, 28*(3), 565–580.

Henderson, J. C. (2002). Heritage attractions and tourism development in Asia: A comparative study of Hong Kong and Singapore. *International Journal of Tourism Research, 4*(5), 337–344.

King, B. (2015). Introduction. In B. King & B. Lord (Eds.), *The manual of museum learning* (pp. 3–10). Lanham, MD: Rowman & Littlefield.

Klein, L. (1998). Evaluating the potential of interactive media through a new lens: Search versus experience goods. *Journal of Business Research, 41*, 195–203.

Knudsen, D. C., Rickly, J. M., & Vidon, E. S. (2016). The fantasy of authenticity: Touring with Lacan. *Annals of Tourism Research, 58*, 33–45.

Kolar, T., & Zabkar, V. (2010). A consumer-based model of authenticity: An oxymoron or the foundation of cultural heritage marketing? *Tourism Management, 31*(5), 652–664.

Koohang, A., & Paliszkiewicz, J. (2013). Knowledge construction in e-learning: An empirical validation of an active learning model. *Journal of Computer Information Systems, 53*(3), 109–114.

Kozac, M., Baloglu, S., & Bahar, O. (2009). Measuring destination competitiveness: Multiple destinations versus multiple nationalities. *Journal of Hospitality Marketing and Management, 19*, 56–71.

Kumar, J. A., & Ganesh, L. S. (2009). Research on knowledge transfer in organizations: A morphology. *Journal of Knowledge Management, 13*(4), 161–174.

Lee, L., Lajoie, S. P., Poitras, E. G., Nkangu, M., & Doleck, T. (2017). Co-regulation and knowledge construction in an online synchronous problem based learning setting. *Education and Information Technologies, 22*(4), 1623–1650.

Leiper, N. (1979). The framework of tourism: Towards a definition of tourism, tourist, and the tourist industry. *Annals of Tourism Research, 6*(4), 390–407.

Leonard, D., & Sensiper, S. (1998). The role of tacit knowledge in group innovation. *California Management Review, 40*, 112–132.

Liyanage, C., Elhag, T., Ballal, T., & Li, Q. (2009). Knowledge communication and translation – a knowledge transfer model. *Journal of Knowledge Management, 13*(3), 118–131.

López-Guzmán, T., & Santa-Cruz, F. G. (2017). Visitors' experiences with intangible cultural heritage: A case study from Córdoba, Spain. *Journal of Heritage Tourism, 12*(4), 410–415.

Lord, G. D. (1999). *The power of cultural tourism.* A keynote presentation presented at the 1999 Wisconsin Heritage Tourism Conference, Lac du Flambeau, WI.

MacCannell, D. (1973). Staged authenticity: Arrangements of social space in tourist settings. *American Journal of Sociology, 79*(3), 589–603.

MacCannell, D. (1976). *The tourist: A new theory of the leisure class.* New York: Schocken.

MacCannell, D. (1992). *Empty meeting grounds.* London: Routledge.

Nosek, J. T. (2004). Group cognition as a basis for supporting group knowledge creation and sharing. *Journal of Knowledge Management, 8*(4), 54–64.

Olsen, K. (2002). Authenticity as a concept in tourism research: The social organization of the experience of authenticity. *Tourist Studies, 2*(2), 159–182.

Pereira Roders, A., & van Oers, R. (2011). Editorial: Bridging cultural heritage and sustainable development. *Journal of Cultural Heritage Management and Sustainable Development, 1*(1), 5–14.

Peterson, R. A. (2005). In search of authenticity. *Journal of Management Studies, 42*(5), 1083–1098.

Pfeilstetter, R. (2015). Heritage entrepreneurship. Agency-driven promotion of the Mediterranean diet in Spain. *International Journal of Heritage Studies, 21*(3), 215–231.

Prentice, R. (1993). *Tourism and heritage attractions.* London: Routledge.

Prentice, R. C., Witt, S. F., & Hamer, C. (1998). Tourism as experience: The case of heritage parks. *Annals of Tourism Research, 25*(1), 1–24.

Reisinger, Y., & Steiner, C. J. (2006a). Reconceptualizing object authenticity. *Annals of Tourism Research, 33*(1), 65–86.

Reisinger, Y., & Steiner, C. J. (2006b). Reconceptualising interpretation: The role of tour guides in authentic tourism. *Current Issues in Tourism, 9*(6), 481–498.

Rickly-Boyd, J. M. (2012a) 'Through the magic of authentic reproduction': Tourists' perceptions of authenticity in a pioneer village. *Journal of Heritage Tourism, 7*(2), 127–144.

Rickly-Boyd, J. M. (2012b). Authenticity & aura: A Benjaminian approach to tourism. *Annals of Tourism Research, 39* (1), 269–289.

Shackley, M. (1994). When is the past? Authenticity and the commoditization of heritage. *Tourism Management, 15* (5), 396–397.

Szulanski, G. (1996). Exploring internal stickiness: Impediments to the transfer of best practice within the firm. *Strategic Management Journal, 17*, 27–43.

Timothy, D. J. (2011). *Cultural and heritage tourism: An introduction.* Bristol: Channel View Publications.

Timothy, D. J., & Boyd, S. W. (2003). *Heritage tourism.* Harlow: Pearson Education.

Timothy, D. J., & Ron, A. S. (2013). Understanding heritage cuisines and tourism: Identity, image, authenticity, and change. *Journal of Heritage Tourism, 8*(2–3), 99–104.

UNESCO. (2003). *Convention for the safeguarding of the intangible cultural heritage.* Paris: Author.

UNESCO. (2006). *Proceedings. International Conference on the Safeguarding of Tangible and Intangible Cultural Heritage: Towards an Integrated Approach.* Paris: Author.

UNESCO. (2018). *The Nara Document on Authenticity – UNESCO World Heritage Centre.* Retrieved from June 2018 https://whc.unesco.org/document/116018

Van Winkle, C. M., & Lagay, K. (2012). Learning during tourism: The experience of learning from the tourist's perspective. *Studies in Continuing Education, 34*(3), 339–355.

Walter, P. (2017). Culinary tourism as living history: Staging, tourist performance and perceptions of authenticity in a Thai cooking school. *Journal of Heritage Tourism, 12*(4), 365–379.

Wang, N. (1999). Rethinking authenticity in tourism experience. *Annals of Tourism Research, 26*(2), 349–370.

Wang, Y., Severt, D., & Rompf, P. (2006). Examining the nature and dynamics of at-destination recommendations: The local experts' perspective. *Journal of Hospitality & Leisure Marketing, 13*(3–4), 139–160.

Wesener, A. (2017). Adopting 'things of the little': Intangible cultural heritage and experiential authenticity of place in the Jewellery Quarter, Birmingham. *International Journal of Heritage Studies, 23*(2), 141–155.

WTO. (2012). *Tourism and intangible cultural heritage.* Madrid: UNWTO.

Xie, P. F. (2003). The bamboo-beating dance in Hainan, China: Authenticity and commodification. *Journal of Sustainable Tourism*, *11*(1), 5–16.

Xie, P. F., & Wall, G. (2002). Visitors' perceptions of authenticity at cultural attractions in Hainan, China. *International Journal of Tourism Research*, *4*(5), 353–366.

Yang, L., & Wall, G. (2016). *Planning for ethnic tourism*. New York, NY: Routledge.

Zhou, Q. B., Zhang, J., Zhang, H., & Ma, J. (2015). A structural model of host authenticity. *Annals of Tourism Research*, *55*, 28–45.

Zhu, Y. (2012). Performing heritage: Rethinking authenticity in tourism. *Annals of Tourism Research*, *39*(3), 1495–1513.

Development of intangible cultural heritage as a sustainable tourism resource: the intangible cultural heritage practitioners' perspectives

Soojung Kim, Michelle Whitford and Charles Arcodia

ABSTRACT

Authentic intangible cultural heritage (ICH) provides a community with a unique selling point in the globally competitive tourism industry. The process of commodification of ICH, however, has threatened its authenticity and thus sustainable tourism approaches are required to achieve successful transmission and promotion of ICH as a sustainable tourism resource. This paper explores the priorities of ICH practitioners in relation to the development of ICH as a sustainable tourism resource, by utilising South Korea as a case study. The results revealed that from the ICH practitioners' perspectives, authenticity is a holistic notion integrating the transmitted customs, inherited meanings and the practitioners' identities. ICH practitioners agree with the potential positive symbiotic relationship between transmission of authentic ICH and promotion of ICH as a tourism resource. To achieve the positive symbiotic relationship, locals' awareness of ICH, ICH practitioner empowerment and parallel development between tourism development and transmission of ICH are necessary. To date, the practitioner approach to the authenticity of ICH and ICH as a sustainable tourism resource is little explored in the literature, thus this paper makes a valuable addition to the area of sustainable heritage tourism.

Introduction

Globally, intangible cultural heritage (ICH) is fast becoming a significant resource in cultural heritage tourism. ICH refers to oral traditions, performing arts, rituals, and festive events that have been transmitted over generations and are thus recognised by communities as part of their cultural heritage (UNESCO, 2003). ICH represents strong cultural authenticity and facilitates a deep understanding of a destination's culture, which in turn, strengthens the competitiveness of ICH within the broader arena of cultural heritage tourism (Chhabra, Healy, & Sills, 2003; Daniel, 1996; Gonzalez, 2008; Xie, 2003) and creates socio-economic benefits for stakeholders (Esfehani & Albrecht, 2018)

To varying degrees, ICH has been easily commodified into a tourism product that satisfies tourists. Not surprisingly then, this process of commodification has threatened ICH authenticity, when it should be safeguarded for the cultural continuity of communities. Therefore, an approach that facilitates the development of ICH as a sustainable tourism resource has been strongly advised (World Tourism Organisation, 2012) to ensure that the cultural and socio-economic values of ICH are safeguarded. This responsibility falls primarily with the ICH practitioners therefore, their perspectives need to be explored regarding ICH as a sustainable tourism resource. ICH practitioners are the people:

> within or across communities who have distinct skills, knowledge, experience, or other characteristics, and thus perform specific roles in the present and future practice, re-creation and/or transmission of their intangible cultural heritage as, for example, cultural custodians, practitioners and, where appropriate, apprentice. (Asia/pacific Cultural Centre for UNESCO [ACCU], 2006, p. 4)

ICH practitioners are considered the people who automatically and appropriately safeguard and transmit ICH to the next generation (Lenzerini, 2011), thus without these practitioners, transmission of ICH to the next generation cannot be accomplished (Bakar, Osman, Bachok, & Ibrahim, 2014).

In spite of the importance of ICH practitioners in the development of ICH as a sustainable tourism resource, little research has been undertaken to explore ICH from a sustainable tourism resource perspective and even less research has been undertaken to explore ICH practitioner perspectives on ICH as a sustainable tourism resource. To address these research gaps, this paper will explore ICH practitioners perspectives on the development of ICH as a sustainable tourism resource. To achieve this, the first objective is to examine ICH practitioners' perspectives on the authenticity of ICH, the transformation and commodification of ICH. The second objective is to identify the major strategies facilitating ICH to be a sustainable tourism resource. For governments who are interested in safeguarding and promoting ICH as a tourism resource, understanding practitioners' perspectives on the development of ICH as a tourism resource and the identified strategies will support to develop effective policies which benefits the practitioners and attracts tourists looking for enjoying ICH.

Authenticity and ICH

Within the heritage tourism literature, there is little argument that the value of heritage is evaluated based on its authenticity (Bortolotto, 2007). Within the same body of literature, however, there is an ongoing debate as to what constitutes authenticity. Authenticity has been considered as uniqueness and/or distinctiveness from others (Ashworth, 2013; Bessiere, 1998) and providing the cultural identity of communities (Macdonald, 2004). Moreover, authenticity involves traditions, techniques, spirit, feeling and historic and social dimensions of cultural heritage (Munjeri, 2004) which together, represent a sense of historical and cultural continuity (Bortolotto, 2007). Authenticity is diversely constructed by various stakeholders and by the social and political situations in which they exist (Zhu, 2012). For example, when tangible cultural heritage items (e.g. historical monuments) were of international interests, the authenticity of a resource was scientifically interpreted, being defined by materials, design and location of the tangible resource (UNESCO, 1972). However, as intangible values became globally important, scientific authenticity was criticised as being too restrictive for understanding the social value of cultural heritage (i.e. craftsmanship or inherited meanings) (UNESCO, 1996). Therefore, the adoption of a different approach to understanding authenticity was deemed necessary (Bortolotto, 2007).

While most research on authenticity follows three dominant approaches; objective, constructive, and existential (Wang, 1999), a comparatively new approach has emerged. It incorporates the three dominant approaches to complement three other dominant approaches that have limitations, in order to understand the value of cultural heritage (Belhassen, Caton, & Stewart, 2008). The term authenticity and these associated approaches underpin and shape the understanding of ICH authenticity.

Objective authenticity concerns the originality and genuineness of a tourism resource. The authenticity of the resource is interpreted and is clearly distinguished between the original and the fake or the authentic and the spurious (Bortolotto, 2007; Hafstein, 2004). This notion of objective authenticity was introduced in MacCanell's seminal study (1976), claiming that a host community provides a limited range of culture to tourists as 'staged authenticity' on a front stage, while 'genuine authentic culture' occurs in the backstage and to which tourists have limited access. Objective authenticity links with Cohen and Cohen's 'Cool Authenticity' (2012, p. 1298), referring to 'the authenticity of an object, site, custom, role or person is declared to be original, genuine or real, rather than a copy, fake or spurious'.

This raises the significant question of 'who has the power to determine what will count as authentic?' (Bruner & Kirshenblatt Gimblett, 1994, p. 459). According to Cohen and Cohen (2012), objective authenticity or cool authenticity is generally identified by 'some individuals, recognised as "experts", or in certain highly formalised and institutionalised positions' (p. 1306). For example, UNESCO is a typical example of an international agency, which has the expertise and has achieved a hegemonic position in identifying and determining the objective authenticity of ICH. UNESCO established its list of ICH in 2008 with the purpose of increasing awareness of their significance and ensuring better protection. Additionally, national governments have the power to authenticate cultural heritage. For example, the Korean national government designates ICH elements which are regarded as representing authentic Korean culture.

Nevertheless, the designation by an international agency or a national government is often criticised as too much of a top-down, 'Occidentalist' approach (Cohen & Cohen, 2012; Hitchcock, King, & Parnwell, 2010), underpinned with political motives and/or interests (Belhassen et al., 2008; Cohen & Cohen, 2012; Wang, 1999). For example, UNESCO has been criticised for its 'Occidentalist' perspectives when defining and designating the authenticity of cultural heritage (Hitchcock et al., 2010). Moreover, national governments have been criticised by Bendix (1989, p. 132) for identifying tradition and authenticity according to what it '.... will accomplish for them what they intend it to accomplish'. In short, when a national government regards ICH as significant for cultural, social and economic development, then they designate ICH as authentic. Bruner (2005, p. 150) argued that a 'fundamental question ... is not whether an object or site is authentic, but rather who has the authority to authenticate ... [t]his is a matter of power'.

Constructive authenticity depends on individual perspectives and interpretations and maintains that there is no absolute originality of toured elements (i.e. objective tourism) (Bruner, 1994). Post-modernism argues that there is no actual, genuine and objective reality and this notion links to the perspective of constructive and existential authenticity in a tourism resource (Zhu, 2012). From tourists' perspectives, authenticity is constructed and projected by their home cultures; therefore, the authenticity of a toured object is regarded as a symbolic authenticity. Consequently, constructive authenticity is 'a projection of tourists' own beliefs, expectations, preferences, stereotyped images, and consciousness onto toured objects, particularly onto toured others' (Wang, 1999, p. 355). From host community perspectives, authenticity is 'contemporary understanding of the past culture' (Zhou, Zhang, Zhang, & Ma, 2015, p. 30) that is underpinned by constructive authenticity and traditional performances (i.e. ICH) are still authentic even when the language and/or customs are transformed based on contemporary understandings. Host communities evolve in response to social changes, and the changes influence and characterise the feature/s of authenticity (Chhabra, 2009; Zhou et al., 2015).

Existential authenticity places value on people themselves, such as the tourists'/locals' identity (Wang, 1999) and/or their experience (Pons, 2003) rather than showing concern for tourism resources. For example, Wang (1999) argued that tourists' purpose in heritage tourism is to identify their 'real self' through insights into the places associated with their history (i.e. cultural heritage). Moreover, Steiner and Reisinger (2006) stated that 'authenticity is a choice that people make' (p. 309). From this perspective, host communities' reproduction or alteration of their culture (e.g. traditional culture) is still authentic because the host community decides and chooses how to present their culture to others. Additionally, a community's traditional culture is 'entitled to change and evolve in response to their changing circumstances; authenticity always is a self-judgment' (Steiner & Reisinger, 2006, p. 311). While existential authenticity is a state, Zhu (2012) introduced performative authenticity, emphasising the dynamic process of 'becoming' authentic through the ongoing interaction between the traditional performers (e.g. ICH practitioners) and the external world (e.g. tourists). Similarly, Cohen and Cohen (2012) linked existential authenticity with 'hot authentication' referring to 'an imminent, reiterative, informal performative process of creating, preserving, and reinforcing an object's, site's, or events' authenticity' (Cohen & Cohen, 2012, p. 1300). Hot authentication argues the performative reinforcement, such as making offerings or practicing traditional dance, facilitates tourists in feeling their identity and/or feeling cultural authenticity (Cohen & Cohen, 2012).

As the latter two concepts of authenticity (i.e. constructive and existential authenticity) are introduced and adopted in tourism research, objective authenticity has diminished in value because it lacks ontological perspective and thus has limitations in exploring tourists' perspectives and motivations (Reisinger & Steiner, 2006; Wang, 1999). Nevertheless, objective authenticity should continue to carry conceptual value, because abandoning objective authenticity can cause the toured object and its originality to be outweighed by tourists' motivation and it can subsequently lose the inherited idea and distinctiveness of the toured object (Belhassen & Caton, 2006). For many scholars, objective authenticity remains a common reference point, especially in the context of heritage tourism (Chhabra 2010). To reduce the gaps in these three main categories of authenticity, theoplacity authenticity was introduced by integrating the three categories.

Theoplacity, introduced by Belhassen et al. (2008), is an integrated notion of authenticity combining 'the elements of place, belief, action, and self, which exist in dialogue and which act together to produce the complex notion of authenticity' (Belhassen et al., 2008, p. 685). That is, theoplacity argues that tourists seeking existential authenticity tend to prefer them in an objectivist setting (Chhabra, 2010b). For example, authenticity of ICH is a result of interaction between the cultural value of ICH (i.e. objective authenticity) and individuals' beliefs (e.g. locals, tourists, or ICH practitioners) and their performances (e.g. tourists' experiences of practicing traditional craftsmanship, ICH practitioners' experience of interacting with tourists). Moreover, theoplacity recognises the issue of political power, which influences authenticity (Belhassen et al., 2008). For example, if a national government either agrees with or refuses to identify the historical and cultural value (i.e. objective authenticity) of certain ICH, this decision will impact on local perceptions and tourist experiences. Based on the various concepts underpinning the authenticity of ICH, this study will explore how ICH practitioners interpret and understand the authenticity.

Authenticity and sustainable tourism resource

Facilitating sustainability has been an imperative in tourism for over two decades, because among other things, tourism activities have been deemed to have an impact on the ecological and socio-cultural environment (Garrod & Fyall, 1998). However, there still is no exact definition of sustainable tourism because sustainable tourism includes a great number of different dimensions, according to the different background and perceptions of those who are defining it (Garrod & Fyall, 2000; Saarinen, 2006). Nevertheless, it is normally agreed and accepted that sustainable tourism is a dimension of and contributes to, sustainable development. Sustainable development is the 'development that meets the needs of the present without compromising the ability of future generations to meet their own needs' (Brundtland et al., 1987, p. 43). Sustainable tourism then implies that tourism activities satisfy the social and economic needs of the present, but does not result in the serious degradation of the natural and cultural environment, in order for future generations to have equitable access to them (Garrod & Fyall, 1998).

Sustainable tourism can be understood with both community-based and resource-based approaches which are not mutually exclusive and impact each other. Community-based approaches advocate tourism which brings a better quality of community (Hunter, 1997; Saarinen, 2006; Tsaur, Lin, & Lin, 2006) and importantly contributes to community empowerment and self-reliance (Chambers, 1994). Community-based approaches strongly advise community participation in tourism decision making because communities need to reflect their interests in decisions so that benefits from the decision can be distributed (Hall & Richards, 2002; Robinson, 1999). A lack of financial resources and inequal power relations among stakeholders (e.g. government and local community) discourage community participation, nevertheless community participation is fundamental to achieve community empowerment and self-reliance.

A resource-based approach by contrast, focuses on the transmission of economic, cultural and social values of ICH. Resource-based approaches tended to follow the notion of carrying capacity, which argues to limit tourist numbers experiencing cultural heritage (e.g. ICH) to protect it from unacceptable degradation (e.g. loss of authenticity) (Saarinen, 2006). Carrying capacity, however, is a too limited approach which does not follow holistic views integrating economic, social and cultural dimensions, in which sustainable development advocates (Saarinen, 2006). In other words, safeguarding ICH and tourism development have the potential to have positive and constructive relationships (Loulanski & Loulanski, 2011). A resource-based approach therefore, is concerned not only with the authenticity of ICH but also with the economic and social values pertaining to ICH.

Authenticity and sustainable tourism then can either contribute to and/or detract from each other. Modern tourists are seeking 'pure', real and authentic culture, rather than 'staged' authenticity (MacCannell, 1976). A culturally authentic resource then is both culturally and economically valuable (Cohen, 2002). Given that interests in preservation and/or restoration of cultural heritage may be dependent on the economic value of the cultural heritage as a tourism resource (Cohen, 2002), authenticity may contribute to the sustainability of the resource. In contrast, however, a commodified ICH tourism resource may transform cultural heritage (e.g. traditional performances) and create a threat to the unique features of cultural heritage (i.e. authenticity), which in turn, perpetuates the problems associated with the authenticity of cultural heritage resources (Cohen, 2002). Thus, underpinned by the notion of sustainability and the relationship between authenticity and sustainability, ICH as a sustainable tourism resource aims to meet the economic and social needs of communities while maintaining and transmitting the cultural, economic and social values of ICH. Based on this notion of sustainable tourism resource, this study will explore the strategies facilitating ICH as a sustainable tourism resource, from ICH practitioners' perspectives.

Research method

Case study

This paper reports on a case study of South Korea as a single representative study. South Korea has a well-established reputation for developing and safeguarding ICH. For example, one public organisation called the Cultural Heritage Association, designates ICH elements, and currently, there are 138 national ICH in South Korea. Moreover, Korea has a systemised ICH apprenticeship system. The practitioner training system is offered at four levels, Beginners, Advanced, Assistant Instructors and Living Human Treasures. In 2017, the Cultural Heritage Association had designated a total of 6171 'Advanced' practitioners, a total of 286 'Assistant Instructors' and a total of 170 Living Human Treasures. Moreover, the Cultural Heritage Association established the National Intangible Heritage Centre in 2014 which is mainly responsible for safeguarding, inheritances, exchanges and the revitalisation of ICH. The National Intangible Heritage Centre protects successors' intellectual property rights and develops educational programs as well as hosting ICH exhibitions and/or events. Due to these efforts, following initiatives in China and Japan, Korea possesses the third-highest number of registered ICH with UNESCO. Furthermore, the UNESCO-accredited NGO for safeguarding the intangible cultural heritage of the Asia-Pacific region (ICHCAP) was established in Korea in 2011.

South Korea has promoted ICH to both domestic and international tourists. For example, 'Korea House', operated by the public organisation *Cultural Heritage Foundation,* provides tourists with opportunities to experience making and tasting traditional cuisine and/or watching UNESCO registered performances such as 'Pansori' (e.g. Korean traditional musical storytelling) or 'Arirang' (e.g. Korean traditional song) (Korea House, 2015). Moreover, ICH based regional festivals have been hosted and promote the regional ICH, such as Hansan Moshi (Weaving of fine ramie in the Hansan region) or Taekkeyon (Korean traditional martial arts).

Samples, data collection and analysis

A total of 25 interviews with ICH master practitioners took place between June 2016 and July 2016. By employing a purposive sampling, which selects potential respondents based on their expertise in the phenomenon (Cavana, Delahaye, & Sekaran, 2001), this study limited the scope of ICH practitioners to be interviewed into Assistant Instructors and Living Human Treasures as they are regarded as practicing ICH with higher functional and artistic skills than other levels of practitioners.

The researcher was able to access contact details of Assistant Instructor and/or Living Human Treasures through the Korean Heritage Administration web page. The researcher initially sent interview invitation emails to the potential participants. In most cases, however, the replies were delayed or were not given, thus they were contacted via a phone call to inform them of the research project, to personally invite them to participate in an interview and set schedules for the interviews. The final 25 interview participants are described in Table 1.

The interviews were digitally recorded and the recorded data were transcribed and translated from Korean into English by the researcher. The transcriptions were entered into the QSR NVivo data management program. The analysis process was a combination of content and thematic analysis as explained by Bowen (2009). Both content and thematic analyses include the process of coding and developing themes and sub-themes (Vaismoradi, 2013). The differences are that content analysis is more focused on quantitative counts of codes (Downe Wamboldt, 1992). In contrast, the thematic analysis aims to identify and report the patterns within the data by comparing codes and themes derived from the data (Braun & Clarke, 2006). This study considered both quantitative counts of codes and the patterns and relationships between codes and themes by adopting the combination of content and thematic analysis.

Results/discussions/implications

Authenticity of ICH from the practitioners' perspectives

This study revealed that ICH authenticity, from the practitioners' perspective, is a complicated notion that integrates the traditional custom of ICH, the inherited meaning and the practitioners' identity. Authenticity of ICH was divided into three categories: the emphasis on maintaining the original version of ICH [ICH 8, 9, 11, 21, 25], the emphasis on maintaining/safeguarding the meaning of ICH [ICH 1, 3, 4, 5, 6, 16], and the emphasis on the practitioners' identity [ICH 2, 3, 11, 16, 23]. Importantly, these three categories were not mutually exclusive, but rather interactive and converging into a complex notion of authenticity.

The practitioners who emphasised the need to maintain authentic ICH placed importance on training and on mastering the performance of original versions in order to ensure that commodified and transformed versions of performances maintain levels of authenticity. This understanding of ICH is shaped by objective authenticity, which places importance on customs and objects declared to be original (Cohen & Cohen, 2012). For example, one respondent [ICH8] said that:

> ICH should keep the original form … the commodified version of ICH is too much focusing on entertainment purpose … in order to minimise the risk of losing authenticity, the practitioners firstly should learn and acquire the original form of ICH. Then, they can show the transformed ICH by targeting the audiences.

Moreover, practitioners advocating safeguarding the original customs, gestures, languages, and performance time were concerned that the transformation of ICH would lead to the extinction of ICH and one [ICH25] stated that 'if we follow the audiences wants, ICH at the end will be disappeared … I think we should follow the tradition and original form, although it is boring'.

The practitioners who emphasised the meaning and message of ICH admitted that social changes affect ICH. In other words, socio-cultural shifts in society influence changes in languages, in the masks and the clothes used in performances and also in the needs of audiences. Therefore, the

Table 1. Profile of interview participants.

Labelled in result	Positions/ levels	National ICH No.	Title	Description
ICH1	Living human treasure	No.62	Jwasuyeong eobang nori	Reproduction of fishing performance in Jwasuyeong village
ICH2	Living human treasure	No. 18	Dongnae yaryu	Masked dance in Dongnae village, satirising higher social group
ICH3	Living human treasure	No.43	Suyeong yaryu	Masked dance in Suyoung village, satirizing higher social group
ICH4	Living human treasure	Regional ICH	Suyeong jisin balki,	Ritual event wishing communities health and wellness
ICH5	Living human treasure	Regional ICH	Suyeoung nong chung nori	Reproduction of farming performance in Suyeoung area
ICH6	Assistant instructor	No. 76	Taekkyeon	Korean traditional martial art
ICH7	Living human treasure	No. 76	Taekkyeon	Korean traditional martial art
ICH8	Assistant instructor	No3.	Namsadang nori	All male composed folk performance which have been practicing by travelling in Korea, and have been kept by professional troupes
ICH 9	Assistant instructor	No. 34	Gangnyeong talchum	Mask dance in Gangnyeong region, which has more singing than other mask dance
ICH 10	Assistant instructor	No. 17	Bongsan Talchum	Masked dance handed down from the Bongsanregion, Hwanghae Province in North Korea
ICH11	Living human treasure	No. 104	Seoul Saenam gut	Reproduction of exorcism by shaman performers especially for the dead who was higher social class, in Seoul city
ICH12	Assistant instructors	No.1	Jongmyo jeryeak	A royal ancestral Confucian ceremony practices which bring together song, dance and music
ICH13	Living human treasure	No. 79	Baltal	Puppet placed on and manipulated by the foot
ICH14	Assistant instructor	No. 79	Baltal	Puppet placed on and manipulated by the foot
ICH15	Living human treasure	No. 17	Bongsan talchum	Masked dance handed down from the Bongsanregion, Hwanghae Province in North Korea
ICH16	Living human treasure	No. 17	Bongsan talchum	Masked dance handed down from the Bongsanregion, Hwanghae Province in North Korea
ICH17	Living human treasure	No. 13	Gangneung Danoje – shamanistic ritual	A festival in the Gangneung region, including a shamanistic ritual, mask drama, oral and narrative poetry
ICH18	Assistant instructor	No. 13	Gangneung Danoje – mask drama	A festival in the Gangneung region, including a shamanistic ritual, mask drama, oral and narrative poetry
ICH19	Assistant instructor	No. 13	Gangneung Danoje	A festival in the Gangneung region, including a shamanistic ritual, mask drama, oral and narrative poetry
ICH20	Living human treasure	No. 30	Gagok	Korean traditional lyric song
ICH21	Living human treasure	No. 40	Hagyeon hwadae hapseolmu	Royal dance composed of bird- and flower-dances
ICH22	Assistant instructor	No.99	Sobanjang	Korean traditional wooden tray-table carpentry
ICH23	Assistant instructor	No. 4	Gatiljang	Making Korean traditional hat for higher social class in Joseon dynasty
ICH24	Living human treasure	No. 34	Gangnyeong talchum	Mask dance in Gangnyeong region, which has more singing than other mast dance
ICH25	Living human treasure	No3.	Namsadang nori	All male composed folk performance which have been practicing by travelling in Korea, and have been kept by professional troupes

meaning of the languages and performance is more important for safeguarding authenticity. ICH 16 argued that

> I don't think there is 'original version' of ICH, and although there is, I haven't seen it. For example, the mask and clothes have been changed. The original version means what we are doing in contemporary culture, founded on what our trainers was teaching.

The importance of the meaning of ICH was also emphasised by ICH 6, who said that 'in the training of Takkyeon (No. 76 Korean national ICH, martial art), we concern a lot of politeness, toward nations, parents, or instructors ... without the politeness and spirit, it is just fighting and cannot be martial arts'. This understanding of ICH authenticity is shaped by constructive authenticity, suggesting authenticity as 'contemporary understanding of the past culture' (Zhou et al., 2015, p. 30) which is influenced by social changes.

Last, some respondents emphasised their identity for the authenticity of ICH. For them, a transformed version is still authentic because they are experiencing their identity while practicing the transformed version. One respondent [ICH11] mentioned that the 'transformed version does not mean it is not my ICH ... although we show the transformed performance we still feel our identity and the performance still shows authenticity'. This understanding of ICH authenticity is in accordance with existential authenticity, suggesting authenticity focuses on individuals' identities and their performative experiences, which may enhance an object's authenticity.

Although these three categories of authenticity were developed, they are not mutually exclusive. The respondents who emphasised the transmission of the original version still considered the transformed performance as a part of ICH because they feel authentic when dancing. Moreover, the respondents who emphasised self-identity and the meaning of ICH still identified the importance of the original form of ICH. One respondent stated that 'the beginner practitioners can realise and acquire the spirit and message of this martial art only through continuous training of the original version of ICH ... when practitioners master the original version of ICH, they can achieve self-realisation'.

The combined categories of authenticity endorse the notion of 'theoplacity authenticity'. Theoplacity authenticity, as suggested by Belhassen et al. (2008), suggests that authenticity is a complex notion affected by multiple factors such as the place (e.g. the place where traditional dance performs), tourists'/practitioners' beliefs, action, and themselves. That is, the authenticity of ICH does not depend on one aspect only, such as gesture or spirit; rather, it is comprehensively affected by a practitioner's cultural identity, performances, and a belief about audiences. The respondents perceived ICH authenticity as a compound notion that is affected by its transmitted performance, meaning, and message underpinning ICH and the practitioners' identity.

Commodification and transformation of ICH

One interesting finding of this study was that overall, the majority of respondents showed a positive attitude towards the commodification and transformation of ICH. ICH practitioners are the people most responsible for safeguarding the authenticity of the resource (Lenzerini, 2011). Thus it is often assumed that they would be opposed to the commodification of ICH (Yim, 2004) as purportedly, it is a potential threat to the loss of ICH authenticity (Halewood & Hannam, 2001; Taylor, 2001). A total of 11 ICH practitioner respondents in this study, however, showed a positive attitude towards the commodification and transformation of ICH as a means to create increased interest for tourists. Commodification and transformational changes include shortening presentation times [ICH 3, 5, 17, 18], combining ICH with other modern performances (e.g. modern and contemporary music with traditional dances; modern materials with traditional craftsmanship) [ICH 1, 6, 7] and modifying lyrics or gestures to increase interaction with audiences [ICH 1, 2, 4, 5]. One respondent [ICH 1] mentioned that:

> There is a regular 'Eobang' festival in Gwangan Beach in Busan and we performed in this year's festival (in 2016). The performance was combined with Busan city musical orchestra instead of using traditional instrument for background music and the combined performance was successful. Audiences were happy with it

... I think adding extra factors to increase audience enjoyment is good for marketing and promoting our ICH ...

The main reasons for the positive attitudes of ICH practitioners toward the commodification of ICH were because of their concern that the original version of ICH might be boring for audiences [ICH 2, 3, 4, 9, 10] and/or less understandable [ICH 1, 3, 18]. For example, ICH 2 argued that 'some degree of transformation is effective for transmitting ICH as it helps understanding of audiences and increase interests in ICH'. Similarly, ICH 10 said that 'the original version takes three hours. The whole performance may be too boring for the audiences and too hard to play for us as well'. Moreover, ICH 1 mentioned that 'the words in original ICH are very strong dialectal, in which the audiences cannot understand ... thus we use easy languages which all the audiences can understand' while ICH 18 mentioned that 'our mask dance is mime performance without voices ... to ensure the inherited meaning of gestures and performances conveyed to the audiences, we sometimes add voices ... ICH changes based on the target audiences ... '.

For the practitioners, the transformation of ICH is a way of disseminating its value and thus they showed positive attitudes towards it. This endorses the partnership between tourism and ICH developments in which ICH, transformed to suit the interest of tourists, not only contributes to the dissemination of ICH as a valuable resource but also attracts more tourists to the region which in turn, contributes to community development.

Develop ICH as a sustainable tourism resource

This study identified the major priorities of ICH a sustainable tourism resource include: (1) the promotion of ICH to locals, (2) ICH practitioners' empowerment and (3) parallel development between tourism and safeguarding ICH.

Promotion of ICH to locals

The promotion of ICH to locals, especially the younger generation, is fundamental given the survival of ICH is vulnerable unless it is identified and utilised by locals (Bortolotto, 2007). Early and Seitel (2002) emphasised the importance of locals in safeguarding ICH by the statement 'No folklore without the folk'. Moreover, ICH is not a material object, but a living performance thus locals' continuous practice and awareness is required to safeguard and transmit ICH. Promoting the value of ICH, including running compulsory educational programs, establishing ICH hub or centres, and/or hosting tourism activities such as events, festivals, and performances contributes to the transmission of ICH and increases the economic, social, and cultural value of ICH.

The majority of respondents pointed out that current generations, especially the younger generation, has a lack of interest in, awareness of, and respect for, practicing ICH, which leads to lower desire to be practitioners and threats to the transmission of ICH [ICH 1, 5, 15]. For example, one respondent [ICH 5] worried about a lack of interest by the younger generation in ICH and said that 'the biggest problem is that the present generation does not wish to learn and transmit ICH ... most of this generation has difficulties in understanding the value, which makes it more difficult in accepting and transmitting it'. According to Inglehart and Baker (2000), the younger generation, particularly in the nations that have had substantial economic growth since 1950 (e.g. South Korea), have a much more 'secular–rational worldview' and are less interested in traditional cultures (Nas et al., 2002).

Nevertheless, in accordance with the existing studies (Chhabra, 2010a; Vecco, 2010; Youn & Uzzell, 2016), this study also reiterated the importance of increasing ICH awareness in the younger generation. One respondent was adamant that 'increasing the younger generation's interest in ICH is the most significant issue that ICH is facing now. The individual ICH associations and the government organisations should make an effort to attract their interest in ICH' [ICH1]. The younger generation is the group responsible for the future of cultural heritage (Vecco, 2010). Importantly, their lack of interest in ICH leads to a lack of potential ICH practitioners, which may lead to failure of ICH transmission given that ICH practitioners are mainly responsible for safeguarding ICH and transmitting ICH to the next generation (Lenzerini, 2011). The active promotion of ICH to locals is expected by the practitioners to increase interest in ICH, thus contributes to the transmission of ICH.

Promotion to locals also contributes to the enhanced economic, social, and cultural value of ICH. When locals have awareness of the value of ICH, they will visit in order to experience ICH, which in turn will facilitate the growth of the ICH tourism market. According to Nuryanti (1996), the majority of heritage tourists are domestic tourists due to their identification of their own culture. The increased awareness of and interest in ICH by locals should facilitate growth in the ICH tourism market. This in turn will encourage locals to show respect in practicing ICH and assist in developing a stronger cultural identity. One respondent [ICH 18], who is a practitioner of one ICH element attracting international and domestic tourists mentioned that:

> although it is so crowded and there are traffic jams in the festival season, locals understand it and sometimes seem to feel proud of the festival ... the festival can become bigger and more popular because the locals support and identity with it.

Empowerment of ICH practitioner and each ICH associations

Empowering ICH practitioners is necessary in facilitating ICH to be a sustainable tourism resource, because it enables the development of strategies that suit each ICH. Currently, however, a prevalent top-down development approach leads to a lack of empowerment in safeguarding and promoting ICH. Currently, in Korea, the development of ICH is controlled by the Korean government's Cultural Heritage Administration. For example, the head of the Cultural Heritage Administration has the authority to examine and decide on who becomes ICH practitioners. The respondents criticised this system and argued that the Master ICH practitioner's right and power to examine each practitioner does not belong to the Cultural Heritage Association. For example, ICH 3 stated:

> the government should give us the responsibility of finding ways in which ICH can be transmitted to future generations ... for example, designating ICH practitioners, increasing financial support (or income) ... all are decided by the government, not by each ICH association, and so each ICH practitioner and the associations have less power and are discouraged from self-reliance.

Moreover, as a Living Human Treasure, a person expects to have the authority to research, train and transmit ICH based on the feature of each ICH. However, ICH practitioners are required to train and transmit ICH based on policies and guidelines created by public organisations. Therefore, for self-reliance, each ICH association and each ICH practitioner should have their own organised system in terms of training, attracting potential ICH practitioners and promoting financial income opportunities. For example, ICH 17 argued:

> As the effect of historical military government, public organisations have too much authority to control ICH. We cannot wait until the government sets effective and organised systems for Living Human Treasures. We need to find the way for self-reliance. Each ICH association should have organised systems to be self-reliable in safeguarding ICH authenticity and transmitting ICH.

The respondents' desire for empowerment is supported by the literature (Fraser, Dougill, Mabee, Reed, & McAlpine, 2006; Greer, 2010; Lyons, 2001) which argues for increased community empowerment in sustainable tourism. Community is one of the sustainability indicators and communities must have the capacity to manage their cultural heritage (Fraser et al., 2006). *Empowerment* can be understood as the process of giving community a relevant legal authority (Lyons, 2001) or as the transfer of control to communities over decisions on resources (World Bank, 1996). The aim of empowerment for communities is self-reliance, and independence from the external government so that they can formulate their own goals and aims (Lyons, 2001). This is the Korean ICH practitioners' desire, as ICH 17 claimed 'we need to have our own power to manage this ICH, safeguarding and promoting ... however, a predominant top-down approach makes empowerment difficult to realise'. Empowering ICH practitioners can enhance their capacity to control cultural heritage, and it enables and supports them in solving problems in the long term (Garrod & Fyall, 2000).

Parallel development

The respondents suggested the need for separated ICH development based on its purpose (e.g. tourism purpose, or safeguarding purpose). They argued that it is important to separate roles of relevant ICH associations according to their purpose, to safeguard/transmit, or to commodify to satisfy tourists [ICH 6, 8, 9, 11]. For example, ICH6 stated that 'The parties who are responsible for safeguarding ICH have to focus on safeguarding it; on the other hand, the parties who are utilising and promoting it have to focus on that'.

This strategy can be supported by the parallel existence between tourism and cultural heritage management, introduced by McKercher, Ho, and du Cros (2005). Parallel existence advocates see clear, distinct roles between/in cultural heritage development and tourism development. For example, the cultural heritage development sector is responsible for the ownership and day-to-day management of the asset, while the tourism sector assumes the product development and marketing (McKercher et al., 2005). Parallel relationships are common in mature destinations where two sectors (e.g. cultural heritage development and tourism development) have complementary goals, but their roles are different (McKercher et al., 2005). Parallel relationships can take many forms, from exclusive relationships (i.e. no contact with each other) to symbiotic (i.e. a certain degree of collaboration) relationships between cultural heritage and tourism development. Although the relationship suggested by ICH practitioners was not articulated as succinctly as this, a parallel relationship strategy could achieve the safeguarding of ICH cultural values while concomitantly facilitating the socio-economic value of ICH via the commercial promotion of ICH.

Conclusion and recommendations

This study explored the priorities of ICH practitioners in relation to the development of ICH as a sustainable tourism resource. The authenticity of ICH has been identified as a key component to developing ICH as a sustainable tourism resource. The practitioners believed authenticity is a holistic notion integrating the transmitted custom, inherited meanings and the practitioner identity. Arguably then, the development of ICH as a sustainable tourism resource requires a positive and constructive symbiotic relationship between safeguarding ICH authenticity and increasing the socio-economic value of ICH. The potential outcome of this approach is the increased community self-reliance. To achieve this, it is necessary for practitioners to be cognisant of the negative impacts of tourism (e.g. commodified transformation of ICH) as ICH develops. Perhaps more importantly, however, it is necessary during ICH development that there is local interest in and awareness of ICH, that ICH practitioners are empowered and that there is parallel development between tourism development and the transmission of ICH.

Future research on the development of ICH as a sustainable tourism resource is required in different cultural and/or political contexts. Cultural heritage and sustainability are influenced by political, social and cultural changes, therefore ICH practitioners' from other cultures may have different perspectives to those from South Korea. Therefore, research in different cultural and political contexts will provide us with a more nuanced understanding of the development of ICH. Furthermore, there is room for future studies to focus on each ICH category, such as traditional dance, ritual event, festival, or traditional craftsmanship. this study adopts a holistic approach to ICH and thus covers all the elements of ICH, however, differences exist among the ICH elements therefore, a focus on each ICH element will provide more explicit and specific findings that can contribute to the ongoing development of ICH as a sustainable tourism resource. Moreover, further studies need to explore public organisations policies pertaining to facilitating ICH as a sustainable tourism resource. Public organisations are the institutions which initiate laws, guidelines and strategies for safeguarding and utilising ICH (Du Cros, Bauer, Lo, & Rui, 2005), thus public organisation policy analysis will facilitate the development of better informed public organisational strategies and policy. Additionally, not only is the perspectives of each stakeholder important, but the integration of their perspectives is significant in the development of ICH as a sustainable tourism resource. Loulanski and Loulanski (2011) also pointed out the lack of research on the demand side and there are even fewer studies on the integration of supply and demand on a sustainable tourism resource development. Therefore, the integrated perspectives of the stakeholders, such as tourists, ICH practitioners, local communities and public organisations will contribute to the research area of the development of ICH as a sustainable tourism resource.

Disclosure statement

No potential conflict of interest was reported by the authors.

ORCID

Charles Arcodia http://orcid.org/0000-0002-9196-9591

References

Ashworth, G. J. (2013). From history to heritage–from heritage to identity: In search of concepts and models. In G. Ashworth & P. Larkham (Eds.), *Building a new Heritage: Tourism, Culture and Identity in the New Europe* (pp. 13–30). London: Routledge.

Asia/Pacific Cultural Centre for UNESCO [ACCU]. (2006). *Expert meeting on community involvement in safeguarding intangible cultural heritage: Towards the implementation of the 2003 convention.*

Bakar, A. A., Osman, M. M., Bachok, S., & Ibrahim, M. (2014). Analysis on community involvement level in intangible cultural heritage: Malacca cultural community. *Procedia - Social and Behavioral Sciences, 153*, 286–297.

Belhassen, Y., & Caton, K. (2006). Authenticity matters. *Annals of Tourism Research, 33*(3), 853–856.

Belhassen, Y., Caton, K., & Stewart, W. P. (2008). The search for authenticity in the pilgrim experience. *Annals of Tourism Research, 35*(3), 668–689.

Bessiere, J. (1998). Local development and heritage: Traditional food and cuisine as tourist attractions in rural areas. *Sociologia Ruralis, 38*(1), 21–34.

Bortolotto, C. (2007). From objects to processes: UNESCO's 'intangible cultural heritage'. *Journal of Museum Ethnography, 14*, 21–33.

Bowen, G. A. (2009). Document analysis as a qualitative research method. *Qualitative Research Journal, 9*(2), 27–40.

Braun, V., & Clarke, V. (2006). Using thematic analysis in psychology. *Qualitative Research in Psychology, 3*(2), 77–101.
Brundtland, G., Khalid, M., Agnelli, S., Al-Athel, S., Chidzero, B., Fadika, L., ... de Botero, M. M. (1987). *Our common future.*
Bruner, E. M. (1994). Abraham Lincoln as authentic reproduction: A critique of postmodernism. *American Anthropologist, 96*(2), 397–415.
Bruner, E. (2005). Abraham Lincoln as authentic reproduction. In E. Bruner (Ed.), *Culture on tour* (pp. 145-168). Chicago: University of Chicago Press.
Bruner, E. M., & Kirshenblatt Gimblett, B. (1994). Maasai on the lawn: Tourist realism in East Africa. *Cultural Anthropology, 9*(4), 435–470.
Cavana, R. Y., Delahaye, B. L., & Sekaran, U. (2001). *Applied business research: Qualitative and quantitative methods.* Milton: John Wiley & Sons Australia.
Chambers, R. (1994). The origins and practice of participatory rural appraisal. *World Development, 22*(7), 953–969.
Chhabra, D. (2009). Proposing a sustainable marketing framework for heritage tourism. *Journal of Sustainable Tourism, 17*(3), 303–320.
Chhabra, D. (2010a). Back to the past: A sub-segment of generation Y's perceptions of authenticity. *Journal of Sustainable Tourism, 18*(6), 793–809.
Chhabra, D. (2010b). Branding authenticity. *Tourism Analysis, 15*(6), 735–740.
Chhabra, D., Healy, R., & Sills, E. (2003). Staged authenticity and heritage tourism. *Annals of Tourism Research, 30*(3), 702–719.
Cohen, E. (2002). Authenticity, equity and sustainability in tourism. *Journal of Sustainable Tourism, 10*(4), 267–276.
Cohen, E., & Cohen, S. A. (2012). Authentication: Hot and cool. *Annals of Tourism Research, 39*(3), 1295–1314.
Daniel, Y. P. (1996). Tourism dance performances authenticity and creativity. *Annals of Tourism Research, 23*(4), 780–797.
Downe Wamboldt, B. (1992). Content analysis: Method, applications, and issues. *Health Care for Women International, 13*(3), 313–321.
Du Cros, H., Bauer, T., Lo, C., & Rui, S. (2005). Cultural heritage assets in China as sustainable tourism products: Case studies of the Hutongs and the Huanghua section of the great Wall. *Journal of Sustainable Tourism, 13*(2), 171–194.
Early, J., & Seitel, P. (2002). UNESCO draft convention for safeguarding intangible cultural heritage: "No folklore without the folk". *Talk Story,* (22), 19.
Esfehani, M. H., & Albrecht, J. N. (2018). Roles of intangible cultural heritage in tourism in natural protected areas. *Journal of Heritage Tourism, 13*(1), 15–29.
Fraser, E. D. G., Dougill, A. J., Mabee, W. E., Reed, M., & McAlpine, P. (2006). Bottom up and top down: Analysis of participatory processes for sustainability indicator identification as a pathway to community empowerment and sustainable environmental management. *Journal of Environmental Management, 78*(2), 114–127.
Garrod, B., & Fyall, A. (1998). Beyond the rhetoric of sustainable tourism? *Tourism Management, 19*(3), 199–212.
Garrod, B., & Fyall, A. (2000). Managing heritage tourism. *Annals of Tourism Research, 27*(3), 682–708.
Gonzalez, M. V. (2008). Intangible heritage tourism and identity. *Tourism Management, 29,* 807–810.
Greer, S. (2010). Heritage and empowerment: Community-based Indigenous cultural heritage in northern Australia. *International Journal of Heritage Studies, 16*(1–2), 45–58.
Hafstein, V. T. (2004). *The making of intangible cultural heritage: Tradition and authenticity, community and humanity.* Berkeley, CA: University of California.
Halewood, C., & Hannam, K. (2001). Viking heritage tourism: Authenticity and commodification. *Annals of Tourism Research, 28*(3), 565–580.
Hall, D., & Richards, G. (2002). The community: A sustainable concept in tourism development? In G. Richards & D. Hall (Eds.), *Tourism and sustainable community development* (pp. 19–32). London: Routledge.
Hitchcock, M., King, V. T., & Parnwell, M. (2010). *Heritage tourism in Southeast Asia.* Copenhagen: Nias Press.
Hunter, C. (1997). Sustainable tourism as an adaptive paradigm. *Annals of Tourism Research, 24*(4), 850–867.
Inglehart, R., & Baker, W. E. (2000). Modernization, cultural change, and the persistence of traditional values. *American Sociological Review, 65,* 19–51.
Korea House. (2015). *The best performance in Korea.* Retrieved from http://www.koreahouse.or.kr/eng/?en_skin = performance.html
Lenzerini, F. (2011). Intangible cultural heritage: The living culture of peoples. *European Journal of International Law, 22*(1), 101–120.
Loulanski, T., & Loulanski, V. (2011). The sustainable integration of cultural heritage and tourism: A meta-study. *Journal of Sustainable Tourism, 19*(7), 837–862.
Lyons, M. (2001). Participation, empowerment and sustainability: (How) do the links work? *Urban Studies (Edinburgh, Scotland), 38*(8), 1233–1251.
MacCannell, D. (1976). *The tourist: A new theory of the leisure class.* London: University of California Press.
Macdonald, S. (2004). A people's story. In G. Corsane (Ed.), *Heritage, museums and galleries: An introductory reader* (pp. 272–290). London: Routledge.

McKercher, B., Ho, P. S., & du Cros, H. (2005). Relationship between tourism and cultural heritage management: Evidence from Hong Kong. *Tourism Management, 26*(4), 539–548.

Munjeri, D. (2004). Tangible and intangible heritage: From difference to convergence. *Museum International, 56*(1–2), 12–20.

Nas, P. M., Talal, H. P., Claessen, H. M., Handler, R., Kurin, R., Olwig, K., … Nas, P. M. (2002). Masterpieces of oral and intangible culture: Reflections on the UNESCO World Heritage List. *Current Anthropology, 43*(1), 139–148.

Nuryanti, W. (1996). Heritage and postmodern tourism. *Annals of Tourism Research, 23*(2), 249–260.

Pons, P. O. (2003). Being-on-holiday: Tourist dwelling, bodies and place. *Tourist Studies, 3*(1), 47–66.

Reisinger, Y., & Steiner, C. J. (2006). Reconceptualizing object authenticity. *Annals of Tourism Research, 33*(1), 65–86.

Robinson, M. (1999). Collaboration and cultural consent: Refocusing sustainable tourism. *Journal of Sustainable Tourism, 7*(3–4), 379–397.

Saarinen, J. (2006). Traditions of sustainability in tourism studies. *Annals of Tourism Research, 33*(4), 1121–1140.

Steiner, C. J., & Reisinger, Y. (2006). Understanding existential authenticity. *Annals of Tourism Research, 33*(2), 299–318.

Taylor, J. P. (2001). Authenticity and sincerity in tourism. *Annals of Tourism Research, 28*(1), 7–26.

Tsaur, S.-H., Lin, Y.-C., & Lin, J.-H. (2006). Evaluating ecotourism sustainability from the integrated perspective of resource, community and tourism. *Tourism Management, 27*(4), 640–653.

UNESCO. (1972). *Convention concerning the Protection of the World Cultural and natural Heritage*. Retrieved from https://whc.unesco.org/archive/convention-en.pdf

UNESCO. (1996). *Our cultural diversity*. Retrieved from https://unesdoc.unesco.org/ark:/48223/pf0000101651

UNESCO. (2003). *Convention for the safegaurding of the Intangible Culturall Heritage* [Press release]. Retrieved from https://ich.unesco.org/en/convention

Vaismoradi, M. (2013). Content analysis and thematic analysis: Implications for conducting a qualitative descriptive study Qualitative descriptive study. *Nursing & Health Sciences, 15*(3), 398–405.

Vecco, M. (2010). A definition of cultural heritage: From the tangible to the intangible. *Journal of Cultural Heritage, 11*(3), 321–324.

Wang, N. (1999). Rethinking authenticity in tourism experience. *Annals of Tourism Research, 26*(2), 349–370.

World Bank. (1996). *World Bank participation sourcebook*. Washington, DC: World Bank.

World Tourism Organisation. (2012). *Tourism and intangible cultural heritage*. Madrid: UNWTO.

Xie, P. F. (2003). The bamboo-beating dance in Hainan, China: Authenticity and commodification. *Journal of Sustainable Tourism, 11*(1), 5–16.

Yim, D. (2004). Living human treasures and the protection of intangible culture heritage: Experiences and challenges. *ICOM News, 4*, 10–12.

Youn, S. H., & Uzzell, D. (2016). The young generations' conceptualisation of cultural tourism: Colonial heritage attractions in South Korea. *Asia Pacific Journal of Tourism Research, 21*(12), 1324–1342.

Zhou, Q. B., Zhang, J., Zhang, H., & Ma, J. (2015). A structural model of host authenticity. *Annals of Tourism Research, 55*, 28–45.

Zhu, Y. (2012). Performing heritage: Rethinking authenticity in tourism. *Annals of Tourism Research, 39*(3), 1495–1513.

Time, authenticity and photographic storytelling in *The Museum of Innocence*

Kevin Hannam and Edward Ryan

ABSTRACT
Although an individual may recollect an event, such remembering is influenced by the wider social environment to which the individual belongs. Heritage tourism research has focused on the active contestation of performances of collective memories through specific material affordances such as photographs and souvenirs. More recent work has also examined the kinds of pictures and objects that people carry with them and use to reassemble memories, practices and even landscapes, thus remaking the materiality of places. However, memories are also reconstructed through intangible practices of storytelling, and the telling of a story can confer added authenticity to a material place. This paper explores these conceptual ideas through an examination of the intertextuality of the novel by Nobel Prize winning author Orhan Pamuk, *The Museum of Innocence* which has subsequently been turned into a museum in Istanbul dedicated to the characters depicted in the book. Based upon visual ethnographic fieldwork at the museum we argue that the story of the Museum of Innocence as well as the actual museum help us to understand how conceptualisations of time are interwoven with how we experience and perform authenticity.

Introduction

Individual memories are influenced by the presence of others, by the social and cultural worlds we inhabit and are imaginative reconstructions of the past. Although an individual may recollect an event, such remembering is influenced by the wider social environment to which the individual belongs (Hannam & Yankovska, 2017). Thus various 'sites of memory' may hold communal identities together or divide them depending upon the perceived authenticity of the site (Crang & Travlou, 2001). Heritage tourism research has focused on the active contestation of performances of collective memories through specific material affordances such as photographs and souvenirs (Crang, 1996; Hannam, 2006). More recent work has also examined the kinds of pictures and objects that people carry with them and use to reassemble memories, practices and even landscapes, thus remaking the materiality of places (Basu & Coleman, 2008). However, memories are also reconstructed through intangible practices of storytelling, and the telling of a story can confer added authenticity to a material place. Memories are also enveloped within our understandings of time and temporalities. Thus in this paper, we consider the temporalities and related authenticities involved in the creation of a novel and a museum as well as the retelling of a story using photography.

Specifically, this paper explores these conceptual ideas through an examination of the intertextuality of the novel by Nobel Prize winning author Orhan Pamuk, *The Museum of Innocence* (2008) which has subsequently been turned into a museum in Istanbul dedicated to the characters depicted in the book. The story of the *Museum of Innocence* explores ideas of love, obsession, collecting, materialities, memories, photography, authenticity, and time within the specific urban spatial context of Istanbul. Visitors to the actual museum in Istanbul based upon the novel, meanwhile, have been invited to co-produce the museum by donating objects of personal value with the memories they carry to be displayed in the museum's temporary exhibition space. Based upon visual ethnographic fieldwork at the museum we argue that the story of the Museum of Innocence as well as the actual museum help us to understand the complexity of authenticity as it is provoked through storytelling such that we may better understand the nature of temporalities in the construction of heritage tourism experiences.

Authenticity, time and photographic storytelling

Tourism studies have long debated issues of authenticity (Halewood & Hannam, 2001; Rickly-Boyd, 2013). MacCannell (1973) famously argued that the notion of staged authenticity may lead to the development of a distinct tourism space separate from the immediate locality and this separation largely prevents any experience of authenticity. Alternative tourism, on the other hand, was seen as journeys into 'uncharted territory beyond the limits of the "tourist space", to have "authentic' experiences" (Cohen, 1995, p. 13). Such a binary distinction between the authentic and the inauthentic has been deconstructed such that authenticity is seen as negotiable and integrated into everyday life (Cohen, 1995; Halewood & Hannam, 2001). Nevertheless, various tourism commodities, such as souvenirs, may be socially constructed as 'authentic' due to a focus on the uniqueness and originality of a product, its workmanship, its cultural and historical integrity, its aesthetics, and/or its functions and use. Academic expertise may also be utilsed to confer a quality assurance of authenticity. Similarly, shopping at places where goods are made, allows tourists to actually view authenticity being conferred to the object (Littrell, Anderson, & Brown, 1993). Various labels are also often placed on goods to make them seem more authentic, to add a quality assurance tag, and even explain their wider context, making explicit their exchange value (Halewood & Hannam, 2001). Moreover, time can confer authenticity, something that simply looks old may be deemed to be more authentic than something that is new.

Wang (1999) has championed an existential approach to understanding tourist's experiences of authenticity as going beyond objects to focus on activities or practices instead and how these give or afford various meanings. Rickly-Boyd (2013) has further developed this insight in terms of the sense of place that authenticity may afford touristic performances. Thus Knudsen and Waade (2010, p. 12) argue that a performance approach to authenticity in tourism 'not only signifies that we do and perform places by our actions and behaviours, but that places are something we authenticate through our emotional/affective/sensuous relatedness to them.' For example, in her study of lifestyle climbers, Rickly-Boyd (2013, p. 683) found that 'existential authenticity was experienced through the lifestyle aspects of their dedication, including the challenges of life on the road, community gatherings at campgrounds, and the considerable amount of time spent in nature. Thus, place matters in existential authenticity.' If place matters in existential authenticity, then so does time. Hence we need to examine the concept of time more closely.

Hans Ramo (1999) discusses how the ancient Greek philosopher Aristotle conceptualises time in terms of the differences between *chronos* and *kairos*. Chronos refers to time as change which can be measured as a sequence or an order, it is literally chronological as in the passing of time indicated on a clock. Kairos, meanwhile, refers to specific life-changing moments in time, a critical or decisive time to act, time that is taken or grasped, or a perfectly timed opportunity which has value. In relation to authenticity we can see that both *chronos* and *kairos* are significant. The former in terms of the aging of material objects to confer meaning and authenticity and the latter in terms of the meaning gathered through the 'time spent' in the pursuit of the touristic challenges that Rickly-Boyd (2013) refers to. Mike Crang (2005) has further discussed the notion of temporality in relation to tourism – where time is not experienced as a linear flow but more in terms of cycles. Tourism is frequently experienced and organised through various temporal rhythms, repetitions, routines and rituals. Moreover, it is hardly surprising that we find rituals in particular as being socially constructed as having authenticity and meaning as they contain *kairos*.

Tourist's experiences of time, authenticity and places are also emphatically mediatised – particularly through the use of photography (Crang, 1997). Hughes (1995, pp. 782–783) has argued that often tourists, '... do not contrast the staging of their authenticity ... against direct experience of the original, but rather with a mental image of that original which has already been 'corrupted' by mediating influences.' This rather misses the point though as experiences of authenticity are not necessarily 'corrupted' but interwoven to co-create new emotional responses to touristic places and landscapes (Rickly-Boyd, 2013). The invention of photography, and its ability to mechanically reproduce other works of art (and for that matter a scenic view) have reconfigured our relationships with our environments. The camera lens is capable of bringing out details that were unobtainable to the naked eye. It can also put the copy of the original object into situations that would be out of reach for the original (Benjamin, 1935). For instance, a photograph – a miniaturised version of the scenic view – can then be displayed in tourists' homes (Thompson, Hannam, & Petrie, 2012). Rickly-Boyd (2012) draws upon the work of Walter Benjamin (1935) to illustrate the complexity of artistic reproduction and its importance for understanding the social and political construction of authentic experiences. She argues that the concept of 'aura' highlights that the unique value of an 'authentic' work of art always has its basis in ritual and that 'aura' is an experience, an engagement, defined as a 'strange tissue of space and time: the unique apparition of a distance, however near it may be' (Benjamin, 1968, p. 23; cited in Rickly-Boyd, 2012, p. 270). In relation to urbanisation and urban landscapes, in particular, Benjamin's insights have led to an emphasis on the ritualised character of tourist's experiences – time again experienced as *kairos*. Thus Benjamin argues that photographic representations cannot strip the aura from cities; they always retain their uniqueness because the landscape requires more than vision to experience it, the other senses contain the potential for the recovery of memory (cited in Rickly-Boyd, 2012, p. 276; Savage, 2000, p. 46). Moreover, artistic interventions allow disruptions to everyday habits and routines such that tourists and indeed residents may find new ways to reimagine and co-create experiences.

Photography has thus been explored as one form of both everyday as well as artistic practice that connects ritual with the co-creation of authenticity in tourism. As Rickly-Boyd (2012, p. 281) also notes:

> Photographs, as powerful communicative technologies, construct identities and subjectivities by bridging the individual, experiential, and private realms with collective, public ones ... Photographs, and souvenirs, result from the desire to capture the aura of the tourism experience, an aura which is made manifest through the collective tourism ritual.

She further argues that: '... photographs have "enduring afterlife," as they "become a vital part of people's life-stories and spaces of everyday" (Haldrup & Larsen, 2003, p. 42), they go on, open for re-interpretation, recall of memories, and recuperation of experience.' (Rickly-Boyd, 2012, p. 283). In what follows we develop a methodological approach which uses photography as a way of understanding the multiple temporal dimensions of the fictional and museum work-in-practice – *The Museum of Innocence* – developed by the Nobel prize winning author and curator Orhan Pamuk. While contemporary research has begun to investigate how storytelling is a powerful co-creative behaviour in tourism (Chronis, 2012; Mossberg, 2008; Pera, 2017; Tung & Ritchie, 2011), we focus on how a photographic intervention can further help storytelling as a means to understand the temporalities of touristic experiences.

Methodological process

Scarles (2010) has argued that using visual methods in tourism research allow us to unpack the intricate performances and the mobilising of knowledge exchange so that the complexities of embodied tourist experiences are more fully understood. As Pink (2007, p. 21) argues: '"visual research methods" are not purely visual. Rather, they pay particular attention to visual aspects of culture. Similarly, they cannot be used independently of other methods; neither a purely visual ethnography nor an exclusively visual approach to culture can exist.' Thus visual methods need to be joined up with other insightful strategies. We argue that artistic methods may also be useful in this vein. Peters (2018) suggests that we need to move beyond the dualism of art versus science where 'art becomes a paragon of unmethodological, autonomous and intuitive work, while science appears uncreative, methodological and articulate.' Both social science research and art have to be performed through multiple and collaborative practices. Thus the 'journey of making' becomes the interpretative methodological process through which we verify the story of research rather than criteria of validity and reliability (Thompson et al., 2012). In this paper, there is a collaboration between an academic tourism researcher (author A) and a contemporary artistic photographer and design academic (author B). Author B conducted visual autoethnography at the Museum of Innocence in Istanbul in February and December 2017. This involved participant observation at the museum and its surroundings, conversational interviews with tourists and museum staff as well as photography.

In this paper, we use photography to retell the story of the book and the museum rather than use interview data. We were interested in photographing the museum in the same manner as the story – creating a series of artistic images that play on the central concept of Aristotelian time, where each vitrine had been designed to illustrate the path of the protagonists' relationship as *kairos*. As Chan-fai Cheung (2009, v) has written:

> Photography is a play of time and light. The amount of time allowing light to get into the camera determines the quality of the photograph. The speed meter of the camera is commensurate with chronological time. Hence, most photographs are taken as records of external events. However, if photography is seriously considered as art, then the clicking of the shutter by the conscientious photographer for a particular phenomenon though his photographic seeing is what Cartier-Bresson called 'the decisive moment', i.e. *kairos*. All creative photographic works are products of *kairos*.

In terms of previous academic research, the Museum of Innocence has been studied from both an architectural (Allmer, 2009) and a design (Ogut, 2017) perspective but not in terms of tourism and not using this collaborative methodological approach. In the discussion below we have developed a co-creative approach using visual ethnography to understand the consumption and production of authenticity in terms of multiple temporal layers, or rather connected moments. The images denote emotional and affective responses to particular content in specific vitrines and run in chronological order, following the chapters of the story and layout of the museum.

Discussion – The Museum of Innocence, Istanbul

The physical Museum of Innocence in Istanbul is based upon the 2009 book of the same name by Orhan Pamuk and has been funded from his Nobel Prize. The synopsis of the story is as follows:

> The Museum of Innocence – set in Istanbul between 1975 and today – tells the story of Kemal, the son of one of Istanbul's richest families, and of his obsessive love for a poor and distant relation, the beautiful Fusun, who is a shop-girl in a small boutique. In his romantic pursuit of Füsun over the next eight years, Kemal compulsively amasses a collection of objects that chronicles his lovelorn progress – a museum that is both a map of a society and of his heart. The novel depicts a panoramic view of life in Istanbul as it chronicles this long, obsessive love affair; and Pamuk beautifully captures the identity crisis experienced by Istanbul's upper classes that find themselves caught between traditional and westernised ways of being. (Faber, 2009, n. p.)

The story illustrates the tensions between *chronos* and *kairos*, in that while experiencing chronological time, the collecting of objects becomes *kairos* – the opportunity to grasp time. Pamuk subsequently built the museum in the house in which his hero's fictional family lived, to display Kemal's fictional collection of objects associated with Fusun and their relationship – the house opened to the public in 2012 in the Beyoglu district of Istanbul. In his museum catalogue, *The*

Innocence of Objects, Pamuk (2013, p. 18) discusses the relationship between his novel and his museum in terms the affinity between memory and imagination:

> There is, of course, a strong bond that holds the novel and the museum together: both are products of my imagination, dreamed up word by word, object by object, and picture by picture over a long period of time. This is perhaps also why the novel and the museum each tell a story. The objects exhibited in the museum are described in the novel. Still words are one thing, objects another. The images that words generate in our minds are one thing: the memory of an old object used once upon a time is another. But imagination and memory have a strong affinity, and this is the basis of the affinity between the novel and the museum.

Here Pamuk seeks to illustrate the power of material objects in conveying meaning and a sense of authenticity – however, contrived this may be – and in this case, the authenticity is entirely fictional.

Pamuk (2013, p. 51) then discusses how his idea for the museum actually preceded the writing of the novel and was inspired by visits to small museums in the backstreets western European cities as well as visits to various collectors or hoarders of local artefacts in Istanbul:

> I kept seeking out more small museums in my travels. What I found most enthralling was the way in which objects removed from the kitchens, bedrooms, and dinner tables where they had once been utilized would come together to form a new texture, an unintentionally striking web of relationships. I realized that when arranged with love and care, objects in the museum ... could attain a much greater significance than they had before.

His 'journey of making' then involved considerable research into heritage tourism and the ways in which everyday artefacts contain elements of *kairos*, significant time.

In the novel, the main protagonist, Kemal, also reflects upon the concept of time:

> In 'Physics' Aristotle makes a distinction between time and the single moments he describes as the 'present'. Single moments are – like Aristotle's atoms – indivisible, unbreakable things. But Time is the line that links these indivisible moments. Though Tarık Bey asked us to forget Time – that line connecting one present moment to the next – no one except for idiots and amnesiacs can succeed in forgetting it altogether. (Pamuk, 2008, p. 395).

The point being made here is that we do not forget moments of kairos, as these are decisive moments, turning points and rituals that connect the present to the past. Similarly, in the catalogue to the actual Museum, Pamuk (2013, pp. 252–253) writes that 'just as the line that links moments together forms Time, so the line that ties objects together creates a story. This ... is the greatest happiness a museum can bring to see Time turning into Space.' The story told is about how the collecting of everyday objects becomes a routine, a ritual for the protagonist and here we have the concept of time as *kairos* – as opportunity – being used in terms of the museum.

Photography is a medium that instantly consigns it's subject and content to the past, as that moment – fictional or otherwise – can never be repeated in quite the same way again. It is a recording of a fleeting moment of time, a capture of an incident, feeling, story or position lost to us forever but for the physical existence of that photograph. We can thus look on our photographs of the Museum in Istanbul as images of indivisible moments of Aristotelian time. This concept of time is visually introduced to us in the foyer of the Museum though we may not recognise it until we reach the upper floors and look back down into the stairwell below.

The *kairos* of Aristotelian time is projected onto the floor next to the vitrine containing all 4213 of Fusun's cigarette ends (Figure 1), collected by Kemal over the time of their acquaintance and graphically illustrating the concept as we enter. We encounter the idea yet again at the top of the first flight of stairs in the Museum, in the vitrine illustrating chapter one of the novel and containing Fusun's lost earring (Figure 2), a butterfly whose wings are made of the same Aristotelian spiral of time.

We engage with a range of fictional assemblages throughout the museum, from the elevated yellow shoe in the window of the Sanselize Boutique (Figure 3), to the curtain coming down on Kemal's engagement to Sibel at Fuyae (Figure 4). Kemal's obsession with the missing Fusun is graphically illustrated in 'The Shadows and Ghosts I Mistook for Fusun' (Figures 5 and 6), two images

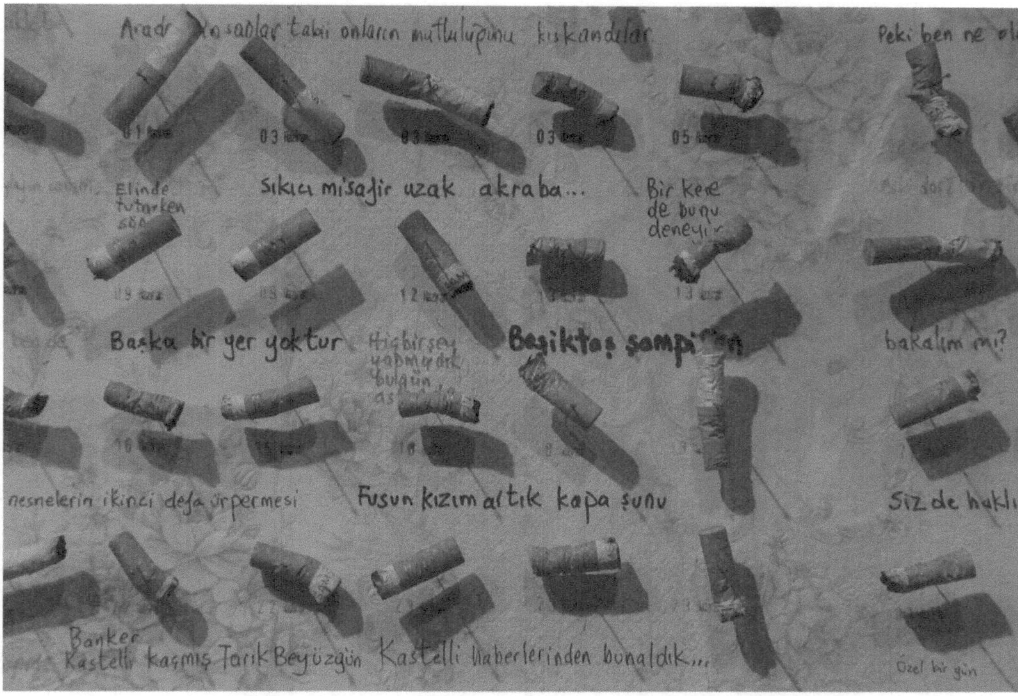

Figure 1. Fusun's cigarette ends.

portraying the places throughout the city he thought he had encountered her, the figure casting its shadow across the city and his life.

Between the depiction of the Fuyae Restaurant and the vitrine containing the China dogs that Kemal purloined from the Keskin household over seven years and ten months (Figure 7), Fusun's

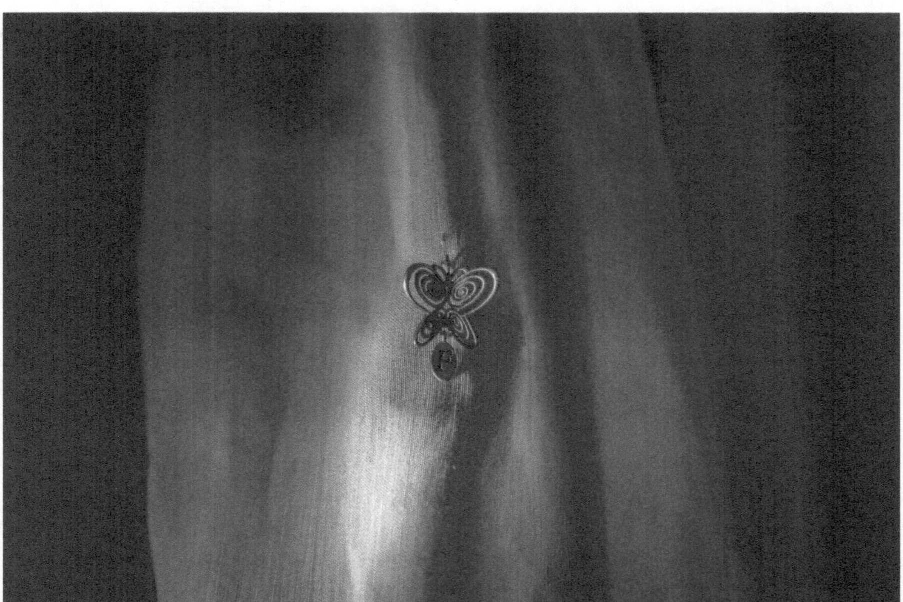

Figure 2. Fusun's lost earring here.

Figure 3. The Sanselize boutique.

father Tarik Bey asks us to 'forget' time, but being asked to forget time in the Museum of Innocence is impossible to do. Each fictional object, image, newspaper clipping, figurine, game piece or piece of film, tie Kemal to moments of *kairos*.

Figure 8 foreshadows the tragic end of the novel, and displays Fusun's driving licence as a historical document alongside pieces of her jewellery, the recurring spiral motif in the butterflies and the collected objects from their trips when Fusun had learned to drive. Figure 9 is made at the top of the museum in the room where Kemal (fictionally) lived and narrated his story to Orhan Pamuk, alongside handwritten and sometimes illustrated manuscript pages from the novel. The images photographed on the wall relate to the life Kemal and Fusun once enjoyed, a time now past and documented on the floors below his room.

Conclusions

Time is often conceptualised in terms of events as a rite of passage that people pass through, something that is experienced in a linear fashion (Hannam, Mostafanezhad, & Rickly, 2017). Aristotle developed the notion of linear time through his search for regular movements which could be measured in terms of *chronos*. However, our experience and consciousness of time as *kairos* is not necessarily that straightforward. In his work on residential mobility, Alan Metcalfe (2006, p. 243) uses the concept of *kairos*, as meaning the 'right time' to act, arguing that 'people who move house narrate their moving experiences in such terms: they saw an opportunity to move

Figure 4. Fuyae restaurant.

Figure 5. Shadows and ghosts.

home, an opportunity that arose at just the right time and their timely actions meant that they seized the moment.' Similarly, it is through narratives of *kairos* that the story of the museum of innocence, its objects and ultimately meaningful tourism experiences are created.

Figure 6. Fusun's location here.

Figure 7. China dogs here.

In this paper, we have sought to discuss how time, authenticity and storytelling come together in Orhan Pamuk's novel and museum – The Museum of Innocence. Through photography, we have sought to demonstrate how the retelling of the story of the Museum of Innocence as well as the actual museum itself help us to understand the complexity of authenticity such that we may better

Figure 8. Fusun's driving Licence.

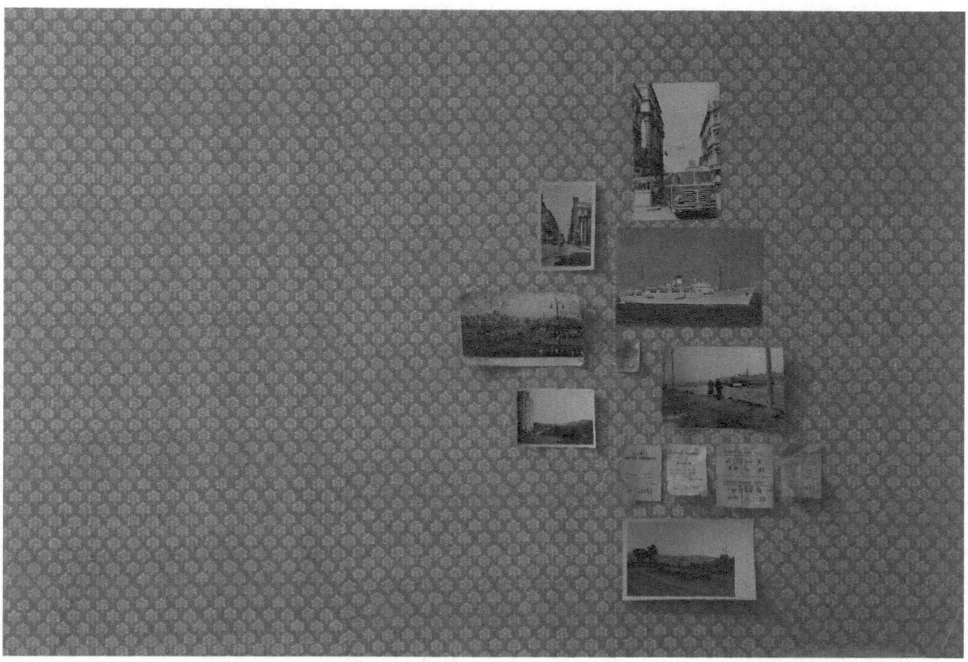

Figure 9. Kemal's room.

understand the nature of temporalities in the construction of heritage tourism experiences. In particular, through the example of the Museum of Innocence we can begin to think of authenticity as a series of stories that are told, layer upon layer, in a mimetic process where the past, present and future become connected into a perfomative texture. Authenticity then becomes not just important in terms of places and experiences but also in terms of an ongoing story about time.

Disclosure statement

No potential conflict of interest was reported by the authors.

References

Allmer, A. (2009). Orhan Pamuk's 'museum of Innocence': On architecture, narrative and the art of collecting. *Architectural Research Quarterly, 13*(2), 163–172.
Basu, P., & Coleman, S. (2008). Introduction: Migrant worlds, material cultures. *Mobilities, 3*(3), 313–330.
Benjamin, W. (1935). *The work of art in an age of mechanical reproduction.* Retrieved from http://www.arthistoryarchive.com/arthistory/modern/The-Work-of-Art-in-the-Ageof-Mechanical-Reproduction.html.
Benjamin, W. (1968). *Illuminations.* New York: Schocken Books.
Cheung, C.-F. (2009). *Kairos: Phenomenology and photography.* Bucharest: Zeta Books.
Chronis, A. (2012). Tourists as story-Builders: Narrative construction at a heritage museum. *Journal of Travel & Tourism Marketing, 29*(5), 444–459.
Cohen, E. (1995). Contemporary tourism. Trends and challenges: Sustainable authenticity or contrived Post-modernity? In R. Butler & D. Pearce (Eds.), *Change in tourism: People, places, Processes* (pp. 12–29). London: Routledge.
Crang, M. (1996). Magic kingdom or a quixotic quest for authenticity. *Annals of Tourism Research, 23*(2), 415–431.
Crang, M. (1997). Picturing practices: Research through the tourist gaze. *Progress in Human Geography, 21*(3), 359–373.
Crang, M. (2005). Time: Space. In P. Cloke & R. Johnston (Eds.), *Spaces of geographical thought: Deconstructing human geography's binaries* (pp. 199–217). London: Sage.
Crang, M., & Travlou, P. S. (2001). The city and topologies of memory. *Environment and Planning D: Society and Space, 19*, 161–177.
Faber. (2009). *The Museum of innocence - about book.* Retrieved from https://www.faber.co.uk/9780571237005-the-museum-of-innocence.html.
Haldrup, M., & Larsen, J. (2003). The family gaze. *Tourist Studies, 3*(1), 23–45.
Halewood, C., & Hannam, K. (2001). Viking heritage tourism: Authenticity and commodification. *Annals of Tourism Research, 28*(3), 565–580.
Hannam, K. (2006). Contested Discourses of War and heritage at the British Residency, Lucknow, India. *International Journal of Tourism Research, 8*(3), 199–212.
Hannam, K., Mostafanezhad, M., & Rickly, J. (2017). *Event Mobilities.* London: Routledge.
Hannam, K., & Yankovska, G. (2017). You can't Go home again - only Visit: Chernobyl Resident's memories and tourism Mobilities. In S. Marschall (Ed.), *Tourism and memories of home* (pp. 53–67). Bristol: Channel View.
Hughes, G. (1995). Authenticity in tourism. *Annals of Tourism Research, 22*, 181–203.
Knudsen, B. T., & Waade, A. M. (2010). Performative authenticity in tourism and spatial experience: Rethinking the relations between travel, place and emotion. In B. T. Knudsen & A. M. Waade (Eds.), *Re-Investing authenticity: Tourism, place and Emotions* (pp. 1–21). Bristol: Channel View Publications.
Littrell, M., Anderson, L., & Brown, P. (1993). What makes a craft souvenir authentic? *Annals of Tourism Research, 20*, 197–215.
MacCannell, D. (1973). Staged authenticity. *American Journal of Sociology, 79*(3), 589–603.
Metcalfe, A. (2006). 'It was the right time to do it': Moving house, the life-course and *kairos*. *Mobilities, 1*(2), 243–260.
Mossberg, L. (2008). Extraordinary experiences through storytelling. *Scandinavian Journal of Hospitality and Tourism, 8*(3), 195–210.
Ogut, S. T. (2017). The Struggle of objects and meaning: Design, Representation and material culture in the everyday objects of Orhan Pamuk's 'museum of Innocence'. *The Design Journal, 20*(1), 45–66.
Pamuk, O. (2008). *The museum of Innocence.* London: Faber.

Pamuk, O. (2013). *The Innocence of objects*. New York: Abrams.
Pera, R. (2017). Empowering the new traveller: Storytelling as a co-creative behaviour in tourism. *Current Issues in Tourism*, *20*(4), 331–338.
Peters, P. (2018). On becoming a parcel: Artistic interventions as ways of knowing mobile worlds. In A. A. Kjaerulff, S. Kesselring, P. Peters, & K. Hannam (Eds.), *Envisioning networked urban mobilities: art, performances, impacts* (pp. 26–37). London: Routledge.
Pink, S. (2007). *The future of visual Anthropology: Engaging the senses*. London: Routledge.
Ramo, H. (1999). An Aristotelian human time-space manifold. *Time and Society*, *8*(2), 309–328.
Rickly-Boyd, J. M. (2012). Authenticity & aura: A Benjaminian approach to tourism. *Annals of Tourism Research*, *39* (1), 269–289.
Rickly-Boyd, J. M. (2013). Existential authenticity: Place matters. *Tourism Geographies*, *15*(4), 680–686.
Savage, M. (2000). Walter Benjamin's urban thought: A critical analysis. In M. Crang & N. Thrift (Eds.), *Thinking space* (pp. 33–53). London: Routledge.
Scarles, C. (2010). Where words fail, visuals ignite: Opportunities for visual autoethnography in tourism research. *Annals of Tourism Research*, *37*(4), 905–926.
Thompson, F., Hannam, K., & Petrie, K. (2012). Producing Ceramic Art through tourism research. *Annals of Tourism Research*, *39*(1), 336–360.
Tung, V., & Ritchie, J. R. B. (2011). Exploring the essence of memorable tourism experiences. *Annals of Tourism Research*, *38*(4), 1367–1386.
Wang, N. (1999). Rethinking authenticity in tourism experience. In S. Williams (Ed.), *Tourism: Critical concepts in the social sciences* (pp. 210–234). London: Routledge.

Fairytale authenticity: historic city tourism, Harry Potter, medievalism and the magical gaze

Jane Lovell

ABSTRACT

This article makes an original contribution to debates about authenticity by asking how tourist experiences of the medieval historic environment are linked to fairytales, providing a new way for tourists to imaginatively authenticate heritage. The architecture of some historic cities is preponderantly medieval, an era which is strongly associated with fairytales. Magical-historical double affectiveness has been compounded in the collective imagination by modern fairytales such as the fantasy Harry Potter and Game of Thrones which employ historic city locations and faux-medieval settings, establishing a fluid magi-heritage simulacrum. This is concretised by the appearance in many historic cities of evidence of magical placemaking and staged magical authenticity, such as wizarding shops. The study used a visual methodology to examine 14 historic cities including Oxford, Cambridge, Bath, York, and Canterbury, demonstrating how the magical gaze employs fairytale schemata to imaginatively authenticate places. The findings illustrated how heritage tourists serendipitously encountered the medieval-fairytalesque, unfolding the agency of monumental cathedrals and castles and discovering stories and the historicisation of mythology within the extraordinary-ordinary streetscape. The research findings imply that in an era when the fantasy genre is increasingly popular, the experiential authenticity of heritage tourists may be enhanced by the 'heritage marvellous.'

Introduction

This article makes an original contribution to debates about heritage authenticity by exploring authentically imaginative experiences, defining magical realities and linking the medieval historic environment to fairytales. The research question examines the ways in which the marvellous manifests in tourist experiences in historic cities, many of which are illuminating case studies when discussing authenticity because the historic environment contains a substantial amount of original and pastiche medieval heritage (Tuan, 1977/2001). The medieval era continues to remain a popular object of fascination (Eco, 1986, p. 68) and is strongly associated with fairytales (Ortenberg, 2006). Fairytales continue to evolve; recent fantasy texts include the books and televised adaptations of *A Discovery of Witches* by Deborah Harkness and *His Dark Materials* by Philip Pullman, both filmed in 2018, which converge in parallel fantasy and heritage versions of the historic city of Oxford. These fantasies use settings of castles, alleyways and landmarks which possess significant historical 'architectural agency' (MacDonald, 2009, p. 157) such as the Bodleian library. In contrast, dramas like *Game of Thrones* remodel the medieval era by historicising mythology using genuine and faux pastiche settings and tropes (Larrington, 2016).

Capital cities such as New York or London have been denoted 'cinematic' (Shiel & Fitzmaurice, 2001) and some tourists feel that heritage sites resemble movie sets (Willson & McIntosh, 2007). This study was initiated because when researching the extent of staged authenticity in historic cities, rather than the sensation of being on a film set, unexpectedly, heritage tourists conveyed the feeling of inhabiting a fairytale. The implications for research and practice are that with a plethora of gaming, film and TV fantasy influences, tourists may increasingly encounter the 'heritage marvellous' or 'magi heritage' in historic cities. Magical placemaking may augment the spectrum and quality of visitor experiences, by expanding the opportunities to imaginatively authenticate the historic environment.

Literature review

Magical realities

A key element of this paper demonstrates how magic and fairytales can be applied to heritage, tourism and authenticity. Magical reality was first used to describe post-colonial Latin American literature juxtaposing the technological magic of the new world and the functional spirituality of the old (Faris, 2004). To deconstruct magical reality further, according to Bowers (2004, p. 20): '... in marvellous and magical realism "magic" refers to any extraordinary occurrence' and realism is what can be 'detected through the senses.' While the phrase magical reality suggests polarity, Faris (2004, p. 1) resolved the duality by stating that magical reality combines a perceptual: '... realism and the fantastic, so that the marvellous seems to grow organically within the ordinary, blurring the distinctions between them.' In the same vein, Strecher (1999, p. 267) brought the separate elements of magic and reality together by outlining the '... marvellous-yet real-place' drawing on Russia's literary tradition of the maravilloso (the marvellous real). These definitions encapsulate the paradigm used in this article, where magical realities embody the imagination (including wonder, the extraordinary, marvellous, fantastical and fairytalesque) and reveal the 'heritage marvellous' or 'magi-heritage' in the actual world.

Parallels exist between tourism, authenticity and magic. The drive to fulfil a fantasy or unobtainable quest (Crang, 1996, p. 415; Knudsen, Rickly, & Vidon, 2016) motivates tourists seeking 'experiential authenticity' (MacCannell, 1976; Wang, 1999). Folklore tourism is regarded as a sub-set of heritage tourism that offers tourists something 'beyond the ordinary' (Timothy, 2011, p. 424) and the desire to escape the everyday and experience the fantasy could be said to underpin much tourism activity (MacCannell, 1973). Leal (1995, p. 101) submitted that magical realism is '... an attitude toward reality' and postmodern authenticity (Wang, 1999) is supposedly a more playful viewpoint which is substantiated by the tourist pursuit of imaginary worlds and enchantment (Hennig, 2002; Robinson & Picard, 2009). Authenticity is an applicable concept in themed magical environments; Waysdorf and Reijnders (2018) and Lovell and Bull (2017) observed how tourists authenticate the Wizarding World of Harry Potter, for example using the theme park's 'official' endorsement by JK Rowling.

Transformational authentic experiences are sought at living history sites, re-enactment festivals, cos-play events and at fantasy film locations (Beeton, 2016; Buchmann, Moore, & Fisher, 2010; Carnegie & McCabe, 2008; Everett & Parakoottathil, 2018). Kim and Jamal (2007, p. 198) implied that during these activities, tourists construct an 'alternative reality.' This research suggests that rather than tourists adopting alternative realities, medieval historic environments stimulate tourists to perceive magi-heritage as the embodiment of the imagination in the actual world.

Authenticity is a liquid term and it is important to contextualise its use. It could be argued that in addition to postmodern authenticity, objective authenticity (Wang, 1999) often employed by heritage tourists, resembles the magical in its focus on the auratic, cultic qualities of remoteness, value and rarity (Benjamin, 1936/2008). When also researching authenticity, Rickly-Boyd (2012, p. 129) remarked on the use of the word 'magic,' used by tourists to describe the wonder of heritage reproductions. The elusiveness of aura means that while people travel to find it, it remains ever-fugitive and yet exerts a magnetic force. Chhabra's (2010, p. 806) work on Generation Y indicates an interest in object-related authenticity rather than theme parks, expressing a preference for 'true to the original and historically endorsed objects.' Thus, Generation Y are more likely to visit the auratic material architecture of historic cities, however, once there, the proximity of heritage may evoke magical qualities. Magical realities have been positioned by Lovell and Bull (2017, p. 8) within debates about authenticity, suggesting that tourists both attribute magical qualities to places and also experience places in magical states including the 'dreamlike, poetic, otherworldly, rescaled, phantasmagorical and uncanny.' They extended Fjellman's (1992, p. 255) descriptors of Walt Disney World: 'fake fake, fake real, real real and fake fake,' to include the unreal, hyper real and magically real. While resembling the inversions, copies and exaggerations of hyperreality (Baudrillard, 1981; Eco, 1986), magical realities differ, within this paper, because they are underpinned by stories. Building further on conceptual intersections, fairytales have been defined by Swann (1995, p. 9) as encompassing any story incorporating the magical or marvellous. For the purposes of this research, magical realities, marvellous realities, and the fairytalesque are viewed as permeable terms, encapsulating the fantasies which tourists seek.

The 'Fairytale Route' in Germany (Bendix & Hemme, 2004; Hemme, 2005) is a popular fantasy tourist destination, as are folklore festivals and re-enactment events. Storytelling has always been perceived as an essential part of historic interpretation (Smith, 2006) and fairytales provide recognisable schemata which enable tourists to relate to the past. Fairytales are significant to tourism (Järv, 2010); Larrington (2015, p. 7) observed how people are attracted to: 'tales which draw their energy from the places where we live or where we travel.' Some tourists seek to understand the myths of origins of places (Lovell & Bull, 2017) and Larrington (2015, p. 9) argued that legends offer answers '... through a kind of metaphorical thinking, through structures and patterns which, in their stripped-down clarity, show us what's really important in an unfamiliar light.' Larrington went on to describe (pp. 16–30) how Anglo-Saxons explained the ruins of Roman buildings in Britain as the work of giants, demonstrating how multi-layered historic environments have traditionally been explained by fairytales. It has been demonstrated by Lovell and Bull (2017) that heritage tourists coolly use facts to 'mechanistically authenticate' historic sites. When tourists 'imaginatively authenticate' medievalness with fairytales, they may also make meaning and attribute origin stories in a warmer, more playful postmodern manner.

As part of the process of authentication, historic cities are framed by a 'magical gaze' which takes Urry's (2002) original, romantic 'tourist gaze' further into the realm of the imagination. Historic cities are inchoate canvases, peppered with material and atmospheric traces of the Roman and medieval landscape, in which tourists can detect the poetic 'reverberations' (Bachelard, 1994) of the past. Fairytales help the process of reconstructing the past, by entwining collective memories with the collective imagination in a simulacrum of medievalness. Historic and film re-enactors actively pursue experiential authenticity: 'Both require accurate foundations; it is only when their two worlds are aligned that their fantasy performances can take place' (Lovell & Bull, 2017, p. 155). Heritage tourists may unexpectedly encounter magical realities due to factors such as the resonance of historic sites, the vertiginous abstractness of the past and its materialisation in monumental structures such as city walls. The auratic encounter with vestiges of the distant past may seem a source of wonder to the 'imaginative eye' (Massey, 2005) and a state of 'heritage flow' merge with a 'magical flow' (adapted from Lovell & Bull, 2017, p. 11). Rather than a reading of historic cities as texts, a state of magical flow unfolds the extra-textual, 'the inside of the outside or outside of the inside' (Derrida, 1976/2016, p. 32). Openness to the imagination is necessary for tourists to experience the creativity and fluidity of space and poetics (Bachelard, 1994; Barthes, 1980/2000; Massey, 2005; Relph, 1976; Tuan, 1977/2001). Flow also necessarily absents the gazer, who adopts the 'imagining attitude' (Sartre, 2004, p. 190), which is assumed when mentally recreating the stories within the composition of paintings, or when reading fiction. Magical realities are described by Lovell and Bull (2017, p. 8) as an 'evaporating' rather than a hot form of authentication, because of this abstraction of the imaginative experience. When magic and reality are aligned in historic cities, the imagination is allowed to flow, unfolding marvellous realities.

Once upon a time in historic cities – magical placemaking

Historic cities have long been considered as significant tourist destinations; Ashworth and Tunbridge defined the term 'tourist-historic city' (2000), emphasising the issues of congestion and commodification which epitomised over-tourism in the historic cities of the early 1990s. They are meaningful sites in which to study authenticity, incorporating the ongoing tension between preservation and development. The layout of historic cities may vary, but tends toward a physically compact palimpsest of different built eras, with a Roman grid plan, and walls and a winding medieval cluster of streets centred on a cathedral or church (Orbaşli, 2000, p. 9). While the built heritage of historic cities is seemingly static and immutable, the city walls, cathedrals, castles, timbered buildings, narrow lanes and jetties and cod-medieval new builds are also soft, phenomic places of legend and memory (Nora, 1984–1992; Smith, 2006). The material heritage environment provides visual metaphors such as ruins, which allow tourists to displace the present and mentally reconstruct the past. Official versions of authentication, such as World Heritage Centre designation in Bath, 'frame and elevate, enshrine and reproduce' (MacCannell, 1976, pp. 43–45) as part of the sacralisation process, enfolding physical buildings in a magical envelope of constructed authenticity.

Intangible cultural heritage is nurtured by historic cities because it contributes extraordinary, locally distinctive elements to the cultural capital. In 2005, a report, *City of Imagination* (Yellowbook, 2005), emphasised Canterbury's links to authors such as Geoffrey Chaucer. It could be said that historic cities invent traditions (Hobsbawm & Ranger, 1983) which embellish and augment elements of the fairytale-medieval; designing medieval parades and pageants, generating historic simulacra and reinventing old mythologies. Lovell and Griffin (2018) have argued that light installations and festivals, such as Durham Lumiere, are magically real and irreal events, using illusion to encase immanent historic structures, evoking affective atmosphere and sensations of disbelief and wonder and attracting fairytale tourism (see Image 1).

Image 1. St Augustine's Abbey Light Installation, 2018.

Placemaking builds on the monumental and vernacular architecture of historic cities which is primarily connected with the medieval period (Relph, 1976). This era is specifically associated with folklore according to Ortenberg (2006, p. 40): 'The literature of folklore, of which fairytales were regarded as an essential component, went hand in hand with scholarly interest in the medieval past.' Debord (1967/2014, pp. 74–75) made the point that while belief in myth ended with the Middle Ages, the Middle Ages has become a mythic period of history. In the essay, *Dreaming of the Middle Ages*, Eco (1986, p. 66) asserted that: 'immediately after the official ending of the Middles Ages, Europe was ravaged by a pervasive medieval nostalgia' which, he argued, continues today. New generations of tourists are emerging for whom Zipes's (1988, p. 148) declaration that fairytales 'pervade our lives' is highly relevant. That historic cities embody fantasy culture was evident in Will Self's description of Canterbury at a book reading in Canterbury in 2007: 'It is Hobbiton.'

This fairytale-medievalness is symptomatic of the emergent, constructive and postmodern authenticity (Bruner, 1994; Cohen, 1988; Wang, 1999) reflected in cyclical social taste and the metahistorical. Collective memory is a selective, unreliable narrator, focusing on popular eras of history such as medieval and Roman (Eco, 1986) and tending toward the sensationalism of 'mythhistoricus' (Cornford, 2014) which blends history and artistry in the telling. Eco (1986, pp. 63–65) observed that the medieval is on 'continuous return,' but it is the spectacularly medieval which is repeated in trends such as pre-Raphaelitism. Historical storybookism was treated in an acerbic manner by Benjamin (cited in Boyer, 1996, p. 135), who remarked that: 'once upon a time ... resides in the brothel of historicism.' The mid-to-late Victorian revival of fairytales portrayed a heightened, romanticised version of the faux-medieval, associated with artisanship and authenticity. Ultimately, according to Eco (1986, p. 67), 'the rediscovery of the medieval would be the work of twentieth century mass-media.'

Some mass-media reinterpretations of historic themes extended postmodern authenticity and provoked some critics to cite 'fakelore' (Crang, 1996, p. 429) and ultimately, 'Distory' or 'Disney realism' (Fjellman, 1992, p. 60). Eco (1986, p. 67) described medieval pastiche as 'fantastic neomedievalism,' which is exemplified by the spectacle of *Game of Thrones* (2011–), blending medieval European history with the Celts, Anglo-Saxons and Vikings (Larrington, 2016). The potential effect of fantasy on heritage tourism is suggested by the recent explosion of films and television series about the supernatural addressed earlier. Growing numbers of media platforms, games such as *Assassin's Creed*, the increasingly sophisticated use of virtual and augmented realities and special effects square the 'hermeneutic circle' (Jenkins, 2003) of medievalism. Mixed realities are not simply technological, but imaginative. Fairytales also continue to evolve as living traditions using intertextual referencing and formats, for example the artwork of Paula Rego, and the *Game of Thrones* tapestry in Ulster, feeding the collective imagination and potentially leading to the reappraisal of medieval sites by tourists.

Magical placemaking, historicising mythology, has occurred in some historic cities. Connections to fantasy can be tangential, for example, even urban myths about the ubiquitous modern fairytale, *Harry Potter* add locations to guided tours: key historic alleyways in London, York, Exeter, Edinburgh and Chepstow all share the title of the 'inspiration for Diagon Alley.' The wizarding establishment, *The Shop With No Name* opened in 2017 in the Shambles in York as a result attracting several others and there are wizarding shops in Edinburgh, including *The Boy Wizard* and *Diagon House* in Victoria Street. These historic cities follow Kings Cross's Platform Nine and Three Quarters in the move towards staging extra-textual, physical versions of the Potterverse. Oxford is a fulcrum of magical geographies, with tours of *Harry Potter* filming locations, the parallel realities of *Lyra's Oxford* and *Narnia*, plus growing interest in the sites of the book and televised adaptation of *The Discovery of Witches*. The tour guides mix factual heritage and fantasy content when visiting sites such as the Pitt Rivers Museum (Coffey, 2017). Canterbury Cathedral was selected as the original location for Hogwarts in the Harry Potter films, but eventually Gloucester and Durham Cathedrals, Alnwick Castle and Lacock Abbey acted as an assemblage of the wizarding school. Regardless of which cathedrals were chosen, *Harry Potter* contributed to the lexicon of magi-heritage turrets, gothic halls and cloisters, let alone mysterious alleyways, crooked buildings, rambling pubs, and cobblestones. This article investigates how the built medieval (and neo-medieval) heritage of historic cities may be authenticated by tourists as innately magical, prior to placemaking.

To conclude this section, Eco (1986) listed 10 contemporary versions of the Middle Ages and if an eleventh were added today, it may be entitled: 'The fairytale-neomedieval tourist destination.'

Methodology

The research employed a visual methodology, which is appropriate because photography has been described as a way of making magic (Robinson & Picard, 2009). Larsen (2008, p. 149) argued that photography is an organic way of processing experiences and Visitor-Employed Photography (VEP) (Dodman, 2003) emerged as a sensory, self-directed research tool, permitting the mobility essential for a spatial study of tourism. Using photography enabled participants to perform a placemaking and storytelling activity of their own (Pink, 2006). An initial VEP study into authenticity was conducted in 2009–2010. This foundation was extended into a longitudinal study and further data collected in September 2016 and June–August 2018 through semi-structured interviews with tourism and heritage practitioners. A convenience sampling strategy was adopted which involved approaching placemaking experts, obtaining the views of an informed research population. The VEP study distributed disposable cameras and diaries (photo-diaries) to tourism managers from the historic cities of Bath, Brighton, Cambridge, Canterbury, Chester, Chichester, Durham, Lancaster, Lincoln, Oxford, Rochester, Shrewsbury, Winchester and York. It is worth noting that this study involved English historic cities, but the findings are equally internationally applicable. Twenty-four placemakers have also taken part (including archivists, stonemasons, architects, development managers, planning officers and museum curators). In total, 64 tourists from Canterbury were chosen using the pragmatic criterion-based sampling on arrival at the Visitor Information Centre. Pseudonyms are used to protect the anonymity of participants. This established a representative range of participants from all ages and 23 nationalities, while it is a small sample of the approximately approximate 4.2 million tourists visiting the city. The Visitor Information Centre not only legitimised the project but allowed easy, city-centre return of the camera packs. Altogether, 1203 photo-diary entries have been assessed. While disposable cameras are dated, the retro method caught the attention, increasing the likelihood of a significant response.

Participants were asked: 'To what extent is this place authentic or inauthentic?' and Lightroom software provided a method of searching and theming, intertwining image and text equally, to further understand the phenomic, experiential meaning of the photo-diaries (Pink, 2006) (see Image 2). After pure content analysis (counting castles) was deemed overly quantitative for a visual approach, the method of assessing the photo-diaries strove for a richness and depth appropriate for a qualitative study. The four-stage method developed by Collier (2001) suggested that the researcher worked from the individual photographs upwards. This meant that rather than working with 98 participants, the researcher was working with 1203 views of historic cities. To establish coherence, the researcher used the structure of Fjellman's (1992) categories of fake and real to reassemble the historic cities into four typologies.

The longitudinal study has explored a 'participatory' (Guba & Lincoln, 2008, pp. 192–197) paradigm, recognising the 'interweaving of viewpoints, for the incorporation of multiple perspectives.' Different perspectives are inherent in visual methodologies; the possibility of attribution is recognised at various stages of the process, including the interpretation of the photographer and the subjectivity and reflexiveness of the researcher (Stevenson & Inskip, 2008). To emphasise the co-creation, 'studium' (Barthes, 1980/2000, pp. 20–28) was employed to avoid photographs being 'inert' or 'polite' under the researcher gaze, by animating images with the agency of 'affective intentionality.' Using the practice of studium – perhaps a magical form of deeper analysis – a grouping emerged from the categories of fake and real as a fairytalesque assemblage of magical realities and formed the inspiration for the article.

Image 2. Lightroom software displaying Sir John Boy's House in Canterbury.

Findings

Gingerbread spaces in Wonderland

The research findings focused on three aspects of magical realities: the suggestions and affordances of material heritage, the relationship of tourists and placemakers to unseen 'medieval hosts' and myth-historicus, or performed, staged medievalness.

That the architecture of historic cities yields medieval and magical atmospherics, was remarked on by participants visiting Canterbury, for example, Tourist 43: 'Everything is magical' and Tourist 27: 'I like the medieval feeling of the city.' The medieval era was by far the most popular epoch mentioned in the study. The miracles (and fakery) worked on pilgrims visiting the shrine of the murdered Thomas Beckett, arguably give Canterbury an enduring magical atmosphere and tourists visiting the city with this in mind may predisposed to the marvellous. As sites of meaning, historic environments can incline visitors towards storytelling, for example Stevenson and Inskip (2008) described the semiotic power of clock faces and after moving to the city, a tourism practitioner (Canterbury 16), was struck by the 'storybook' blue clock faces on heritage buildings.

The heritage environment portrayed in the photo-diaries seemed to the researcher to unfold and fold in a Derridian manner as visitors observed the built streetscape. Spatial fairytales were suggested by the depth of photographic compositions, where narrow streets and lanes and jetties loomed over the observer. The effect created a Tom Thumb perspective, shrinking the viewer in a giant environment, where the tall buildings returned the gaze. Monumental medieval structures were designed to dominate (Relph, 1976); cathedrals, castles, towers, and city walls were constructed to fortify cities and convey temporal and spiritual power, underlining how: 'the castle is so marvellous a place of human design, that marvels seem especially suited to it' (Thomas, 1986, p. 129). There were multiple photo-diary entries of St George's Clocktower in Canterbury and Clifford's Tower in York. Towers are tropes of fairytale settings (Thomas, 1986) follies in the city, from which Rapunzel could let down her hair. It is not only the medieval, but also Gothic and Neo-Gothic architecture which celebrated a storybook feel during Romantic revivalism. Photo-diaries expressed the overwhelmingly 'wonderful,' 'marvellous' and 'really real' impressions of the Gothic spires of cathedrals and Kings College chapel Cambridge. Winchester was said by the practitioner to be a 'city of gates' with primarily symbolic resonance due to their position in the city centre as fragments of a vanished boundary. Some photo-diaries featured the river through the bars of the fence, or the churchyard glimpsed through a wooden gate, unfolding an innately romantic, Gothic narrative of the forbidden: the barred gate, the closed door, the cloister.

The medieval vernacular layout of the historic core is also fairytalesque, forming an impression of what some tourists called 'oldyworldy,' 'medievally' and 'otherworldly' and another participant Canterbury 24, referred to as: 'the medieval pattern of the city.' The winding motion of central medieval lanes in Canterbury's historic core was unusual to participants used to grid streetscapes, spiralling them deeper into their authentic selves:

> I find the narrow medieval streets sweet. They give character to Canterbury. They make me feel like wandering around randomly doing nothing, just walking slowly absorbing the positive energy that I perceive around me, walking around the same places where people from medieval times walked by. (Tourist 43)

Experiential authenticity and magical flow are evident in this comment, as the effects of architectural agency (MacDonald, 2009, p. 157) are substantiated by the participant's statement that the streets 'make' her behave in specific ways. Tourists 5, 44 and 48 used a variant of the magical gaze, the 'Grimm gaze,' to discover the 'romantic' Hansel and Gretel-style 'hidden house' in All Saints Lane, which seemed concealed in plain sight, as Tourist 5 confirmed: 'Hidden gem - nice peaceful street that no-one seemed to notice.' The agency of the historic environment is further indicated by a pottery 'hidden' in the Ginnels (passageways) in Lancaster. As Pullman (2012, p. xix) stated: 'A fairytale is not a text. The fairytale is in a perpetual state of becoming and alteration' and these photo-diaries evinced a state of magical flow, disclosing the magically quantum activities of historic cities which reassemble themselves, hiding and placing the subconscious in plain view. Space was fluidly creative (Bachelard, 1994; Massey, 2005), revealing and concealing suggestions to tourists.

Participants also considered the 'hidden' urban bucolic in Winchester, Shrewsbury and Chester, and Canterbury 6 remarked on a garden in Canterbury Cathedral grounds, the stout, high city walls protecting what became a storied space from the outside world in a manner reminiscent of Oscar Wilde's story of *The Selfish Giant*. Further folds of historic cities revealed the urban uncanny (Freud, 1940/2004) where the storybook has come to life. Participants photographed the 'English eerie' (MacFarlane, 2015), the process of medieval entropy encapsulated by the ruins of St Augustine's Abbey and also an overgrown wildflower meadow which houses the seemingly miniature, ancient Greyfriars Chapel, described by Canterbury 1 as: 'a last surviving fragment of the Franciscan monastery.'

Magical realism has been linked to uncanny sensations of defamiliarity (Royle, 2003, pp. 160–161) which suggest storybook spaces to tourists authenticating historic places. Photographs of Sir John Boy's House on Palace Street in Canterbury (see Image 2), the Little Crooked House on Lancaster Quay and Old Chesil Rectory in Winchester, showed defamiliarised leaning structures with sunken foundations conveying the vertiginous passing of time (Lovell & Bull, 2017, p. 33). Tourist 8 observed of Sir John Boy's House that: 'My husband thought it could not be real as it was obviously part of a set from Alice in Wonderland.' A Wonderlandian subconscious turning of the imagination inside out, can be surmised from the focus on the small doors and gates of the city, as expressed by Canterbury 13, when looking at Mint Yard Gate (see Image 3): 'Such a small gate made for people a lot smaller than we are now.' In contrast, some participants considered the exaggerated scale of an outsized pilgrim's inn in Longmarket, Canterbury, dating from 2002. According to participant Canterbury 6, the architects who came to view the building declared: 'It looks Disneyesque!' The magical gaze also observed staged, 'fake real' imitative 'gingerbread architecture' (Hannigan, 1998, p. 68). Historic cities are a mixture of original features and new builds and this example of larger-than-life pastiche further entwines the built environment with the fairytalesque, unfolding more Wonderland schemata.

The landscape was augmented by backstories, invented by tourists who detected mysteries. The magical gaze added a veneer of suspense to a trap door for Tourist 44, 'Trap door, love the secrecy of where that door leads to.' As did some ancient graffiti identified by Canterbury 3: 'How authentic is

Image 3. The Mint Yard Gate.

"Iheny" meaning purity, how old? There is a mystery behind these carefully carved letters.' Tourist 28 discovered a mysterious, Harry-Potterish lost diary in the Cathedral cloisters. Both the lost diary and the ancient graffiti acted as examples of the 'punctum,' which Barthes (1980/2000, pp. 26–27) described as a poetic, poignant detail which draws the attention in a scene. Hidden houses and streets, tiny doors, oversized and weirdly leaning structures, the punctum of found objects and the single word 'purity,' all combined to suggest the possibilities of the magical gaze.

Fairytale flâneurie

Material heritage has the capacity to inspire stories which fill the absences left by time. People-watching and inventing a narrative for strangers is typical flâneur behaviour and fits into Eco's (1986, p. 68) concept of the medieval period as a 'mythological stage on which to place contemporary characters.' Fairytales are a genre of folk tales, which portray ordinary people, with similar aims and desires (Swann, 1995, p. 9). Crang (2006, p. 55) remarked how tourist sites '... are shot through by absences, where distant others, removed in spaces and time, haunt the sites.' According to Hemme (2005, p. 75): 'travellers have a need for narratives and imaginaries with which to individually enliven and animate landscapes and thus experience them afresh.' Rather than ghosts, medieval hosts were cast as authentic actors in an imagined mis-en-scène, giving the interplay intersubjective, kinaesthetic immediacy. The experientially authentic state of marvel and wonder at the heritage-marvellous skills of past and contemporary unseen craftsmen, was demonstrated by the York practitioner observing the stained-glass Rose window of the Minster.

The magical gaze made a proscenium arch of windows and gateways framing scenes which occurred throughout the historic cities. When the fairytale consciousness, is raised, it is not simply the Gothic, but all medieval buildings of stone, wood and brickwork possess a viscerally magical carapace, acting as a 'heritage time-turners' (adapted from *Harry Potter and the Order of the Phoenix* by Lovell & Bull, 2017, p. 39), enabling experiential authentication. The fantasy sensation of time-travelling has been established as a commonality of tourism (Laing & Frost, 2012, p. 11; Rickly-Boyd, 2012, p. 129) and was a frequent observation made by many participants: Tourist 42: 'Something that attracts me to Canterbury is that it is a medieval city. And (in a way) I feel transported in time.' Time-travelling tourists found that medieval hosts inhabited metaphysical edgelands where habitual, familiar simple gestures were being repeatedly reinscribed on the space, such as opening windows, passing through gateways, or drinking pints of beer. A picture of an open mullioned window was taken by Tourist 19 (see Image 4). The medieval host was poetically just out of reach; traces of movement in space glimpsed in the peripheral vision, a diffuse presence of a person who had just vanished from view, looking back, occupying the parallel worlds of a Philip Pullman novel.

One participant (Canterbury 9) focused the 'imaginative eye' (Massey, 2005), observing: 'Verona type of window. I love this place. You expect Romeo and Juliet to appear.' Fantasy literary geographies make popular tourist sites, but of particular relevance to this paper was a comment by a tourism manager in Oxford, whose photo-diary depicted the King's Arms 'where the Inklings met.' Tolkien wove a 'mythology for England,' using the 'romantic fairy story,' and other interconnected legends (Ortenberg, 2006, p. 180). A research participant from Canterbury (9) serendipitously discovered a hint of another pivotal author, Boccaccio, in Canterbury Cathedral herb garden: 'On a hot day, you would be in a Decameron Tale with naughty people in Italian medieval dress behind the wall.' The remark transforms and subverts the peaceful garden with an earthy scene from the

Image 4. Opened mullioned window.

Decameron, which served as a source for Giovanfrancesco Straparola and Giambattista Basile's authorship of the first stories of the fairytale genre (Swann, 1995, p. 8).

Storytelling is central to flâneurie and participants recast ordinary people as extraordinary fairy-tale characters; Canterbury 9:

> I start the day at Neros at half seven and at a quarter to eight a woman magically appears on the scene with a bundle of medieval clothes and sews there on that sofa and she has to finish a few more stitches.

The fairytalesque is implied in the unexplained 'magical appearance' of the woman with her bundle of medieval clothes, like the helpers in Anderson's *The Elves and the Shoemaker*. The woman is also

Image 5. Carving on shop in Mercery Lane in Canterbury.

Image 6. Green man roof boss, Canterbury Cathedral, courtesy of Canterbury Cathedral.

reminiscent of the phrase 'ordinary and then ... ' (Burness & Griswold, 1982) which was used to describe PL Travers, the writer of *Mary Poppins.* Probing by the researcher revealed that the woman is a medieval reenactor and sews her costumes in the Tudor café, before work, preparing to inhabit her marvellous heritage another time.

Mythhistoricus

Fairytales incorporate tall tales (Swann, 1995, p. 11) and the search for authentic backstage views may involve mythmaking, apocryphal tales and urban legends. The magical cultural heritage of historic cities can sometimes resemble staged authenticity when poetic licence is used in order to reinvent cultural heritage for each era. Examples include the thirteenth century 'round table' hanging in the Great Hall in Winchester, supposedly made for a Round Table Tournament and thought to be Arthurian by Caxton (Lacy, Ashe, Ihle, Kalinke, & Thompson, 1991). Tourist (55) pointed out how a tour guide referred to an Inn in Canterbury, staging the unstaged with the words: 'Hotel where four

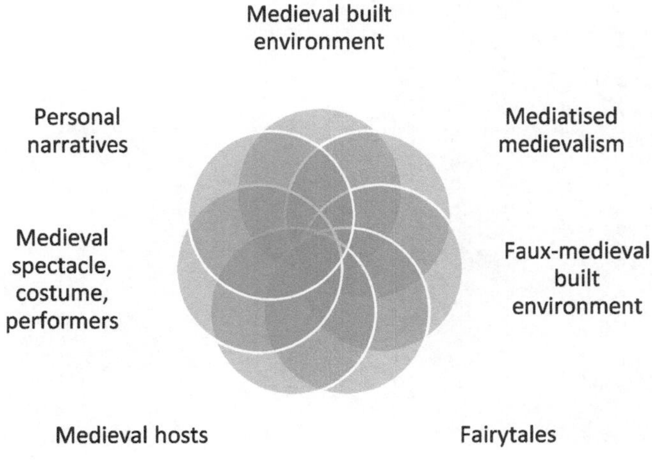

Figure 1. Impressions of fairytale-medievalness in historic cities.

Table 1. Impressions of tangible magi-heritage in historic cities.

Qualities	Illustrated by
Fairytale settings	Castles, cathedrals, cottages, lanes
Anthropomorphism	Towers, clocks
Architectural agency	Winding streets, looming structures, hidden houses and lanes
Medieval hosts	Drinking beer, opening windows, buying fruit
Scale	Small doors, small chapel
Disorientation	Leaning buildings
Uncanny	Poignancy of ruins
Tall tales	Apocryphal stories in tours, renamed street signs
Personal narratives	Dressing up in costume, making up names, inhabiting characters
Pagan/folklore	Green man, Morris dancing, devilish carvings
Literary fairytale figures	Inklings, Boccaccio
Punctum/mystery	Ancient graffiti, lost diary

knights might have stayed.' The Oxford practitioner declared that Oxford 'is full of apocryphal stories.' Some places seem essentially marvellous, and others are *made* marvellous, for example, as mentioned earlier, the York practitioner pointed out that the lanes were once called The Great Flesh Shambles because they were an open-air slaughterhouse. Grope Lane in Shrewsbury has also been renamed. What seems to be historic is not always a reliable indicator of authenticity; some subjects are considered too dark to be palatable for modern sensibilities. Sanitising street signs perpetuates a fairytale past, while militating against the unsettling and often crude violence of the fairystory world. While reinterpretations of the past could be said to be forms of staged authenticity (MacCannell, 1973) they contain their own truth; as Chhabra, Healy, and Sills (2003) observed, '… what is staged is not superficial since it contains elements of the original tradition.' Preserving the myth includes retaining arcane signs as symbols of adventure, an example at the Bell and Crown pub in Canterbury,

Image 7. Lemn Sissay's Cantarion poem projected onto the bridge over the river Stour in Canterbury.

photographed by Tourist 6: 'Vagabonds, dog stealers, horse thieves, rapscallions, scoundrels, liars and especially bursars! Will not be served on these premises!'

The personal narratives of tourists spin history into fairytales, using archetypal characters, such as witches and knights; Tourist 55 described The Weavers, the timbered café beside a (Victorian and therefore fake-medieval) witch's ducking stool as: 'The Dunking House,' 'weaving' their own version. Travellers imbue their journeys with fantasy by using the structures of fiction; a holiday becoming a quest (Laing & Frost, 2012) and dressing up can facilitating a transformation of self, allowing visitors to assume a different identity (Everett & Parakoottathil, 2018). After a family (Tourist 63) had visited the Canterbury Tales visitor attraction, one of the children went on to wear a plastic souvenir knight's helmet throughout the visit; inhabiting the quest.

The seeking of staged authenticity spectacles is illustrated by photo-diaries featuring costumed buskers and re-enactors in medieval clothing in Canterbury, Chester, Rochester and, as the Shrewsbury practitioner described, the 'darker and wilder' Border Morris dancers. Wilder and earthy forms of magic were also embodied in the demonic carvings on a timbered medieval pilgrim's inn (and,

Image 8. Lemn Sissay's Cantarion poem projected onto the bridge over the river Stour in Canterbury, Courtesy Griffin.

reputedly, a brothel) in Mercery Lane observed in Canterbury by Tourist 10 (see Image 5). Gargoyles and the green man roof bosses in Canterbury Cathedral (see Image 6) provided a mystical, pagan example of magical reality, unfolding the inside of the subconscious to the outside: 'There are more than 70 examples of "green men" sculptures and carvings in Canterbury Cathedral' (Tourist 21). They are also called 'foliate heads' (Larrington, 2015) and depict a mask-like face, surrounded by leaves, with branches sprouting from the mouth. Green men can be found throughout Europe, decorating churches and cathedrals, including Winchester and Cambridge. Fairytales can tap into the diffuse atavistic fears, archetypes and deep-seated fears of the subconscious (Freud, 1940/2004) and, as Larrington notes, the story behind this pagan figure is unknown: a mysterious cipher for the imagination. Interestingly, a green man carving above the much-photographed Canterbury chip shop *didn't* attract the imaginative eye. Unobserved, it is an unexplained presence looking down on the scene. Canterbury Cathedral shop now use the Green Man as a marketing motif, emphasising the mixed myths and sometimes conflicting narratives of heritage buildings.

The research findings bring together elements of fairytale-medievalness, or magi-heritage, in historic cities (see Figure 1), which are stimulated by different forms of built and intangible, recreated, reproduced and revived heritage. Table 1 lists the qualities of the overall magi-heritage assemblage. The findings conclude with a tale of two medieval authenticity palimpsests; the first intangible, the second tangible. The poet Lemn Sissay was asked to write a piece for Canterbury in 2018. *Cantuarian* used poetic licence to reimagine a knight cleaning his weapons in the River Stour after murdering Thomas Becket, although the events of the night were unknown. The poem was projected onto a bridge spanning the river by Canterbury Cathedral and local Marlowe Theatre in June 2018. The reinscription of the imagined past generates a medieval-fantasy simulacrum (see Images 7 and 8) composed of imagination, words, light, brickwork and reflection and the reflected moon in the river is a fairytalesque touch. The second example is a marvellous medieval metaphor. As observed by Canterbury (21), a pinnacle and buttress on the North Side of Canterbury Cathedral has 'a Romanesque base, with Early English, Early Gothic, Later Gothic interventions, then a 1920s and 1930s version of Gothic, which borders on Art Deco.' The whole is an assemblage of styles, holding up an iconic building and, when viewed with a magical gaze, adds up to a spectacular tall tale of fairytale-medievalness.

Conclusion

The research findings indicate that the magical gaze offers an imaginative way of authenticating heritage environments with fairytale schemata. The medieval topology of historic cities may be perceived as innately fairytalesque, suggesting that the blend of magi-heritage is becoming less separate for tourists. 'Fairytale qualities' have been attributed by tourists to the Island of Fyn in Denmark, the birthplace of Hans Christian Andersen (Knudsen & Greer, 2011, p. 95), and the increasing popularity of the fantasy medieval landscape indicates that a similar associative process is likely to increase in historic cities. The separation between magical and actual worlds were less marked in historic cities than in theme parks and tourists located the fantasy without signposting. Through affective intentionality, photo-diaries revealed spatial fairytales, the magical gaze of participant and researcher unlocking the intersubjective flow of storybook tropes of looming castles and winding streets. When magic and material heritage aligned in historic cities, some participants assumed an optimal state of magical flow, turning historic cities inside out, perceiving the collective imagination under the stones. Other experientially imaginative states included the Grimm gaze which located the hidden cottage and lane and authenticated historic cities by locating them within fairytale landscapes, such as *Alice in Wonderland*. Fairytale flâneurie subverted the auratic remoteness of the past, permitting participants to glimpse a parallel world of medieval hosts, as they walked through gates, opened windows, ate and drank, depicting the extraordinary ordinariness of folk tales. This past and present mis-en-scène is interspaced with folkloric Green Men, pagan dancing and demonic gargoyles. Postmodern authenticities were apparent in the playfully observed apocryphal stories, fake-real pastiche architecture and sanitised, revised street signage, perpetuating a fairytale version of the past without crude violence.

A limitation of this research is that it initially emerged as distinctive thread from a study of staged authenticity in the historic environment. The authenticity of magi-heritage merits further specific research; the enduring rootedness of fairytales such as *Harry Potter* implies that locating the fantasy in medieval historic cities may become less serendipitous and more purposeful, not simply for folklore and fairytale tourists, but for heritage tourists. Oxford's magical success will inevitably be replicated, and future research directions could explore extra-textual magical heritage by investigating the effect of magical placemaking (the growth of themed wizarding shops and zones in historic alleyways) on the aura of historic cities. Chhabra et al.'s (2003) view that staged authenticity contains refractions of the originals could be explored in the context of how these extra-textual magical geographies are authenticated in varying degrees by placemakers and their fans.

Finally, the sheer pervasiveness of storyworlds is encapsulated in a last example. The author took a class of 37 Level 4 events management students on a walking seminar in Canterbury in September 2018. The group paused in Mercery Lane to examine the grotesque carvings (see Image 5) the jetties overhead, the hanging signs and cobblestones underfoot. When asked 'What does this lane make you think of?' The class responded: '*Harry Potter.*'

Disclosure statement

No potential conflict of interest was reported by the author.

References

Lacy N. J., G. Ashe, S. N. Ihle, M. E. Kalinke, & R. H. Thompson (Eds.). (1991). *The new Arthurian encyclopedia: New edition*. New York, NY: Routledge.

Ashworth, G., & Tunbridge, J. (2000). *The tourist-historic city* (2nd ed.). London: Belhaven.

Bachelard, G. (1994). *The poetics of space*. Boston: Beacon Press.

Barthes, R. (1980/2000). *Camera Lucida*. London: Vintage.

Baudrillard, J. (1981). *Selected writings: Simulacra and simulation*. Cambridge: Polity Press.

Beeton, S. (2016). *Film-induced tourism*. Bristol: Channel view publications.

Bendix, R., & Hemme, D. (2004). Fairytale activists: Narrative imaginaries along a German tourist route. *Folkloreostika svetur, 21*, 187–197.

Benjamin, W. (1936/2008). *The work of art in the age of mechanical reproduction*. London: Penguin.

Bowers, M. N. (2004). *Magic(al) realism*. Abingdon: Routledge.

Boyer, M. (1996). *The city of collective memory: Its historical imagery and architectural entertainments*. Cambridge: MIT Press.

Bruner, E. (1994). Abraham Lincoln as authentic reproduction: A critique of postmodernism. *American Anthropologist, 96*, 397–415.

Buchmann, A., Moore, K., & Fisher, D. (2010). Experiencing film tourism: Authenticity & fellowship. *Annals of Tourism Research, 37*(1), 229–248.

Burness, E., & Griswold, J. (1982). *P. L. Travers, the art of fiction no. 63*. Retrieved from https://www.theparisreview.org/interviews/3099/p-l-travers-the-art-of-fiction-no-63-p-l-travers

Carnegie, E., & McCabe, S. (2008). Re-enactment events and tourism: Meaning, authenticity and identity. *Current Issues in Tourism, 11*(4), 349–368.

Chhabra, D. (2010). Back to the past: A sub-segment of generation Y's perceptions of authenticity. *Journal of Sustainable Tourism, 18*(6), 793–809.

Chhabra, D., Healy, R., & Sills, E. (2003). Staged authenticity and heritage tourism. *Annals of Tourism Research, 30*(3), 702–719.

Coffey, H. (2017). *Lyra's Oxford: New Philip Pullman-inspired walking tour launches to celebrate book of dust trilogy.* Retrieved from https://www.independent.co.uk/travel/uk/lyras-oxford-walking-tour-philip-pullman-book-of-dust-trilogy-la-belle-sauvage-northern-lights-his-a8005131.html

Cohen, E. (1988). Traditions in the qualitative sociology of tourism. *Annals of Tourism Research, 15*, 29–46.

Collier, M. (2001). Approaches to analysis in visual anthropology. In T. Van Leeuwen & C. Jewitt (Eds.), *The handbook of visual analysis* (pp. 35–60). London: Sage.

Cornford, F. M. (2014). *Thucydides mythistoricus* (Routledge revivals). Abingdon: Routledge.

Crang, M. (1996). Magic kingdom or a quixotic quest for authenticity? *Annals of Tourism Research, 23*(2), 415–431.

Crang, M. (2006). Circulation and emplacement: The hollowed-out performance of tourism. In M. Minca, & T. Oakes (Eds.), *Travels in paradox: Remapping tourism* (pp. 47–64). Lanham: Rowman and Littlefields.

Debord, G. (1967/2014). *The society of the spectacle.* (K. Knabb, Trans.). Berkley, CA: Bureau of Public Secrets.

Derrida, J. (1976/2016). *Of grammatology.* (G. Chakravorty-Spivak, Trans.). Baltimore, MA: Johns Hopkins University Press.

Dodman, D. (2003). Shooting in the city: An autophotographic exploration of the urban environment in Kingston, Jamaica. *Area, 35*, 293–304.

Eco, U. (1986). *Faith in fakes: Travels in hyperreality.* London: Picador.

Everett, S., & Parakoottathil, J. (2018). Transformation, meaning-making and identity creation through folklore tourism: The case of the Robin Hood festival. *Journal of Heritage Tourism, 13*(1), 30–45.

Faris, W. (2004). *Ordinary enchantments: Magic realism and the remystification of narrative.* Nashville, TN: Vanderbilt University Press.

Fjellman, S. (1992). *Vinyl leaves: Walt Disney World and America.* Boulder, CA: Westview Press.

Freud, S. (1940/2004). The uncanny. In D. Sandner (Ed.), *Fantastic literature: A critical reader* (pp. 74–101). Westport, CT: Greenwood.

Guba, E. G., & Lincoln, Y. S. (2008). Paradigmatic controversies, contradictions and emerging confluences. In N. K. Denzin & Y. S. Lincoln (Eds.), *The landscape of qualitative research* (Vol. 1, pp. 97–128). London: Sage.

Hannigan, J. (1998). *Fantasy city: Pleasure and profit in the postmodern metropolis.* London: Routledge.

Hennig, C. (2002). Tourism: Enacting modern myths. In G. M. S. Dann (Ed.), *The tourist as a metaphor of the social world* (pp. 169–89). Wallingford: CABI.

Hemme, D. (2005). Landscape, fairies and identity: Experience on the backstage of the fairy tale route. *Journal of Tourism and Cultural Change, 3*(2), 71–87.

Hobsbawm, E., & Ranger, T. (Eds.). (1983). *The invention of tradition.* Oxford: Blackwell.

Järv, R. (2010). Fairy tales and tourist trips. *Fabula, 51*(3–4), 281–294.

Jenkins, O. (2003). Photography and travel brochures: The circle of representation. *Tourism Geographies, 5*(3), 305–328.

Kim, H., & Jamal, T. (2007). Touristic quest for existential authenticity. *Annals of Tourism Research, 34*(1), 181–201.

Knudsen, D. C., Rickly, J. M., & Vidon, E. S. (2016). The fantasy of authenticity: Touring with Lacan. *Annals of Tourism Research, 58*, 33–45.

Knudsen, D., & Greer, C. (2011). Tourism and nostalgia for the pastoral on the island of Fyn, Denmark. *Journal of Heritage Tourism, 6*(2), 87–98.

Laing, J., & Frost, W. (2012). *Books and travel.* Bristol: Channel View.

Larrington, C. (2015). *The land of the green man: A journey through the supernatural landscapes of the British Isles.* London: IB Tauris.

Larrington, C. (2016). *Winter is coming: The medieval world of Game of Thrones.* London: I.B. Tauris.

Larsen, J. (2008). Practices and flows of digital photography: An ethnographic framework. *Mobilities, 3*(1), 141–160.

Leal, L. (1995). Magic realism in Spanish America. In L. P. Zamora & W. Faris (Eds.), *Magic realism: Theory, history, community* (pp. 119–124). London: Duke University Press.

Lovell, J., & Bull, C. (2017). *Authentic and inauthentic places in tourism: From heritage sites to theme parks.* Abingdon: Routledge.

Lovell, J., & Griffin, H. (2018). Fairy tale tourism: The architectural projection-mapping of irreal and magically real lightscapes. *The Journal of Policy Research in Tourism, Leisure and Events.* doi:10.1080/19407963.2018.1556674

MacCannell, D. (1973). Staged authenticity: Arrangements of social space in tourist settings. *American Journal of Sociology, 79*(3), 589–603.

MacCannell, D. (1976). *The tourist: A new theory of the leisure class.* New York, NY: Schocken Books.

MacDonald, S. (2009). *Difficult heritage: Negotiating the Nazi past in Nuremberg and beyond.* Abingdon: Routledge.

MacFarlane, R. (2015, April 10). *The eeerieness of the English countryside.* Retrieved from https://www.theguardian.com/books/2015/apr/10/eeriness-english-countryside-robert-macfarlane

Massey, D. (2005). *For space.* London: Sage.

Nora, P. (1984–1992). *Les Lieux de Memoire.* Paris: Gallimard.

Orbaşli, A. (2000). *Tourists in historic towns: Urban conservation and heritage management*. London: Taylor and Francis.

Ortenberg, V. (2006). *In search of the Holy Grail: The quest for the middle ages*. London: A&C Black.

Pink, S. (2006). *The future of visual anthropology: Engaging the senses*. Abingdon: Routledge.

Pullman, P. (2012). *Grimm tales for young and old*. London: Penguin Classics.

Relph, E. (1976). *Place and placelessness*. London: Pion.

Rickly-Boyd, J. M. (2012). 'Through the magic of authentic reproduction': Tourists' perceptions of authenticity in a pioneer village. *Journal of Heritage Tourism*, *7*(2), 127–144.

Robinson, M., & Picard, D. (2009). Moments, magic and memories: Photographing tourists, tourist photographs and making worlds. In D. Picard & M. Robinson (Eds.), *The framed world: Tourism, tourists and photography* (pp. 1-37). Abingdon: Routledge.

Royle, N. (2003). *The uncanny*. Manchester: Manchester University Press.

Sartre, J. P. (2004). *The imaginary: A phenomenological psychology of the imagination*. (J. Webber, Trans.). London: Routledge.

Self, W. (2007). *Visit to Waterstone's Canterbury*. Author present.

Shiel, M., & Fitzmaurice, T. (2001). *Cinema and the city: Film and urban studies in a global context*. Oxford: Blackwell.

Sissay, L. (2018). *Cantuarian*. Retrieved from https://www.canterbury-cathedral.org/whats-on/news/2018/06/12/a-poem-for-canterbury/

Smith, L. (2006). *Uses of heritage*. Abingdon: Routledge.

Stevenson, N., & Inskip, C. (2008). Visualising London. *London Journal of Tourism, Sport and Creative Industries*, *1*(1), 3–12.

Strecher, M. C. (1999). Magical realism and the search for identity in the fiction of Murakami Haruki. *Journal of Japanese Studies*, *25*(2), 263–298.

Swann, J. S. (1995). *The fairy tale—The magic mirror of imagination*. New York, NY: Wayne Publication.

Thomas, J. (1986). Woods and castles, towers and huts: Aspects of setting in the fairy tale. *Children's Literature in Education*, *17*(2), 126–134.

Timothy, D. J. (2011). *Cultural heritage and tourism: An introduction*. Bristol: Channel View Publications.

Tuan, Y. (1977/2001). *Space and place* (Reprint ed.). Minneapolis, MN: University of Minnesota Press.

Urry, J. (2002). *The tourist gaze* (2nd ed.). London: Sage.

Wang, N. (1999). Rethinking authenticity in tourism experience. *Annals of Tourism Research*, *26*(2), 349–370.

Waysdorf, A., & Reijnders, S. (2018). Immersion, authenticity and the theme park as social space: Experiencing the wizarding world of Harry Potter. *International Journal of Cultural Studies*, *21*(2), 173–188.

Willson, G. B., & McIntosh, A. J. (2007). Heritage buildings and tourism: An experiential view. *Journal of Heritage Tourism*, *2*(2), 75–93.

Yellowbook. (2005). *Canterbury: City of imagination*. Canterbury City Council.

Zipes, J. (1988). *The Brothers Grimm: From enchanted forests to the modern world*. London: Routledge.

OPEN ACCESS

'The smell of death and the smell of life': authenticity, anxiety and perceptions of death at Varanasi's cremation grounds

Nitasha Sharma and Jillian Rickly

ABSTRACT

This paper contributes to an understanding of existential authenticity and existential anxiety in tourism studies through an investigation of tourists' perceptions of death, the Self, and 'others' at the Hindu cremation grounds in Varanasi, India. Encounters with death at dark tourism sites serve as reminders of one's own mortality affecting one's attitude towards death, perception of self, and even challenging one's personal values. Existentialists assert that anxiety is a condition of existential authenticity, and therefore moments of the existentially authentic experience are not always pleasurable. This paper argues that confrontation with death, as exemplified by the Aghori rituals and the cremation grounds in Varanasi, offers tourists an opportunity to examine the inevitability that life will end and to engage with this existential predicament and anxiety in an embodied sense, thereby pushing some of them towards life changes in the pursuit of existential authenticity.

Introduction

The concept of authenticity in dark tourism has mostly been discussed from a destination perspective where degrees of authenticity are attributed to shades of 'darkness' (see Strange & Kempa, 2003). Among those few studies that go beyond a destination perspective to consider authenticity and visitor experience, Roberts (2018) observes that encounters at in-situ dark tourism sites with multisensory 'rememberers', or storytellers, are potentially self-actualizing and enhanced by attitudes of empathy. Indeed, Cohen (2011) contends that tourists may perceive an authentic or 'self-actualization' experience during the process of visiting dark tourism destinations. Conversely, however, Bruner (1991) and Galani-Moutafi (2000) posit that tourists' desire for self-transformation through empathetic encounters with 'authentic' cultures is problematized at atrocity and genocide sites that memorialize the consequences of planned obliteration of cultures. Such sites can trigger emotional reactions, anxiety and moral panic (Biran, Liu, Li, & Eichhorn, 2014). Thus, these experiential challenges inspired Heuermann and Chhabbra (2014) to investigate the role of ethics in dark tourism management and marketing, suggesting that crafting an existentially authentic experience for visitors may support behavior associated with ethical consumption (Guignon, 1986; Wang, 1999) instead of voyeuristic or deviant behavior (Guignon, 1986).

Researchers have argued for a broadly experiential approach to dark tourism research via an integrated supply-demand perspective (Biran, Poria, & Oren, 2011). Yet, there is a dearth of studies examining existential authenticity and anxiety at dark tourism sites. Despite the strong experiential nature of dark tourism and the way it relates to identity politics and inspires self-reflection, there is little empirical research that directly examines the association between existential authenticity and perception of death among tourists. Moreover, there are rich theoretical perspectives linking death-related thoughts, anxiety, and existential authenticity that have yet to be applied to the field. Existential authenticity is a particularly useful theoretical construct for understanding the relations of the embodied nature, identity politics, social relations, and being of tourists. Indeed, research suggests that despite its subjectivity, place matters for the experience of existential authenticity (Rickly-Boyd, 2013b), and that tourism can often function as a catalyst for making life changes post-travel in order to enact ideals of existential authenticity in everyday life (Brown, 2013). Further, an existentialist perspective has been enriched by research focused on the role of existential anxiety in tourism motivation and experience (Kirillova, Lehto, & Cai, 2016, 2017; Vidon & Rickly, 2018). Thus, this paper empirically examines some fundamental questions of dark tourism research, such as how gazing at the death of others paves the way for authentic experiences in cross-cultural tourism encounters. Based on primary data collected on tourists' perceptions of death and their motivations to encounter and experience death at the Hindu cremation grounds at Varanasi, India, a strong association is observed between tourists' fear of premature death and concerns for their own life choices related to existential authenticity and anxiety. This suggests existential authenticity as an underlying factor in tourists' motivations concerning dark tourism. Finally, the paper uncovers moments where existential authenticity clashes with personal values creating challenges to touristic experience that furthers existential anxiety.

Death, existential authenticity, and existential anxiety

The Otherness of death, 'the most powerful of all Others' owing to its universality, is 'the defining feature of thanatourism' (Seaton, 2009, p. 75). This universal otherness, according to Seaton (2009), creates an auratic quality at death tourism sites. Aura is inherently related to authenticity, argues Benjamin (2008), as an experiential quality that connects both ritual and tradition to conceptualizations of authenticity. Rickly-Boyd (2012a) extends the notion of aura to debates about authenticity and tourism, asserting that aura evidences the relationality of experiences of authenticity. In other words, authenticity 'can be simultaneously measured, experienced, and felt', as it is 'a register for the participation in a tradition (however mediated), its rituals (however secularized), and an experience of aura which is a result of this participation' (2012a, p. 284).

Research on the experiential aspects of authenticity has garnered considerable attention in the last decade. While Bruner (1991) describes tourists' desire for self-transformation through an encounter with 'authentic' cultures, more recently scholars examine the ways tourists understand authentic experiences and their own Being while on holiday (Belhassen, Caton, & Stewart, 2008; Brown, 2013; Buchmann, Moore, & Fisher, 2010; Kim & Jamal, 2007; Kirillova et al., 2016, 2017; Rickly-Boyd, 2012b, 2013b; Vidon & Rickly, 2018; Wang, 1999; Wassler & Kirillova, 2019). Existential authenticity refers to an experience that involves a sense of self identity activated by the liminality of tourism and informed by both interpersonal (family ties, communitas) and intrapersonal dimensions (bodily feelings, self-making) (Wang, 1999). Thus, Steiner and Reisinger (2006) advocate a Heideggerian existential authenticity perspective to explicate the moments of authentic Being that are fleeting and often spontaneous in tourism experiences. In particular, they assert that moments of existential authenticity are most possible when tourists themselves are in situations where they can focus on their own 'mineness' and 'resoluteness'. Further, Brown (2013) extends Heidegger's concept of *spielraum* and Sartre's notion of good faith to examine the ways tourism experiences can act as a catalyst for making lifestyle changes (see also Maoz, 2006).

Existential anxiety

The notion of anxiety is inseparable from existential authenticity because it arises from the presence of four existential concerns (death, alienation, freedom, and meaninglessness). As a result, anxiety is fundamental to our existence as humans and has been the focus of existential thought for centuries, from Kierkegaard (1843/1986) to (Sartre, 1966). It arises when an individual's true self or ontological security is compromised and prompts her/him to reclaim the personal value system (Giddens, 1991; Heidegger, 1982), thereby aiding the process of becoming 'self.' Anxiety is the companion of authenticity as it attunes us to both nothingness and possibility (Todres & Galvin, 2010). According to Sartre (1966), coming to terms with the nothingness of life offers the realization that all meaning is made, which has the potential to inspire personal decisions towards authenticity.

In tourism studies, anxiety is discussed in relation to motivation (see Brown, 2013; Canavan, 2017; Kirillova et al., 2016; Shepherd, 2015; Vidon & Rickly, 2018). While Dann (1977) was among the first to note the implications of 'anomie' for touristic motivation, the concept received little attention until the last decade. Indeed, Vidon and Rickly (2018, p. 65) suggest 'alienation and anxiety act as important drivers in tourist motivation, spurring tourists on in their search for authentic experiences.' According to Kirillova et al. (2017) 'prompted by existential anxiety, individuals are forced to confront the truth about the chaotic nature of life and certainty of death.' (p. 13), thus resulting in specific tourism choices. As will be demonstrated, existential anxiety and one's perceptions of death have significant implications for dark tourism motivations and experience.

Being and death

The consciousness of one's death, the death of others, and the mode of existence, which form the core ideas of dark tourism, are thus also central to existential philosophy. Some existential philosophers maintain that the fear of death is simply a misinterpretation of the anxiety that one is not living life in accordance with personal values (Martin, Campbell, & Henry, 2004). Whereas Heidegger (1982) contended that the path to authentic living is the full acknowledgement of death, De Carvalho (2000) and Carstensen, Isaacowitz, and Charles (1999) suggest that a confrontation with death can be a vehicle to authentic becoming as individuals are made more self-aware of their limited time in the world. Martin et al. (2004) assert that when individuals think about their own death, they open up to a more evaluative mode of processing guided by their self-knowledge, and this results in a shift away from the pursuit of culturally derived goals toward the pursuit of personal ones.

According to Heidegger (1982), if we want to understand what it means to be an authentic human being, it is essential that we constantly project our lives onto the horizon of our death, referred to as 'being-towards-death.' The inauthentic Dasein understands the fact of death as an impersonal dying of other people. The phrase 'everybody dies' means 'somebody somewhere dies, but not me, I will die someday, but not now.' This is equivalent to running away from the true meaning of death and from the very essence of existence. Heidegger's conception of being-towards-death is non-relational in nature, suggesting that death cannot be experienced through the death of others, but only through one's self. Thus, facing one's own death is radically different from being concerned with the death of others. For Heidegger, the death of others is secondary to one's own death. One's own death means the end of possibilities, the total disintegration and the end of a person's world. The fear of one's own death comes from the fear of one's extinction as a human being, which therefore leads to death anxiety. However, Heidegger's interpretation of authenticity based on the personal consciousness of death as a precondition of authentic existence is problematic and controversial as it does not accommodate the potential role of the death of others.

Conversely, Levinas' ontological perspective of death offers a useful critique of Heidegger's non-relational death (Budriunaite, 2007). Instead, the death of the other is the essential death. Levinas prioritizes the fear of death of the other over the fear of one's own death. He writes,

> The death signified by the end could not measure the entire significance of death without becoming responsibility for another- by which one becomes oneself in reality: one becomes oneself through this untransferable, undelegatable responsibility. It is for the death of the other that I am responsible to the point of including myself in his death [...] I am responsible for the other in that he is mortal. The death of the other: therein lies the first death. (Levinas, 1993, p. 43)

Accordingly, one's own death reveals itself only by coming into contact with the death of the other. He states, 'we encounter death in the face of the other.' This thinking about one's own death through the death of the other is 'the perception of death in the second person' (Jankélévitch, 1977). Death singularizes Dasein. Levinas opposes Heidegger's idea that death is always one's own by virtue of *mineness*; it is not outside one's self. Levinas further asserts that an encounter with death from outside Being is possible. The death of the Other frees me from anxiety, and 'it subjects me to a love as irrefragable as death' (Levinas, 1993, p. 47). Therefore, death is not separable from the relation with the Other. Fear for death is fear for the Other's death rather than my own, as opposed to Heideggerean ontology of death anxiety. According to Levinas, anxiety is not the fear of the finitude of life, but the realization that 'to-have-to-be is also to-have-to die' (Levinas, 1993, p. 47).

Research design

Geographic context

Varanasi, according to Hindu belief, is a holy city in India that attracts scores of both domestic and foreign tourists. Situated on the banks of the Ganga River, it is known as the 'Great Cremation Ground' (Eck, 1983, p. 30), 'Kashi, the luminous,' 'the Ancient Crossing,' or the 'Microcosm of the Universe' (Parry, 1994, p. 11). It is a religious site where life and death co-exist in public space. Although formally labeled as a Hindu pilgrimage destination, the city has several spaces of death. While Varanasi is also popular among tourists for its rich heritage, temples, music and educational institutes, this study focuses specifically on the dark tourism aspects of the city as a means to examine the relationality of perceptions of death to touristic motivations and experience, particularly existential anxiety and authenticity.

This study analyzes tourists' perceptions of two death-related rituals. The first, the Hindu death ritual, broadly involves burning the deceased over a funeral pyre. The second is a death-related ritual practiced by a group of ascetics, known as the *Aghoris*. This small sect of Hindu ascetics are rigid renouncers and worshippers of the Hindu deity, Shiva. Their rituals include performing austerities at the cremation ground, using skulls as food bowls, smearing one's body with ashes from the dead, coprophagy, necrophagy and meditating on top of corpses. For both, the cremation ground forms an integral part of the ritual space and involves a complex negotiation of sacred and profane. Moreover, both rituals spark an interest among international tourists, supported by several privately owned tour companies and operators who offer walking tours for tourists to witness the cremation grounds, popularly referred to as the 'Burning Ghats', and where they can also meet the Aghoris.

Methodology

This study employed a multi-method approach, which analyzed narratives collected through semi structured interviews, questionnaire-based survey and participant observation, as well as secondary sources of data including background information about the Aghoris, information on Hindu society, death rituals and tourism inflow and outflow in Varanasi. The fieldwork was carried out in May-August 2015 and December 2015– March 2016. During this time, two sub-groups were interviewed: the local people (performers) associated with death-related rituals and tourism (the Aghoris, the funerary workers and priests who perform death rituals at the cremation ground in Varanasi, local businessmen, tour operators and travel guides) and international tourists visiting the cremation grounds to witness these rituals.

Informal semi-structured interviews were audio recorded and transcribed into Microsoft Word and Excel for analysis. A survey was also used to apply the *Multidimensional Fear of Death Scale* to the tourists' experiences in Varanasi. Each interviewee also completed a questionnaire. Thus, a convenience sampling technique was used whereby the sampling population was present during field visits at the specific site. A total of 200 tourists were interviewed, out of which 120 questionnaires were considered for analysis based on completion of all the questions in the questionnaire.

Of the 120 survey participants, there were 62 women and 58 men. The respondents were international tourists predominantly from USA (16%), UK (19%), Australia (15%), Canada (9%) and the rest from countries such as the Netherlands, Germany, Argentina, Italy, Russia, Spain, France, Switzerland, Colombia and Turkey.

The *Multidimensional Fear of Death Scale* (MFODS) (Hoelter, 1979) was chosen as the measure of death anxiety. The scale was developed to investigate the forms of emotional reactions and subjective feelings related to fear of death. Unlike most popular measures of death attitudes, this scale is multidimensional, consisting of 42 variables and comprising eight subscales with different fields of fear of death. Fear of death is defined as 'an emotional reaction involving subjective feelings of unpleasantness and concern based on contemplation or anticipation of any of several facets related to death' (Hoelter, 1979, p. 996). The purpose of using the scale is to measure the general level of death anxiety amongst respondents and to provide a broad context when examining dark tourism experiences and notions of mortality. An assessment of death anxiety levels in the context of dark tourism indicates whether a tourist is fearful of death or not. It provides an idea of the source of fear and also indicates how this fear is related to personal, cultural and contextual factors. The findings suggest that tourists' motivations and experiences at Varanasi relate to several dimensions of existential authenticity and anxiety. However, as the sample was comprised of a diverse group of international tourists, finding may not be generalizable to all tourists that visit Varanasi and other dark tourism sites.

Authenticity and anxiety at Varanasi

Several thanatologists argue that death is a reality that Western society commonly tries to avoid (Becker, 1973/1997; Kubler-Ross, 1997; Yalom, 1980). Through this avoidance or denial of the reality of death, life is a false comfort and therefore inauthentic (May, 1977; Yalom, 1980). Thus, authentic living is the ability to live in congruence and in accordance with the realities of life (Suri & Pitchford, 2010). Similarly, the Aghori rituals can be described as exemplars of the acceptance of death as a vehicle of transcendence and transformation of the 'self' since they demonstrate the principle of non-duality – that there is no distinction between life and death (Suri & Pitchford, 2010, p. 132). According to Aghori philosophy, what prevents us from living authentically is the fear of death, and a confrontation with death paves the way for an authentic living (May, 1977). As such, dark tourism offers an avenue for engagement with death and has implications for theorizing existential authenticity and existential anxiety in tourism studies.

Bodily feelings

Based on Casey's (1996) writings, Feld and Basso (1996, p. 9), suggest that 'place is the most fundamental form of embodied experience – the site of a powerful fusion of self, space, and time.' Tourists derive meaning by participating in the site, the activities there and, through this, they understand both themselves and the landscape in different ways. Therefore, the 'lived experience' of an event or site informs its meaning. This includes the psychological motivations woven together with the body acting as a 'living envelope' of all our intentions (Bullington, 2013, p. 29). As such, the interpersonal dimension of existential authenticity involves attention to the body and the senses and emotions of dwelling in place (see Belhassen et al., 2008; Buchmann et al., 2010; Kim & Jamal, 2007; Rickly-Boyd, 2013b).

Tourists' narratives of Varanasi revealed how sensory perceptions play an inseparable role in understanding their experiences. At the cremation grounds, the smoke from the burning wood pyres overtakes every other smell. Most tourists are unable to describe this smell of death, which is a mix of the sandalwood or general wood, clarified butter or 'ghee' (that is used on the dead body), flowers, smoke, ash, incense sticks and that of the human flesh. The common description of the smell was 'engulfing', 'consuming', 'over-powering', and anything but pleasant, yet, also having a sacred or an authentic character. One tourist described the persistent smell of ashes and the smoke from the cremation grounds as 'overwhelmingly sensual', 'deeply etched in his mind', and that moving away from the cremation ground made him 'understand the difference between the smell of death and the smell of life.' Thus, it is through the body and the body's interaction with Varanasi as place that basic ideas about life and death are affirmed. However, in relation to one's own relationship to and anxiety about death, notions of spirituality, religion, morals and ethics come into play.

Personal values and perceptions of death

Dark tourism, despite its typological, interpretative, political, and moral dilemmas has death – both real and representational – at its core. Thus, dark tourism sites, being emotionally charged spaces, are often referred to as places of symbolic and sacred consumption. However, as tourism spaces, different cultural values and norms interlace as both locals and tourists can be presented with trade-off scenarios. Some values are treated as absolute because they are rooted in individual's moral and ethical principles. As such, these are often non-negotiable and thus are protected from trade-offs with other values (Tanner & Medin, 2004; Tetlock, Kristel, Elson, Green, & Lerner, 2000).

It is observed from previous studies that attempts to protect sacred values from trade-offs against other values, particularly secular values, can be met with strong moral outrage or feelings of emotional distress (Tetlock, 2003). While social and self-imposed regulations contribute to defining and maintaining one's sacred values in moments of trade-offs, there are instances where, through a combination of ritualistic practices or by encountering the Other, an alternate or transformed self is constructed that is willing to trade-off these values. Indeed, the cremation grounds can transform tourists' self-perceptions and lead to a discovery of one's own unrealized perceptions about life and death. This is evidenced by narratives produced from tourists interviewed twice – once after their first encounters with the cremation grounds and then, again, after their second visits.

	After the 1st visit	After the 2nd visit
Tourist 1 (Female, 42, Mexico)	The Ghats was exciting especially the cremation grounds and I am looking forward to meet one of the Aghoris. I have heard so many interesting things about their rituals and this place from my friend.	To be honest, I don't understand what people find 'holy' in here. This is filthy, there is dirt and death everywhere and I didn't find any peace of mind. I have always been fascinated with Hinduism and I have read the Bhagavad Gita too. The Gita has awakened me spiritually but I don't think this place has anything spiritual or sacred about it. This place is dark and does not speak to me. I met an Aghori yesterday and I think what they do is wrong. I am disappointed with this place. I have booked my tickets today and I am leaving tomorrow.
Tourist 2 (Female, 49, USA)	I have been to Tibet and I have seen the sky burial rituals there. I am not affected by the rituals here but I have heard that they are capable of evoking some strong feelings.	Now that I think of it, I think I am impressed by the death rituals here. When my father died, the funeral home used cosmetics to make him look alive and I could barely recognize him. I think this whole process of embalming takes away the sacredness or authenticity of death. Now all I remember of my father is this altered face with make-up on it. I wish I could remember his last appearance as somebody who he actually was. Considering that, I think the Hindu ritual of burning the dead immediately in its natural form without any embalming involved is a better way to go. There is no artificiality involved. I will make sure I tell my kids to cremate me in this manner.

Following her second visit, Tourist 1 experienced a change in perception of the cremation ground and the overall place. While she seemed to be excited after the first visit, the second visit where she met an Aghori was more confrontational. She struggled to trade-off her sacred values regarding the purity of life and death for the 'dirt and death' she perceived at Varanasi and responded with strong moral outrage when the Aghori death-related rituals challenged her self-perception. On the other hand, Tourist 2 was willing to trade-off her previously held values upon witnessing the death rituals in Varanasi leading to a transformed self with an alternate perception of life and death.

The death rituals provide tourists a reflexive opportunity for self-evaluation and recognition that would not have been generated in their everyday lives. Such moments can be described as 'epiphanies.' Denzin (1984) defines such experiences as interactional moments that leave a mark on individuals' lives and have the potential to create transformational experiences. '[S]uch experiences alter how persons define themselves and their relations with the Other; they alter the fundamental meaning structures in a person's life and act as a catalyst for creating new perceptions of self-identity' (1984, pp. 34–39). Thus, epiphanies and self-discovery moments are often observed in tourism experiences and linked to existential authenticity (Brown, 2013).

Death anxiety and self-identity

According to Wearing, McDonald, and Ankor (2016), the concept of existential authenticity could be used to understand a tourist's shift in consciousness and self-identity through the subjective experience of an epiphany. Further, Ankor and Wearing (2013) identify the elements of freedom, anxiety, oneness/connectedness and the Other as contributing experiences that challenge self-identity. These elements can also be identified in the narratives of tourists at Varanasi. The Aghori lifestyle, their philosophy of breaking social hierarchy, norms and taboos and engagement with the concept of death seem offensive, immoral and even hold little spiritual value to most. Yet, for some, this anxiety and discomfort upon encountering the death-related rituals is transformed into learning, creativity, understanding, and accepting of other ways of life, which connects them to the social, cultural, and physical environment in unique and intimate ways. It is in the experience of anxiety stemming from the decision to place oneself in the unknown that one is able to recognize the isolation of the self (Heidegger, 1982) and, through this existential anxiety, change and grow because such feelings are 'a mode of our conscious existence, one of the ways in which consciousness understands [...] its Being-in-the world' (Sartre, 1939, p. 61).

Aghoris exemplify a devotion to the numinous and their monistic or non-dualistic approach to life forms an integral idea of existential authenticity. The word Aghor actually denotes a spiritual stage, or a state of nondiscrimination that is free of hatred, fear and aversion. A person can attain this stage irrespective of any sect or religion to which he/she belongs. It is the foremost mental level of spirituality, and after attaining it a person escapes the cycle of life and death and merges completely into the supreme power that has created the universe. The Aghor philosophy is not specifically bound to Hinduism, but is the state of supreme non-discrimination rooted in non-duality, i.e. there is no distinction between the sacred and the profane or the pure and the impure. Non-duality arises from eternal wisdom inherent in the soul and is the root of liberating knowledge and leading an authentic life. It is knowledge that bestows freedom from the cycle of rebirth. The path of non-discrimination entails becoming indifferent to eating habits, dress, lifestyle, social divisions such as caste and physical appearance. According to the principle of non-duality, everything is but a different manifestation of the same supreme power. Therefore, according to the Aghor tradition, either everything or nothing is sacred. This cognition is the attainment of the Aghora state of consciousness. In the context of tourism in Varanasi, the rawness, forthrightness, and the elements of death and cannibalism in the Aghori rituals adds to the authenticity of the experience for tourists. There is an absence of clearly defined roles and forms of behavior and an opportunity to allow for changes in self-identity by embracing the principle of non-duality. For example, one woman from Canada who adopted the Aghor path 10 years ago said,

> A lot of people have different perceptions of the Aghor initiatory rites. Of course you have to do certain things that might seem filthy to the society, but the power to do so comes from *sadhana* (spiritual practice). Don't

> people eat chicken which is dead or vegetables which are lifeless … everything that we eat is dead, then why differentiate? It is not compulsory to eat the dead but it is a ritual to remind who we are, that everything is equal, from an ant to a dead branch. I don't have anything to show to the world. I live in the shadows and I am comfortable in this. My path might appear dark to the world but I see all the colors here. I have tried being in the light before but this path liberates me.

For the tourists who accept the Aghor lifestyle, death represents a release from the shackles of social institutions and structures. For them, the death-related rituals are the only medium of transcending the world of illusion (Svoboda, 2007). Thus, according to Suri and Pitchford (2010), the corpse upon which the Aghori meditates is a symbol of his own body and necrophagy is a symbol of the transcendence of his lower self and a realization of the greater, all pervading Self. In contrast to people from Western cultures, the Aghoris can be described as exemplars of the acceptance of death as a vehicle of transcendence and transformation of the 'self.' The Aghor philosophy is biased towards individualism and presents a non-conventional approach where the individual can follow an alternate non-dualistic path to salvation, a path where life and death are not separate realities. The freedom of realizing the self's identity with the absolute by embracing the profane through rituals and by transcending social taboos is the realization of non-duality (*advaita*). Thus, in confronting death and the perceived profanity of the Aghoris engagement with death on all scales, provides tourists an opportunity to face not only their fears of death, but also more broadly, their ideals of life, their own lives, and sense of self within their chosen lifestyles. Dark tourism in Varanasi thereby extends arguments about tourism as a catalyst for existential authenticity (Brown, 2013) and evidences the role of existential anxiety in these touristic motivations and experiences (Kirillova et al., 2017; Vidon & Rickly, 2018).

Furthermore, the results of the *Multidimensional Fear of Death Scale* (MFODS) (Hoelter, 1979), as applied in the questionnaire in Varanasi, revealed that these tourists scored high on the subscale *fear of premature death*. In other words, a high fear of death is associated with inability to lead an authentic life and fostered an intention to visit tourism sites related to death. According to Baumeister (1991), the meaning of life can be evaluated in terms of four needs for meaning: purpose (or purposiveness), value, efficacy (control), and self-worth. Since death marks the possibility of disallowing any possibility of undertaking life projects, individuals tend to fear it. However, a confrontation with death in dark tourism makes the individual come to terms with the finitude of life. He further states that death tends to dispel our 'myths of higher meaning' (p. 58) and our awareness of mortality helps to realize that it does not matter if we lived or not. On similar lines, Sartre (1966) also asserted that reflection on death is reflection on the meaninglessness of existence. However, such a nihilistic belief or annihilatory aspect of death is mitigated by meaning-making, or 'imposing meanings on death' (Baumeister, p. 286). This paves the way for 'search of meaning' theories on self-actualization. Neimeyer and Chapman (1980) also provided a positive interpretation of Sartre's thought, suggests conversely that a person who has realized his or her life goals is, to a large extent, less likely to be anxious about death than one whose life projects remain incomplete. Therefore, dark tourism can offer a potentially transformative experience to the tourists by providing an encounter with death and its representation in diverse forms.

Communitas and the death of 'others'

Comparing tourism with pilgrimage, Turner (1973) noted that beyond the normative bonds of home, classlessness ensues and relationships develop based on common humanity, forming what he refers to as *communitas*. He argued that liminality leads to communitas, which is a 'social bond' occurring between those who share a liminal experience. A sense of *communitas* is demonstrated by different groups of tourists in multiple ways with respect to the death-related rituals in Varanasi. Tourists who are interested in the Aghori rituals and spiritual learning can visit the Aghor ashrams or the cremation grounds at the riverbank in pursuit of knowledge, and groups are often seen bonding, interacting, assisting one another, collectively participating in rituals and at times, even maintaining secrecy about the rituals. Irrespective of cultural, economic, and social differences, there is an ambience of acceptance of others and their beliefs. Further, the Aghor philosophy of practicing non-duality that advocates embracing everything in this universe without any class, boundary, or social identity, is reflective of a *communitas* in itself.

There is a growing conviction that individuals are not concerned about the death of others with whom no racial kinship, no linguistic, religious, or economic interests are shared. This is a point of concern in dark tourism in general, and Varanasi as well, where international tourists encounter the death of people who are racially dissimilar. However, Lingis (1994) in his book, *The Community of Those Who Have Nothing in Common,* writes about the mortality that unites all people. He argues the other shows a cultural coding and the feelings of the other mask a structure of hierarchies, the rites of passage of a culture, the polarization of ideologies (Lingis, 1994, p. 25). He reveals that what concerns us in the other is precisely his or her otherness, which appeals to us and contests us face to face. Indeed, one tourist used this encounter with the death of 'others' to reevaluate his understanding of and relationship to death.

> It was so - normal, in this city. No one was crying, sad or phased by the cremations. I really appreciated this accepting view of death (at least this is how I perceived it) - in America it is NOT taken lightly and people dwell for long periods of time - I can imagine perhaps this is because of different views of life after death in Hindu vs Christian religion? I do not identify as a Christian, but it seems to be that "heaven" is obtainable but the living are disconnected from it. So when someone passes, it is more painful, there is more loss. There is less of a connection on a spiritual level to the dead. (Male, mid 40s, USA)

Lingis' approach, to some extent, explains how the death of 'brown' bodies at the cremation ground in Varanasi is capable of evoking an interest among the 'white' tourists as well as challenging their emotions. To perceive the other in the midst of the equivalence and interchangeability of path, is to see one-self bound to one's own place and tasks (p. 170). He states:

> it is the wall of one's own death that circumscribes the zone of possibilities that are possible for oneself and separates them from those that are for others. Another death circumscribes the expanse of possibilities that are possible for the other. In his deferral of his or her death in relationship to one's own, the other is different. The mortality of the other concerns me. Not only in that it is the sense of his mortality that makes me see him as different, destined for a zone of tasks circumscribed by the death coming singularly for him. Such that, as Heidegger says, the best thing I can do for the other if I care about him is to free him for his tasks and his dying, by resolutely pursuing my own. But the tasks that are my own are projected into the world by his passage to his death. I find the shape of my own destiny in the outline of enterprises that the others traced in the world but did not have the time or the power to realize. (p. 171)

Indeed, as this tourist notes, in the presence of death it is nearly impossible to separate oneself from others. Death evokes a visceral reaction, even for those who are unfamiliar with the deceased.

> It was very strange to see something so intimate being so public, to share the pain of their families, I looked at the elder son of one of the dead's body and he was in so much pain, yet he didn't cry and he released his dad into the elements again, it was very powerful. It makes me feel sad thinking about how family members react when a person is gone. (Female, 38, Australia)

Yet, interestingly, in the entanglements of cultural values and personal views on death and afterlife, the body is palpably present – one's own body and the bodies of others, living and dead. Lingis (1994) posits that reconciling the consciousness of one's mortality and the mortality of the other is dependent on the corporeality of the dead body, the body as the locus of meaning. The fear of the annihilation of another's body is inseparable from the fear of annihilation of my own body. Accordingly, the fear of one's own death may evoke the fear of the death of somebody else. It offers the realization, albeit from the perspective of post-nihilist pragmatism, that after the death of meaning all that remains is the body. Thus, returning to the theme of bodily feelings, discussed above, it is possible to understand the existential weight that comes with tourists' remarks on the persistent smell of ashes and smoke at the cremation grounds that signify 'the difference between the smell of death and the smell of life.'

Conclusion

This paper contributes to an understanding of existential authenticity and existential anxiety in tourism studies through an investigation of tourists' perceptions of death, the Self, and 'others' at the cremation grounds in Varanasi. It also supports arguments of tourism as a catalyst for existential authenticity (Brown, 2013; Maoz, 2006), suggesting that dark tourism is capable of transforming tourists' perceptions about death, engaging tourists' existential anxiety, and leading to an emerging self. Representations of death at dark tourism sites serve as reminders of one's own mortality affecting one's attitude towards death, perception of self, and therefore attitude about lifestyle choices. In particular, this was observed as moments of revelation of hidden perceptions about life and death wherein the notion of freedom and social norms were challenged through face-to-face encounters with the Otherness of death. These encounters produce experiences, rooted in epiphany, where the transformation of self has the potential to take place.

Both Heidegger (1982) and Sartre (1966) posit anxiety as a condition of existential authenticity, suggesting that being in the moment of the existentially authentic experience is not always pleasurable (see also Vidon & Rickly, 2018). For tourists confronted with death and in the presence of Hindu death rituals, particularly Aghori practices, existential anxiety and fear of death was also accompanied by moral outrage by some. This does not imply that the notion of existential authenticity indicates a moral or ethical distinction, which is something even Heidegger denies. The Heideggerean notion of authenticity is an entirely non-evaluative and descriptive mode of Dasein's being where there is no fixed moral structure on how to live our lives, but rather the possibility of moral perspectives emerges from the basis of Dasein's universal ontological structures (White, 2005). Thus, the findings of this research suggest that anxiety serves as a reminder when a perceived sense of self is challenged prompting one to reclaim her/his personal value system (Heidegger, 1982). These findings thereby lend support to the growing body of literature in tourism that recognizes the dialectical of authenticity, alienation (Rickly-Boyd, 2013a) and the anxiety that accompanies the process of realizing 'self' (Brown, 2013; Kirillova et al., 2017; Shepherd, 2015; Vidon & Rickly, 2018; Wassler & Kirillova, 2019).

Finally, although the findings of this study are in partial agreement with Heidegger regarding the prioritization of fear of one's own death over the death of others, there is also a sense of communitas observed among certain tourists with respect to the perception of death of others (Levinas, 1993, p. 47). As supported by Lingis (1994) argument, the two fears can co-exist. Thus, confrontation with death, as exemplified by the Aghori rituals and the cremation grounds in Varanasi, offers tourists an opportunity to examine the inevitability that life will end and to engage with this existential predicament and anxiety in an embodied sense, thereby pushing some of them towards life changes in the pursuit of existential authenticity.

Disclosure statement

No potential conflict of interest was reported by the authors.

ORCID

Jillian Rickly http://orcid.org/0000-0002-2150-3294

References

Ankor, J., & Wearing, S. (2013). Gaze, encounter and philosophies of otherness. In O. Moufakkir & Y. Reisinger (Eds.), *The host gaze in global tourism* (pp. 179–189). Boston: CABI International.
Baumeister, R. F. (1991). *Meanings of life*. New York, NY: Guilford Press.
Becker, E. (1973/1997). *The denial of death*. New York, NY: Free Press.
Belhassen, Y., Caton, K., & Stewart, W. P. (2008). The search for authenticity in the pilgrim experience. *Annals of Tourism Research*, *35*(3), 668–689.
Benjamin, W. (2008). The work of art in the age of its technological reproducibility: Second version. In M. W. Jennings, B. Doherty, & T. Y. Levin (Eds.), *The work of art in the age of its technological reproducibility, and other writings on media* (pp. 19–55). Cambridge: The Belknap Press.
Biran, A., Liu, W., Li, G., & Eichhorn, V. (2014). Consuming post-disaster destinations: The case of Sichuan, China. *Annals of Tourism Research*, *47*(1), 1–17.
Biran, A., Poria, Y., & Oren, G. (2011). Sought experiences at (dark) heritage sites. *Annals of Tourism Research*, *38*(2), 820–841.
Brown, L. (2013). Tourism: A catalyst for existential authenticity. *Annals of Tourism Research*, *40*(1), 176–190.
Bruner, E. M. (1991). Transformation of self in tourism. *Annals of Tourism Research*, *18*(2), 238–250.
Buchmann, A., Moore, K., & Fisher, D. (2010). Experiencing film tourism: Authenticity & fellowship. *Annals of Tourism Research*, *37*(1), 229–248.
Budriunaite, A. (2007). The existential experience of one's own death or the 'Dispute' of M. Heidegger and E. Levinas in the eyes of everyman. *Filozofia (Philosophy)*, *8*(62), 704–733.
Bullington, J. (2013). *The expression of the psychosomatic body from a phenomenological perspective*. Berlin and Heidelberg: Springer.
Canavan, B. (2017). An existentialist exploration of tourism sustainability: Backpackers fleeing and finding themselves. *Journal of Sustainable Tourism*, *26*(4), 551–566.
Carstensen, L. L., Isaacowitz, D. M., & Charles, S. T. (1999). Taking time seriously: A theory of socioemotional selectivity. *American Psychologist*, *54*(3), 165–181.
Casey, E. S. (1996). *The fate of place: A philosophical history*. Berkeley: University of California Press.
Cohen, E. (2011). Tourism and land grab in the aftermath of the Indian Ocean tsunami. *Scandinavian Journal of Hospitality and Tourism*, *11*(3), 224–236.
Dann, G. (1977). Anomie, ego-enhancement and tourism. *Annals of Tourism Research*, *4*, 184–194.
De Carvalho, R. J. (2000). The growth hypothesis and self-actualization: An existential alternative. *The Humanistic Psychologist*, *28*(1–3), 59–66.
Denzin, N. (1984). *On understanding emotion*. San Francisco: Jossey-Bass.
Eck, D. L. (1983). *Banaras: City of light*. Princeton, NJ: Princeton University Press.
Feld, S., & Basso, K. H. (1996). *Senses of place*. Santa Fe, NM: School of American Research Press.
Galani-Moutafi, V. (2000). The self and the other: Traveler, ethnographer, tourist. *Annals of Tourism Research*, *27*(1), 203–224.
Giddens, A. (1991). *Modernity and self-identity: Self and society in the late modern age*. Palo Alto, CA: Stanford University Press.
Guignon, C. (1986). Existentialist ethics. In J. De Marco & R. Fox (Eds.), *New directions in ethics* (pp. 73–91). London: Routledge.
Heidegger, M. (1982). *Being and time*. New York: Harper & Row.
Heuermann, K., & Chhabbra, K. (2014). The darker side of dark tourism: An authenticity perspective. *Tourism Analysis*, *19*, 213–225.
Hoelter, J. W. (1979). Multidimensional treatment of fear of death. *Journal of Consulting and Clinical Psychology*, *47* (5), 996–999.
Jankélévitch, V. (1977). *La mort (Champs)*. Flammarion, Paris.
Kierkegaard, S. (1843/1986). *Fear and trembling: Dialectical lyric by Johannes de silentio*. London: Penguin.
Kim, H., & Jamal, T. (2007). Touristic quest for existential authenticity. *Annals of Tourism Research*, *34*(1), 181–201.
Kirillova, K., Lehto, X. Y., & Cai, L. (2016). Existential authenticity and anxiety as outcomes: The tourist in the experience economy. *International Journal of Tourism Research*, *19*(1), 13–26.

Kirillova, K., Lehto, X. Y., & Cai, L. (2017). Tourism and existential transformation: An empirical investigation. *Journal of Travel Research, 56*(5), 638–650.

Kubler-Ross, E. (1997). *On death and dying*. New York, NY: Scribner.

Levinas, E. (1993). *God, death, and time*. Palo Alto, CA: Stanford University Press.

Lingis, A. (1994). *The community of those who have nothing in common*. Bloomington: Indiana Press.

Maoz, D. (2006). Erikson on the tour. *Tourism Recreation Research, 31*(3), 55–63.

Martin, L. L., Campbell, W. K., & Henry, C. D. (2004). The roar of awakening: Mortality acknowledgment as a call to authentic living. In J. Greenberg, S. L. Koole, & T. Pyszczynski (Eds.), *Handbook of experimental existential psychology* (pp. 437–454). New York, NY: Guilford Press.

May, R. (1977). *The meaning of anxiety*. New York, NY: Norton & Company.

Neimeyer, R. A., & Chapman, K. M. (1980). Self/ideal discrepancy and fear of death: Testing an existential hypothesis. *Omega: Journal of Death and Dying, 11*(3), 233–240.

Parry, J. (1994). *Death in Banaras*. New York, NY: Cambridge University Press.

Rickly-Boyd, J. M. (2012a). Authenticity & Aura: A Benjaminian approach to tourism. *Annals of Tourism Research, 39* (1), 269–289.

Rickly-Boyd, J. M. (2012b). Lifestyle climbers: Towards existential authenticity. *Journal of Sport & Tourism, 17*, 85–104.

Rickly-Boyd, J. M. (2013a). Alienation: Authenticity's forgotten cousin. *Annals of Tourism Research, 40*(1), 412–415.

Rickly-Boyd, J. M. (2013b). Existential authenticity: Place matters. *Tourism Geographies, 15*(4), 680–686.

Roberts, C. (2018). Educating the (dark) masses: Dark tourism and sensemaking. In P. Stone, R. Hartmann, T. Seaton, R. Sharpley, & L. White (Eds.), *The Palgrave handbook of dark tourism studies* (pp. 603–637). London: Palgrave Macmillan.

Sartre, J. P. (1939). *Sketch for a theory of the emotions*. London: Routledge.

Sartre, J. P. (1966). *Being and nothingness*. New York: Simon & Schuster.

Seaton, T. (2009). Purposeful otherness: Approaches to the management of thanatourism. In R. Sharpley & P. R. Stone (Eds.), *The darker side of travel: The theory and practice of dark tourism* (pp. 75–108). Bristol: Channel View.

Shepherd, R. J. (2015). Why Heidegger did not travel: Existential angst, authenticity, and tourist experiences. *Annals of Tourism Research, 52*, 60–71.

Steiner, C. J., & Reisinger, Y. (2006). Understanding existential authenticity. *Annals of Tourism Research, 33*(2), 299–318.

Strange, C., & Kempa, M. (2003). Shades of dark tourism: Alcatraz and Robben Island. *Annals of Tourism Research, 30* (2), 386–405.

Suri, R., & Pitchford, D. B. (2010). The gift of life: Death as teacher in the Aghori sect. *International Journal of Transpersonal Studies, 29*(1), 128–134.

Svoboda, R. E. (2007). *Aghora: At the left hand of god*. Delhi: Rupa.

Tanner, C., & Medin, D. L. (2004). Protected values: No omission bias and no framing effects. *Psychonomic Bulletin & Review, 11*(1), 185–191.

Tetlock, P. E. (2003). Thinking the unthinkable: Sacred values and taboo cognitions. *Trends in Cognitive Sciences, 7*(7), 320–324.

Tetlock, P. E., Kristel, O. V., Elson, S. B., Green, M. C., & Lerner, J. S. (2000). The psychology of the unthinkable: Taboo trade-offs, forbidden base rates, and heretical counterfactuals. *Journal of Personality and Social Psychology, 78*(5), 853.

Todres, L., & Galvin, K. (2010). "Dwelling-mobility": An existential theory of well-being. *International Journal of Qualitative Studies on Health and Well-Being, 5*(3), 5444.

Turner, V. (1973). The center out there: Pilgrim's goal. *History of Religions, 12*(3), 191–230.

Vidon, E. S., & Rickly, J. M. (2018). Alienation and anxiety in tourism motivation. *Annals of Tourism Research, 69*(1), 65–75.

Wang, N. (1999). Rethinking authenticity in tourism experience. *Annals of Tourism Research, 26*(2), 349–370.

Wassler, P., & Kirillova, K. (2019). Hell is other people? An existential-phenomenological analysis of the local gaze in tourism. *Tourism Management, 71*, 116–126.

Wearing, S. L., McDonald, M., & Ankor, J. (2016). Journeys of creation: Experiencing the unknown, the other and authenticity as an epiphany of the self. *Tourism Recreation Research, 41*(2), 157–167.

White, C. J. (2005). *Time and death: Heidegger's analysis of finitude*. Aldershot: Ashgate.

Yalom, I. D. (1980). *Existential psychotherapy*. New York, NY: Basic Books.

Using geographical and semiotic means to establish fixed points of a never-ending story: searching for parameters of authenticity in a case study of Australian history

Michael Fagence

ABSTRACT
Recent scholarship has suggested that history-linked and heritage-based tourism, and its engagement in the never-ending telling of stories, is becoming solidly entrenched as a contribution to the popularisation and consumption of the record of history. The essential challenge for tourism is to tell the story by using history-linked sites and objects as cultural 'texts' and as conduits between the past and the present – for providing the experience of 'being there' without 'being there'. Using a story about an episode of Australian history as a case study, this paper experiments with perspectives from geography and semiotics to probe for certainty with fixed points in the story, points which are marked by tangible and visual characteristics and which are at least indicative of important elements which create the identity and significance of the storyscape. A story told through tourism will seldom be permanently fixed, and this circumstance has implications for some of the ideological interpretations of 'authenticity', and although the fundamental shape of the story might not be imperilled, the quality of the experience presented through tourism might be. Important implications of this challenge are addressed in this paper.

Introduction

This paper has been designed to contribute to a niche area tucked away amongst the broad scope of the many commentaries on authenticity and authentication. Its focus is on using selected means of investigation and interpretation to expose and consider fixed points of a never-ending story (Latham, 2016). A particular story about an episode of the history of Australia is used as the case study to test the proposition that by drawing on the opportunities which become available by linking the study processes and tools from geography and semiotics it is possible to create a level of assurance about the authenticity of the events in the episode as they are assembled as contributions to heritage tourism. This level of assurance about authenticity is an important factor as the story becomes transformed into one or more tourism attractions, because it impacts not only on the regard held for the story *per se*, but also – as all good stories have a setting, a character and a plot – on the influence the story and its constituents have as contributions to national (or regional, or local) identity, to its value positions, and to its physical and socio-political heritage.

Whilst drawing on the fundamental strands of thought embedded in the discourses of, for example, Cohen (1988) and Wang (1999), and some of the recent revisionary statements (Cohen, 2007; Cohen & Cohen, 2012), the orientation of this study migrates from such centralist commentaries and associates itself with the initiatives taken by, for example, Chhabra (2005), Chhabra, Healy, and Sills (2003), Grayson and Martinec (2004) and McAuley and Pervan (2014). In doing this it has moved the focus from the broad circumstances of authenticity to the operationalisation of stories from history, and of securing a tourism product which, whilst being flexible, is based on a strongly authentic vein. An important element lying in the background of this study is the contribution which heritage-based tourism is being called upon to make to 'consuming history' (de Groot, 2009) as a means of creating 'prosthetic memories' (Landsberg, 2004), and as a means of facilitating the experience of 'being there' without actually 'being there' (Rickly-Boyd, 2012; see also Kim, 2014). Even with this particular momentum, this study does not overlook the significance of the previously-referenced foundational strands of thought. Rather it draws intellectual strength from them and complements that with the carefully-crafted commentaries and case studies in, for example, Brown (2013), Bryce, Alexander, and Murdy (2017), Pine and Gilmore (2008), Ram, Bjork, and Weidenfeld (2016) and Reisinger and Steiner (2006).

With its focus on deploying 'selected means of investigation and interpretation to expose and consider fixed points of a never-ending story' this study has sought to engage with mechanisms that can be drawn upon to operationalise the authenticism of elements which contribute to stories as they are told through tourism. To help to formalise this position this study has embraced Urry's (1992) advocacies about significance, uniqueness and distinctiveness and the consequence of them for creating and sustaining attractiveness for tourism, and from the advocacies of both Jamal and Hill (2004) and Jamal and Kim (2005) for suitable theoretical underpinnings.

The outcome of being confronted by these various challenges and opportunities has been the drafting of a discourse which uses a case study to 'test' the implications of ascertaining fixed points of a never-ending story. In addition to the intellectual clues emanating from many of the sources listed previously, this study has been influenced especially by the referencing of authenticity with place attachment (Ram et al., 2016), and with 'placeness' (Jamal & Hill, 2004), in which, in both cases, 'place' embraces places *per se*, what happened there, who visited and used them, how they were used, what happened to 'things' (artefacts, tools, documents) associated with them, and so on.

Selected theoretical influences

Although there was references to important issues of backgrounding theory in the Introduction, some are accorded a specially-targeted treatment here in readiness for the application of them in the Case Study. In this targeted treatment the perspective being taken is to explore how particular influences on, and aspects of 'authenticity' respond to the challenge of telling a story through tourism (Chronis, 2012). The aim is to consider a range of fixed elements in what has become a never-ending story about an episode of Australian history, and it follows a trajectory which attracted a significant commentary from Latham (2016). With tourism, as with many other expressions of history through popular culture, the aim is to communicate the circumstances of the story drawing on the benefit of hindsight – to tell the story about 'being there' without 'being there', and to create 'prosthetic memories' for those wanting to experience a 'sense of what happened'. Smith (2006) and others have commented that this form of communication may sacrifice accuracy, credibility and veracity; so, to set telling a story from history in an assessable frame of reference, this discourse proceeds by using particular disciplinary protocols and tools to focus attention on fixed points which may be capable of attracting the approbation of authenticity.

Story-telling and story construction

The first issue to consider is story-telling and story construction. Commentaries about story-telling and tourism tend to differentiate between one type which focuses on the transformation of the physical and psychological evidence into a tourism attraction – as a 'storyscape' (Chronis, 2005) – or a second type which focuses on the stories which emerge from the tales based on tourists' interpretations and experiences (Kim, 2014). Moscardo (2010, 2015) has engaged in observations about both types, perhaps expressing partiality with the second over the first. Gravili and Rosato (2015) and Chronis (2005) have drawn the conclusion that stories come to life when the destination's assets are exposed, and its distinctive personality and identity are revealed. This is the foundation idea of the 'storyscape', and it is this that has been seized for this study. To express it at its most simple level, stories told through heritage-based tourism treat with sites, settings, buildings and structures, behaviour of particular persons, action that has taken place, and with collections of artefacts, documents, and paraphernalia which have an association with the happenings in any selected episode of history. These components become embedded and entangled in the basic features of story construction – setting, character, plot, theme, perspective – and contribute beyond mere descriptions to generating emotional and affective responses, to informing, to entertaining, and to providing explanations and interpretations of events and behaviour. The basic components are the fixed points, and it is these which have the closest eligibility claim for 'authenticity'. There is an abundance of these components in the case study story used later.

Significance

A second important influence to determining the authenticity of a story being told about events in history is 'significance'. This is one of the most contentious issues to be faced in preparing stories about events in history for tourism (see, for example, Kim, Brent Ritchie, & McCormick, 2012; Molleda & Jain, 2013; Tunbridge & Ashworth, 1996). Beyond the academy of scholars, various UNESCO, and national and regional public agencies and organisations have promulgated conventions and protocols to grapple with the issue of 'significance' in the special case of cultural heritage. Many of these have benefitted from the work of ICOMOS (International Council on Monuments and Sites), and one such example is the suite of guiding principles about 'significance' is set out in *The Burra Charter* developed by Australia ICOMOS (2013). In the case of Australia many federal and state government agencies have embedded guiding principles in their heritage legislation, operational guidelines and frameworks (see, for example, Heritage Council of Victoria, 2014, 2015), and the Collections Council of Australia has broadened its interpretation of 'significance' beyond the scope of 'places' to be inclusive of artefacts, events, and people (CCA, 2009). Recently, English Heritage (2017) updated its advice about historic area assessments, explaining that '(t)*he process of assessing significance … enables us to see how and why places are important, for different reasons and from a range of perspectives*' (p. 1). Commonly, 'significance' is attributed to having uniqueness or special characteristics, distinctiveness of identity, and exhibiting the aesthetic, archaeological, architectural, cultural, historical, scientific, social, spiritual or technical values of (and value to) the local community/region/nation.

Cultural heritage landscapes (including buildings, structures, precincts) make their contribution *in situ*; but for some 'items' (such as artefacts and documents) it is most common for them to be domiciled in archives and record offices, art galleries, libraries and museums. The criteria for inclusion at *in situ* sites and within many of these depositories include their distinctiveness, authenticity, intactness, and relevance to the heritage story. In contrast, for some tourism purposes and other expressions of popular culture (art, literature, theatre) a determinant might be their entertainment value. Such is the complexity of the matter that the former Collections Council of Australia advocated a multi-disciplinary approach to determining 'significance' (CCA, 2009).

Discipline

It is the matter of complexity in story-telling that has led to commentaries about improving the capacities of investigative and interpretive processes to progress beyond a single dominant discipline and to engage with suitably-tuned (orchestrated) combinations of discipline-based tool-kits. This has become a general advocacy (Darbellay, 2016; Darbellay & Stock, 2012), and it is being embraced increasingly in studies of tourism and heritage, especially to cope with the systemic interactions in tourism (Cole, 2007; Coles, Hall, & Duval, 2006). A particularly strong combination of disciplines to cope suitably with such matters as places, place attachment, and the signs and symbols of history-based activity associated with those places, would be the disciplines of geography and semiotics, operationalised as an expression of epistemological pluralism (Davies, 2006). At its most simple level of justification, Butler (2004) has made it clear that tourism is an activity which must take place 'somewhere', and that geography, therefore, is inevitably a primary discipline (see also Shurmer-Smith, 2002). To this can be wedded theoretical and conceptual frameworks from 'the gaze' component of semiotics (see, for example, Knudsen, Metro-Roland, Soper, & Greer, 2008; Metro-Roland, 2009, 2011; Waterton & Watson, 2014). These capacities can be used to expose the systemic interactions in tourism by identifying and codifying signs and symbols and their distinctive contributions to telling a story through tourism, especially recognising Urry's (1992) observation that *'it is the distinctiveness of the visual that gives all sorts of activities a special or unique character'* (p.172).

Authenticity

'Authenticity' is the fourth defining influence to be considered here. Rather than indulge in an extensive rejoinder to the various opinions canvassed in many sources the opportunity is taken to acknowledge that vast scope of commentaries, and to take 'as read' the implications of them.

This study fits, albeit clumsily, into the mix of the dominant perspectives on authenticity by engaging somewhat differentially,

- with matters of objectivity and legitimacy;
- with matters associated with the existential realisations of empathy with the circumstances revealed in the story, and the linkage of those circumstances with Australian identity;
- and with the constructivist issues of commodification, marketing and selling heritage, and ownership of the story.

Evidence of each of these influences will be apparent in the case study in the next section.

These four – story-telling, significance, discipline and authenticity – are not the only influences to impact on the communication of a story through tourism. They are used here to merely to demonstrate how the story at what may be referred to as 'baseline of Authenticity 1' – or 'fixed point 1' – will be influenced as it progresses to later baseline levels and become subsequent 'fixed points' as the never-ending story from history unfolds (Figure 1).

Case study: the Ned Kelly story

The story of Ned Kelly, the bushranger-cum-outlaw-cum-folk hero, has attracted exceptional coverage across various forms of popular culture. It offers a case study of the socio-economic and political circumstances in rural areas of the Australian state of Victoria in the final decades of the nineteenth century; and provides evidence of the responses of rural communities to those circumstances as they were agitated by the lingering influences of Celtic and convict heritage, and the allegations about the harsh treatment by government (especially the police and the judiciary) to some sections of the rural communities. A response in those communities was often towards lawlessness and larrikinism. This was the period leading towards the formation of the Commonwealth of Australia (in January 1901). Within that timeframe the Kelly family had its own peak events, especially in the period 1878–1880. It is the legacy of those events which has attracted the attention of scholarship, and some has been captured in art, drama, film, literature. Increasingly, elements of the story have been transformed through commodification into a niche 'industry' broadly expressed through tourism and a range of associated manufacturing, service and travel industries.

As might be expected, the high profile of the story, and especially of its central character and core events, has been confronted with challenges about accuracy of fact and reasonableness of

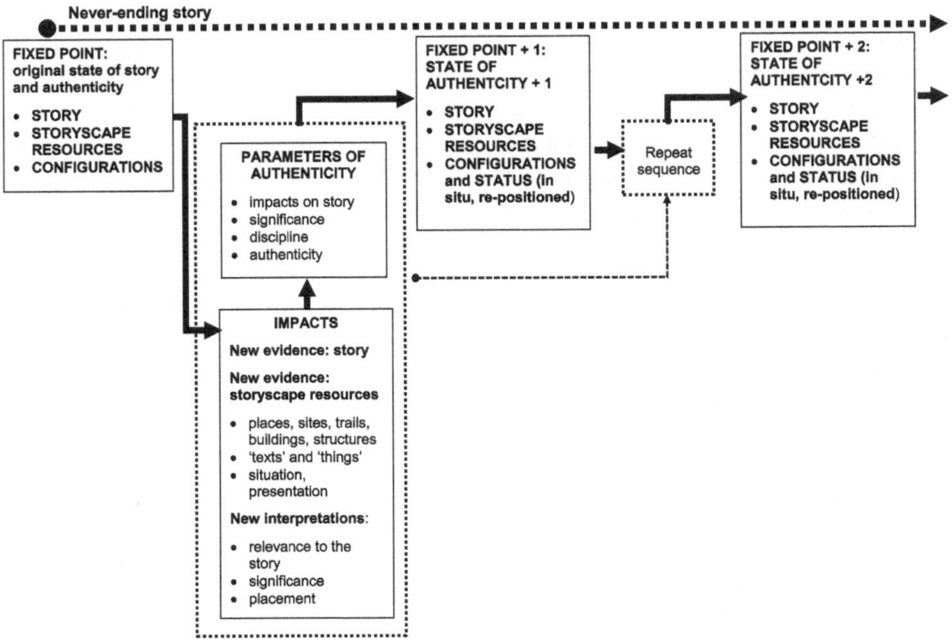

Figure 1. Process of improving the authenticity of a never-ending story.

interpretation. Fortunately, the peak events in the Kelly story took place in the period when newspaper and magazine reporting and the recording of daily events was improving and becoming widespread, and the scope of photographic support for the news reports was increasing. Additionally, the public dissemination of information was becoming more extensive, and this tended to feed the public appetite for more, to nudge it towards taking sides in any confrontation, and in the Kelly case, to contribute to the formation of sympathiser groups in the community. Some scholarship suggests that this, building on the back of the previous convict era, the deprivations and the camaraderie on the goldfields, and the Eureka uprising (December 1854), contributed to the momentum of support for oppressed groups in the emergent Australian society, with its distinctive identity of 'mateship', of entitlement to a 'fair go', and only grudging support for the organs of government and authority. It is this situation which has created the baseline for 'authenticity' in stories about the Kelly period.

True to the commentary of Latham (2016), this baseline, once fixed, has been subjected to tremors and revisions, with previous claims of 'authenticity' challenged. These challenges have come from, for example, improvements to forensic and archaeological techniques of investigation and interpretation. Outcomes have included, for example, clarifications and confirmations of levels of accuracy (of places, of dates – where and when events took place), of ownership and provenance (of the whereabouts of artefacts, documents and weapons), and remarkably, eventual certainty about the whereabouts of the skeletal remains of Ned Kelly. The skull of Ned Kelly is still 'missing', despite a number of claims of ownership. Many of these challenges to 'authenticity' have been well-documented (see, for example, the commentary on 'solving the forensic mystery of Ned Kelly's remains, by Cormick, 2014).

The commentary in the final paragraphs of this section of the paper draws on a number of experiences of treating with matters of 'authenticity', and with the incorporation of changing levels of veracity through revision and new discovery (including, for example, Latham, 2016; and case studies in Garden, 2004; McAuley & Pervan, 2014: Molleda & Jain, 2013; Wood, 2000). Before that, there is a brief account of the Ned Kelly story.

The story of Ned Kelly

The story has a tangible and visible legacy of places, buildings, structures, trails, artefacts and documents, and it is accompanied by an intangible legacy of 'feelings' and sentiments about the experiences of the Kelly family. It is the interweaving in this legacy which gives the story its particular identity, and which contributes to its attractiveness for the purpose of heritage-based tourism.

In summary it is an account of one family's responses to the economic, political and social circumstances and challenges prevailing throughout parts of the State of Victoria in the late Colonial period of Australian history (Jones, 2008; McQuilton, 1979). It is a story, based on ascertainable facts, which has become embellished as it has fallen prey to the expectations of some performing arts (dance, music, theatre), of some artistic interpretations (especially the Sidney Nolan set of paintings), and of a constant barrage of interpretation and counter-interpretation by a number of vested interests including descendants on the Kelly family tree. Heightening the attractiveness of the story for expression through popular culture is the linkage with the facts, fictions and folktales of social banditry (Hobsbawm, 1979), bushranging (McHugh, 2012), and outlawry (Seal, 1996). In the specific case of the Ned Kelly Gang, the focus is most often fixed to a catalogue of dramatic events which took place in a neatly confined period 1878–1880, including two bank robberies, two sieges (in one of which three policemen were killed), an attempt to derail a train, confrontations with the police and the judiciary, statutory proclamations that the members of the Kelly Gang were outlaws, cross-country pursuits by police patrols, the murder of a suspected police informer, and the preparation by Ned Kelly of two quasi-political manifestos. The traction of the story in various forms of popular culture has been almost constant since Ned Kelly's execution in Melbourne in November 1880, and it has drawn on a prospectus of evidence which ranges across 'physical and material reality', 'texts' and 'things', re-presentations and re-positioned presentations, various configurations and morphologies (see Table 1 for the resource categories, and see Figure 2 for the geographical disposition of that evidence).

The research platform

Constructing the research platform for this study has been guided by an approach to a profiling process advocated (Moustakas, 1990; see also Cormick, 2014). A simple process has been formulated (see Figure 1). The crucial element for this study has been to carefully apply suitable 'tests' to an inventory of story-specific information to reach a level of certainty about its 'authenticity', not only at an intrinsic level, but also about its substantive contribution to the telling of the story – a tourism 'storyscape'. In summary the sequence of steps includes:

- the gathering of information from the story being told – relevant to the setting, the cast of characters, and the 'plot';
- the selection of, and then the application of significance and disciplinary 'tests' to the body of evidence;
- the matching of the evidence to spatial configurations and placements.

This process then contributes to a substantive commentary which matches the story and its evidence to fixed or floating points of 'authenticity'. Additionally, it provides a consistent framework which can be used to make adjustments in response to 'new' and/or revised information and interpretations. As each adjustment is made, the 'baseline' of 'authenticity' and the 'fixed point' of the story changes.

Each of these steps has, for this study, relied upon a process of ongoing desk-based research, with complementing fieldwork-based investigations. Inputs to the first step have been accumulated over a period which has extended through a period of more than a decade (since 2007). The original

Table 1. Resource categories; arrangements; interpretations.

Resource categories	Arrangements	Interpretations
'Physical and material reality' • places, spaces, sites • tracks, trails • domestic buildings (homesteads) • public buildings (gaols, courthouses) • structures (bridges) • townships • monuments, memorials, plaques • archaeological remnants • safe havens, lookouts '**Texts', 'things'** • artefacts (tools) • armour, weapons • documents, diaries • correspondence • official public records • photographs, • newspaper and magazines items **Re-presentations, re-positioned presentations** • previous categories relocated to exhibitions, galleries, libraries, museums • monuments, memorials, plaques • cemeteries, gravesites • ceremonies and re-enactments • performance forms and venues (for drama, film, music and other forms) • art galleries	**Configurations,** spatial arrangements in forms, structures as: • 'spot' locations • linear forms • nodal forms • radial forms • concentric forms • irregular forms **Morphologies** as: • land use types • (themed) precincts, districts, enclaves, regional frameworks • townships **Hierarchies,** according to: • location • organisational • accessibility **Defining frameworks**, according to: • natural environment • cultural environment • legend, myth, folktale • presentation practises, marketing • planning and other ordinances • conventions and protocols	**Perspectives,** looking at: • 'foreground' • middle-ground • 'background' **Experiences** • education • information • entertainment • identity • ideology **Interpretations,** according to: • ethnicity, race • nationality • social group • gender • education • experience • ideology • purpose (scholarship, marketing)

baseline of information has not been stable, as both the quantum and the scope have been extended, refined and reconfigured to meet particular study purposes, and in response to new discoveries. Even the story itself has been challenged by occasional flurries of revisions and reinterpretations with the emergence of 'new' facts, increases to the stock of tangible evidence following archaeological discoveries, the recovery of previously 'lost' photographic and documentary evidence as an outcome of forensic investigations, and from deepened or broadened lines of particular discipline-based enquiry. This circumstance of almost constant re-visioning the scope of evidence has challenged some of the previously-nominated and accepted positions on 'authenticity'. Some of the 'fixed points' remain steadfast, while others have taken up 'floating' positions. Even so, 'authenticity' at the broadest scale of the story – the dates, the places, the participants, and the actions in the peak period, 1878–1880 – is largely incontrovertible. It is at the more intimate scale that 'authenticity' is at is most vulnerable level; this is addressed in later paragraphs.

The tourism attraction of the Ned Kelly story: the geographical and semiotic evidence

A specialised inventory of the principal evidence of the Kelly story composed using 'thinking geographically' and 'the gaze' component of semiotics as the deliberately-selected disciplinary perspectives is presented in Table 2 (see also Figure 2). The outcome of this exercise of epistemological pluralism (see earlier) is a reasonable fit with the conceptualisation of 'fixed points' (Latham, 2016), and, as later commentary will reveal, produces a baseline from which subsequent changes to any aspect of the evidence in the story can be judged as being consistent with the expectations of 'floating fixity'.

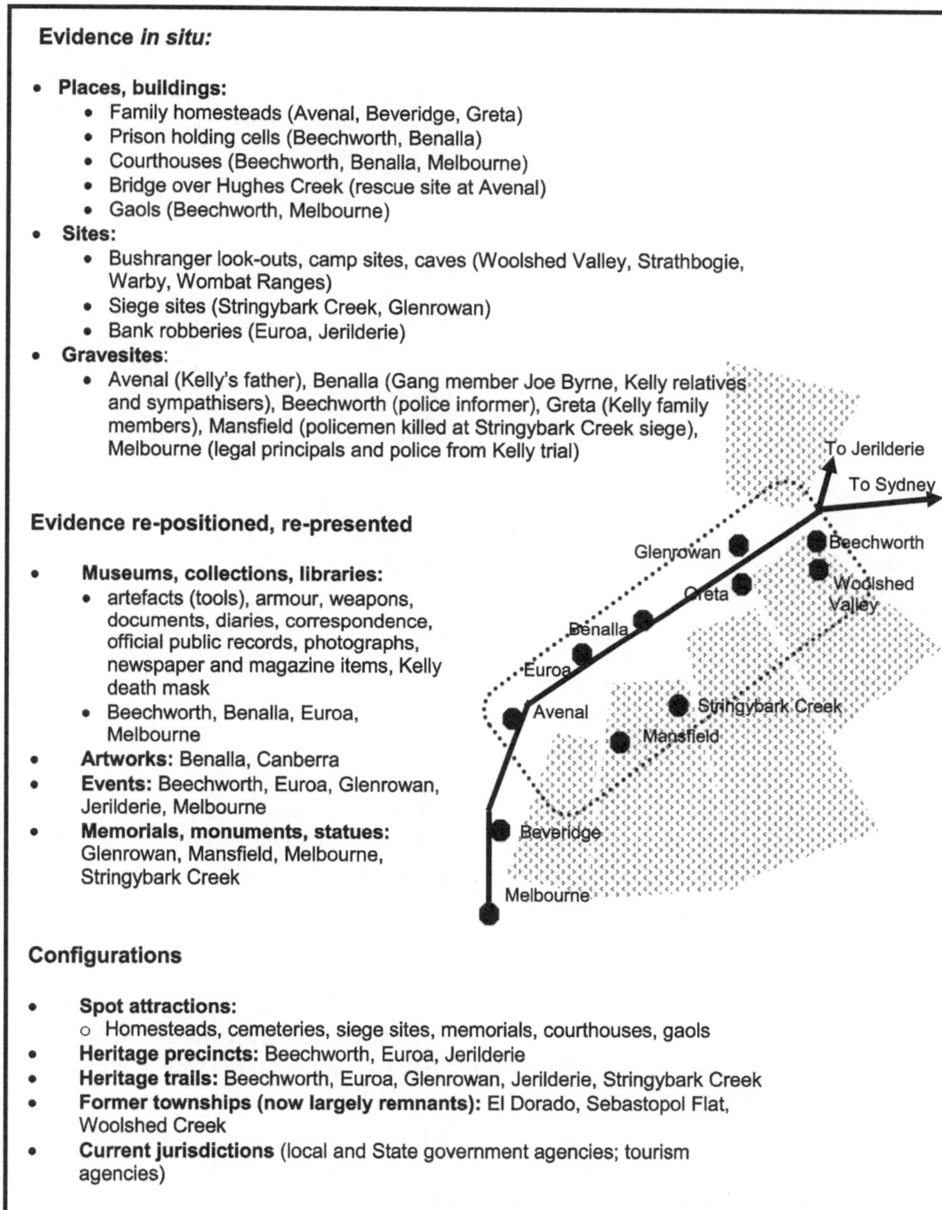

Figure 2. Evidence of the Ned Kelly story.

To reprise briefly and selectively from previous paragraphs, an inventory of the most prominent evidence of the Kelly story would include, for example,

- the sites of the Kelly homesteads, the two bank robberies, the two sieges;
- the proclamation that the members of the Kelly Gang had been declared legally as being outlaws;
- the two quasi-political manifestos authored by Ned Kelly and written by Joe Byrne;
- the sites of the trials, the gaols, and the execution of Ned Kelly;
- the suits of armour and the weapons used by each member of the Kelly Gang at the Glenrowan siege;
- the gravesites of the members of the Kelly family, the sympathisers with the Kelly Gang, and some of the principal judicial and police officers involved in the Kelly trials.

Table 2. Geographical and semiotic elements.

GEOGRAPHICAL ELEMENTS: *'things spatial'*	SEMIOTIC ELEMENTS: *'things symbolic'*	GEOGRAPHICAL and SEMIOTIC ELEMENTS: *'things spatial and symbolic'*
Elements *in-situ* • Sites, places • Structures • Buildings – domestic, commercial, industrial, public • Trails, routes, tracks • Settlements, townships • Landscape, vistas • Remnants – archaeological sites, abandoned sites and buildings **Elements re-positioned, re-presented** • Depositories, collections of: ◦ artefacts, ◦ armour, weapons, ◦ documents, correspondence ◦ effigies, monuments, memorials, statues, plaques ◦ photographs, films, ◦ newspaper reports ◦ artworks • Performance centres: the story told in dance, drama, literature, music – theatres, concert halls, cinemas • Events – ceremonies festivals, re-enactments, pageants, exhibitions	• Authentic, distinct, remarkable, unique • Sensed, experienced ◦ visible ◦ tangible ◦ memorable • Contextual, embedded • Style ◦ vernacular ◦ introduced ◦ elitist ◦ common, familiar • Original ◦ complete, intact ◦ remnant ◦ re-construction • Obsolete, abandoned • Substituted, indicative, representative, refurbished	• Patterns, positioning of resources ◦ spot attractions, ◦ precincts ◦ districts ◦ 'critical mass' ◦ Jurisdiction ◦ organisation • themed attractions • 'sense of place' • physical characteristics • aesthetic and scenic characteristics • associations, linkages • qualities – visibility, tangibility,

Whilst some of this evidence remains *in situ*, some of the sites have been abandoned, cleared, or redeveloped, and others are marked only by remnants. The custodianship of items of material culture (such as documents, correspondence, reports, weapons, armour, newsprint, photographs, and personal items) has been managed more securely, and these have been marshalled into depositories such as museums, libraries, galleries and record offices located in townships across the Kelly district or concentrated in Melbourne.

With the passage of time since the events of the story, each of the elements will have experienced change. This has an impact on the interpretation of authenticity accorded to them. By way of example, most of the sites, buildings, and structures involved in the unfolding Kelly story are no longer in their original state. Some have been cleared and left vacant, others have been physically-changed and subjected to change of use, and still others have been cleared and replaced by major site or building redevelopment. In almost all of these cases the present use seldom reflects the historic significance. A similar circumstance has befallen some of the artefacts and documents which have important contributions to make in the telling of the Kelly story. While some have benefitted from careful curatorial processes, others have languished in various public and private collections and have incurred some physical deterioration. The outcome has been that some of the evidence on display is a replica, copy, facsimile, or in some cases summaries and digests of voluminous studies and reports. Some of the direct and symbolic evidence of the Kelly story has benefitted from being challenged (whether by physical deterioration, relocation, or even the re-telling of the story through popular culture as in drama, films or re-enactments) as these very acts have contributed to heightening public awareness of the story, the potential benefits of conservation, and opportunities for heritage and culture-based tourism. Among the clear examples of catering for increased public interest have been the demarcation of heritage precincts and heritage trails, travelling exhibitions of high profile 'signature' tangible items (such as the Kelly Gang armour used at the Glenrowan siege), and commemorative events (such as the Kelly week-end held at Beechworth). The heightening of popular interest in the Kelly story has flowed from linking it with, for example, the momentum of the socio-political movement towards the formation of the Commonwealth of Australia, to the diasporic links with Ireland, to the formation of a distinctive Australian identity (founded on mateship, mutual support, 'a fair go' and larrikinism), and to the semi-formalisation of public antipathies towards some agencies of government and business. These various traits of Australianism are the existential markers which contribute to the surrogate opportunities of 'being there' without 'being there', and of the creation of 'prosthetic memories'.

Wheeler (2010) has carefully-crafted an assessment of some of constructivist influences on the Kelly-linked tourism product, in her consideration of the various attempts to create a distinctive product, the rivalries to deliver that product, the differences across local government jurisdictions in responding to tourism through their planning and economic strategies, the inconsistencies because of politicisation to the profiling of the regional tourism strategy, and even the antipathies to promoting cultural heritage as a tourism focus.

Despite the scale, scope and dispersion of the evidence of the Kelly story, the difficulties in showcasing that evidence are complicated by the moving target of 'authenticity', and by the occasional flurries of discoveries, interest and revisionism which forge the most recent scenario of acceptability and believability – a clear case of 'floating fixity'.

Conclusion and research directions

The Ned Kelly story may not be exceptional in the opportunities it provides for examining the end-product of striving to achieve the highest possible levels of 'authenticity' through tourism. However, whilst accepting 'as read' the desirability of achieving those levels, this study offers evidence that what is being dealt with is a moving target for which there will almost certainly be a series of challenges, and that each of these will nudge the story towards heightened levels of 'authenticity' as one stage of 'floating fixity' is replaced with another. Another way of expressing this is that as one baseline of evidence is superseded by another which is better informed about particular circumstances in the story, the expression of that story through tourism achieves a heightened status of 'authenticity' (see Figure 1).

This study has been structured progressively to explore the evidence of Latham's (2016) suggestion that perceptions about what is or what is not authentic is influenced by defining fixed points, and to corroborate that by providing evidence that if circumstances in a heritage story change (i.e. new evidence is found, arguments are revised, forensic tests reveal different outcomes) then the previously fixed point will migrate to another position. The case in this study has been that whilst there have been few significant changes to the story *per se* (i.e. the setting, the cast of characters, and the plot have remained intact), there have been a number of significant improvements and additions to the scope of the storyscape resources, and these have been sufficient to nudge the story to new positions of authenticity. To use Latham's expression, 'the point of fixity floats', and previous positions based on less authenticated evidence have become mere stepping stones to the improved position of confidence. Recent small-scale examples from the Kelly story of movement in the body of evidence towards new positions of fixity would include:

- the re-interpretation of a photograph of Ned Kelly, adding confidence to the basic case that Kelly worked for a timber company in the Woolshed Valley after his release from a gaol sentence;
- the recovery of a photograph of Ned Kelly in a pose before his boxing championship fight in Beechworth;
- the confirmation by forensic examination of Ned Kelly's skeletal remains exhumed from a cemetery in Pentridge Gaol (Melbourne);
- the internment of those skeletal remains in a specially-prepared and secure Kelly family grave site in Greta cemetery;
- the improved accuracy for the location of the most likely site of the Stringybark Creek siege in which members of the Kelly Gang were responsible for the murder of three policemen, using new methods of imagery and geographical positioning;

- the confirmation, after archaeological discovery and assessment, of the weaponry used, and the most likely positions of two of the four members of the Kelly Gang inside the eventually burned-down Ann Jones Inn at the siege site at Glenrowan;

Some imponderables remain; for example, one matter that awaits forensic adjudication is whether the two political manifestos (the Cameron and Jerilderie letters) were both authored and written by Ned Kelly, or whether some of the ideas and the penmanship can be attributed to Kelly Gang member Joe Byrne. A second example is the whereabouts of Ned Kelly's skull.

These matters alone will scarcely shake the fundamental shape of the Kelly story. Resolving them or coming to an improved level of 'authenticity', should clarify some of the events in the story, and serve to raise the confidence levels about issues which, without that level of improvement, will continue to jeopardise the acknowledgement given to the story in scholarship and in the domain of public discourse in general and in tourism in particular. This study has engaged with only two (and previously-selected) discipline-based tests, and although it has been used as a convenient test for the Latham (2016) conceptualisation, there are elements of the McAuley and Pervan (2014) trio of tests about (Celtic) marketing, the Grayson and Martinec's (2004) tests of indexical and iconic authenticity, the contextualisation of culture as text in Wood's (2000) Canadian study, and even the provocation of Pearce, Morrison, and Moscardo (2003) about adapting the story of iconic individuals as tourism attractions, which will bear investigation and interpretation. Story-telling, using enigmatic symbols, has the capacity to help with making sense of the world by providing opportunities beyond the mere gathering of information, by generating emotional and affective responses, by entertaining and by providing explanations. Provided the nominally-fixed points in a story are appreciated as being just that, then the presentation of stories from history through tourism will persist as a collection of beneficial experiences of 'being there' without 'being there', and as a momentary step along a continuum of what is a never-ending story.

Disclosure statement

No potential conflict of interest was reported by the author.

References

Australia ICOMOS. (2013). *The Burra Charter: The Australia ICOMOS Charter for the conservation of places of cultural significance* (revised edition). Canberra: Australia ICOMOS.

Brown, L. (2013). Tourism: A catalyst for existential authenticity. *Annals of Tourism Research*, *40*(1), 176–190.

Bryce, D., Alexander, M., & Murdy, S. (2017). Diaspora, authenticity and the imagined past. *Annals of Tourism Research*, *66*, 49–60.

Butler, R. (2004). Geographical research on tourism, recreation and leisure: Origins, eras and directions. *Tourism Geographies*, *6*(2), 143–162.

CCA. (2009). *Signature 2.0.* Adelaide: Collections Council of Australia.

Chhabra, D. (2005). Defining authenticity and its determinants: Toward an authenticity flow model. *Journal of Travel Research*, *44*, 64–73.

Chhabra, D., Healy, R., & Sills, E. (2003). Staged authenticity and heritage tourism. *Annals of Tourism Research*, *30*(3), 702–719.

Chronis, A. (2005). Coconstructing heritage at the gettysburg storyscape. *Annals of Tourism Research*, *32*(2), 386–406.

Chronis, A. (2012). Tourists as story-builders: Narrative construction at a heritage museum. *Journal of Travel and Tourism Marketing*, *29*(5), 444–459.

Cohen, E. (1988). Authenticity and commoditization in tourism. *Annals of Tourism Research*, *15*(3), 371–386.

Cohen, E. (2007). 'Authenticity' in tourism studies: *Apres la Lutte. Tourism Recreation Research*, *32*(2), 75–82.

Cohen, E., & Cohen, S. (2012). Authentication: Hot and cool. *Annals of Tourism Research, 39*(3), 1295–1314.
Cole, S. (2007). The regional science of tourism: An overview. *The Journal of Regional Policy and Analysis, 37*(3), 183–192.
Coles, T., Hall, C., & Duval, D. (2006). Tourism and post-disciplinary enquiry. *Current Issues in Tourism, 9*(4–5), 293–319.
Cormick, C. (Ed.). (2014). *Ned Kelly: Under the microscope*. Collingwood: CSIRO Publishing.
Darbellay, F. (2016). From disciplinarity to postdisciplinarity: Tourism studies dedisciplined. *Tourism Analysis, 21*, 363–372.
Darbellay, F., & Stock, M. (2012). Tourism as complex interdisciplinary research object. *Annals of Tourism Research, 39*(1), 441–458.
Davies, E. (2006). Epistemological pluralism. Retrieved from http://philsci-archive.pitt.edu/3083/1/EPsingle.doc
de Groot, J. (2009). *Consuming history: Historians and heritage in contemporary popular culture*. London: Routledge.
English Heritage. (2017). *Understanding place: Historic area assessments*. London: Historic England.
Garden, M.-C. (2004). *The Heritagescape: Exploring the phenomenon of the heritage site*. PhD Dissertation, Department of Archaeology, University of Cambridge.
Gravili, S., & Rosato, P. (2015). Destination telling: An integrative framework for co-narration practices in tourism destinations. Retrieved from https://www.researchgate.net/publication/275771410
Grayson, K., & Martinec, R. (2004). Consumer perceptions of iconicity and indexicality and their influence on assessment of authentic market offerings. *Journal of Consumer Research, 31*(2), 296–312.
Heritage Council of Victoria. (2014). *Assessing the cultural significance of places and objects for possible state heritage listing*. Melbourne: Heritage Council of Victoria.
Heritage Council of Victoria. (2015). *Landscapes of cultural heritage significance: Assessment guidelines*. Melbourne: Heritage Council of Victoria.
Hobsbawm, E. (1979). *Bandits*. London: Wiedenfeld and Nicholson.
Jamal, T., & Hill, S. (2004). Developing a framework for indicators of authenticity: The place and space of cultural and heritage tourism. *Asia Pacific Journal of Tourism Research, 9*(4), 353–372.
Jamal, T., & Kim, H. (2005). Bridging in the interdisciplinary divide: Towards an integrated framework for heritage tourism research. *Tourist Studies, 5*(1), 55–83.
Jones, I. (2008). *Ned Kelly: A short life*. Port Melbourne: Lothian Books.
Kim, J.-H. (2014). The antecedents of memorable tourism experiences. *Annals of Tourism Research, 44*, 34–45.
Kim, J.-H., Brent Ritchie, J., & McCormick, B. (2012). Development of a scale to measure memorable tourism experiences. *Journal of Travel Research, 51*(1), 12–25.
Knudsen, D., Metro-Roland, M., Soper, A., & Greer, C. (Eds.). (2008). *Landscape. Tourism and meaning*. Aldershot: Ashgate.
Landsberg, A. (2004). *Prosthetic memory: The transformation of American remembrance in the age of mass culture*. New York: Columbia University Press.
Latham, K. (2016). The curious case of floating fixity (and its relationship to authenticity). *Proceedings from the Document Academy, 3 (2)*, Article 2 (7pp), The University of Akron, at http://ideaexchange.uakron.edu/docam/vol3/iss2/2
McAuley, A., & Pervan, S. (2014). Celtic marketing: Assessing the authenticity of a never ending story. *Journal of Consumer Behaviour, 13*, 81–87.
McHugh, E. (2012). *Bushrangers*. Melbourne: Penguin Books Australia.
McQuilton, J. (1979). *The Kelly outbreak: The geographical dimensions of social banditry*. Carlton: Melbourne University Press.
Metro-Roland, M. (2009). Interpreting meaning: An application of Peircean semiotics to tourism. *Tourism Geographies, 11*(2), 270–279.
Metro-Roland, M. (2011). *Tourists, signs and the city*. Farnham: Ashgate.
Molleda, J.-C., & Jain, R. (2013). Testing a perceived authenticity index with triangulation research: The case of Xcaret in Mexico. *International Journal of Strategic Communication, 7*(1), 1–20.
Moscardo, G. (2010). The shaping of tourist experience: The importance of stories and themes. In N. Morgan, P. Lugosi, & J. Ritchie (Eds.), *The tourism and leisure experience: Consumer and managerial perspectives* (pp. 43–58). Bristol: Channel View Publications.
Moscardo, G. (2015). Stories of people and places: Interpretation, tourism and sustainability. In C. Hall, S. Gossling, & D. Scot (Eds.), *The Routledge handbook on tourism and sustainability* (pp. 294–304). Abingdon, OX: Routledge.
Moustakas, C. (1990). *Heuristic research: Design, methodology and applications*. Newbury Park: Sage.
Pearce, P., Morrison, A., & Moscardo, G. (2003). Individuals as tourist icons: A developmental and marketing analysis. *Journal of Hospitality and Leisure Marketing, 10*(1–2), 63–85.
Pine, B., & Gilmore, J. (2008). The eight principles of strategic authenticity. *Strategy and Leadership, 36*(3), 35–40.
Ram, Y., Bjork, P., & Weidenfeld, A. (2016). Authenticity and place attachment of major visitor attractions. *Tourism Management, 52*, 110–122.

Reisinger, Y., & Steiner, C. (2006). Reconceptualizing object authenticity. *Annals of Tourism Research*, *33*(1), 65–86.
Rickly-Boyd, J. (2012). 'Through the magic of authentic reproduction': Tourists' perceptions of authenticity in a pioneer village. *Journal of Heritage Tourism*, *7*(2), 127–144.
Seal, G. (1996). *The outlaw legend*. Cambridge: Cambridge University Press.
Shurmer-Smith, P. (2002). *Doing cultural geography*. London: Sage.
Smith, L. (2006). *Uses of heritage*. London: Routledge.
Tunbridge, J., & Ashworth, G. (1996). *Dissonant heritage: The management of the past as a resource in conflict*. Chichester: Wiley.
Urry, J. (1992). The tourist gaze 'revisited'. *American Behavioral Scientist*, *36*(2), 172–186.
Wang, N. (1999). Rethinking authenticity in tourism experience. *Annals of Tourism Research*, *26*(2), 349–370.
Waterton, E., & Watson, S. (2014). *The semiotics of heritage tourism*. Bristol: Channel View Publications.
Wheeler, F. (2010). *Politics, power and passion: Regional destination branding in North East Victoria*. PhD thesis, Monash University, Melbourne (Australia).
Wood, P. (2000). The historic site as cultural text: A geography of heritage in Calgary, Alberta. *Material History Review*, *52*, 33–43.

The role of authenticity, experience quality, emotions, and satisfaction in a cultural heritage destination

Ana M. Domínguez-Quintero, M. Rosario González-Rodríguez and José Luis Roldán

ABSTRACT

Recent studies have shown the increasing importance of affective and subjective variables, such as experience quality, authenticity, and emotions in the formation of tourist satisfaction. This paper is a pioneer in jointly analysing the influence of authenticity in its double dimension, experience quality, and emotions variables on satisfaction in a cultural context. This study uses the structural equation modelling approach (Partial Least Square) and shows the direct and positive influence of objective and existential authenticity on the quality of the experience, as well as the direct and positive influence of the quality of experience on emotions. It is highly relevant to focus on both cognitive and affective dimensions of authenticity to improve the quality of the tourists' experience. No previous studies in the literature examine the possible relationships between the different dimensions of authenticity on the quality of the experience and on emotions. The work reveals the importance of such variables in generating greater tourist satisfaction with the visited destination.

Introduction

In the field of tourism, recent research has identified that authenticity, quality of experience and emotions are key variables in the process of compounding the satisfaction and loyalty of tourists (Castéran & Roederer, 2013; Chen & Chen, 2010; De Rojas & Camarero, 2008; Kolar & Zabkar, 2010; Lee, Phau, Hughes, Li, & Quintal, 2016; Prayag, Hosany, & Odeh, 2013).

The works of Lee et al. (2016) and Nguyen and Cheung (2016) analysed the direct influence of authenticity as a simple constructor of the satisfaction of cultural tourists. To the best of our knowledge, no previous empirical studies have analysed the possible influence or relationship of authenticity, in its double dimension, on the variable experience quality and on the variable emotions in the context of cultural-heritage tourism. In accordance with this, we consider the following question: Do each of the two dimensions of the authenticity variable exert a certain direct influence on the variables of experience quality and emotions?

Work by Otto and Ritchie (1995, 1996) introduces the concept of *experience quality* of a service and define it as the *affective component* of the experience. Research by Chen and Chen (2010) and Lee et al. (2016) show the direct positive influence of this variable on satisfaction. In relation to this variable, we ask ourselves: does experience quality exert a direct effect on satisfaction in a cultural-heritage context?

Regarding the emotions variable, on one hand, there are numerous studies that analyse the positive or direct influence of this variable on satisfaction (De Rojas & Camarero, 2008; Del Bosque and San Martín, 2008). On the other hand, Zins (2002) analysed the positive and direct influence of the quality of the experience on the variable of emotions, but the results were inconclusive. As a consequence, we pose the following questions: can we confirm with our data that the experience quality exerts a positive influence on the emotions? And, does the emotions variable exert a direct or positive effect on satisfaction in a cultural-heritage context?

In summary, we analyse the relationships between authenticity, experience quality, emotions, and satisfaction. It is argued that the proposed model contributes to the research highlighting the importance of the proposed cognitive–affective variables and their relationships with satisfaction in cultural destinations. The results should lead to recommendations for local Destination Management Organizations (DMOs) concerning the adaptation of their resources and services to those demands and aspects most valued by visitors as an additional tool to improve the overall tourist satisfaction rates.

The structure of this paper is as follows: Theoretical foundations, Methodology, Results, Discussions and Conclusions, Theoretical and Managerial Implications, and Limitations and Future Research.

Theoretical foundations, research model and hypotheses

Authenticity and satisfaction

A review of the academic literature on the subject identifies that there is no consensus among authors on the definition of authenticity. There are various approaches and interpretations of the term upon which the studies of Wang (1999) and of Reisinger and Steiner (2005) conducted a comprehensive review. Wang (1999) summarises the various approaches into three main classifications: The objective or modernist, the constructive or symbolic, and the existential. The first two are related to the objects and the third is related to the activity of the tourist. For Wang (1999), the first two types can coexist, but in his opinion, the existential approach carries greater weight in explaining the experiences of tourists.

This dimension of authenticity plays a dual role in relation to tourism; it recognises the origins of heritage and is synonymous with uniqueness but it also favours the diversity of experiences due to differences between the varieties of tourists visiting a destination. This characterisation of authenticity means it can be considered a key factor in travel related to cultural and heritage tourism (Kolar & Zabkar, 2010; Casterán and Roederer 2013).

In relation to the variable satisfaction, numerous studies have attempted to combine the cognitive and affective approaches in the study of tourist satisfaction (Del Bosque and San Martín, 2008; Lee et al., 2016; Novello and Fernández, 2016). Our work uses this most recent focus in the literature and, according to Del Bosque and San Martín (2008), satisfaction is defined in this research as an individual's cognitive–affective state derived from a tourist experience.

Research in the field of cultural-heritage tourism has examined the relationship between authenticity, considered either as a single variable or in its dual objective-and-existential dimension, and the variable representing tourist loyalty (Kolar & Zabkar, 2010; Shen, Guo, & Wu, 2012). The works by Nguyen and Cheung (2016) and Girish and Chen (2017) confirmed the direct influence of authenticity as a single variable on satisfaction of cultural-heritage tourists, whereas Lee et al. (2016) analysed the direct influence of authenticity as a dual objective-and-existential variable on satisfaction. The latter showed that objective authenticity has a direct effect on satisfaction whereas existential authenticity does not, showing that the direct influence of this variable on satisfaction is not significant. We believe that this double dimension of authenticity is much more enriching and can provide more information about the real relationship between the analysed variables. It is of interest to analyse whether or not our data confirm the positive influence of each of the two dimensions of authenticity on satisfaction. That is why our work considers the two dimensions, objective and existential, of the variable authenticity and we propose the analysis of the following hypotheses:

H1: The higher the object authenticity that the heritage tourists perceive, the higher the level of satisfaction they experience.

H2: The higher the existential authenticity that the heritage tourists perceive, the higher their level of satisfaction.

The aforementioned work by Kolar and Zabkar (2010) and Shen et al. (2012) found that the objective dimension of authenticity positively influences its existential dimension. We believe that in the context of cultural tourism, it is reasonable to think that the high perception of object authenticity, positive evaluation of architecture, material, presentation of resources, activities, all positively influence the perception of existential authenticity, and can favour the feeling of connection and immersion of the tourist in the local culture. To enhance the knowledge of the possible relationship or influence between the two dimensions of authenticity, we propose the contrast of the following hypothesis:

H3: The higher the object authenticity that the heritage tourists perceive, the higher the level of existential authenticity they have.

Authenticity and experience quality

Otto and Ritchie (1995) introduced the concept of 'experience quality' and applied this concept to recreational tourism. They defined experience quality as the affective component of the experience, which includes subjective, emotional, and personal responses to various aspects of service development and leads to overall satisfaction.

Regarding the possible relationship between authenticity and experience quality, Romero (2001) suggests that authenticity can be a key factor in enabling cultural tourists to attain high levels of experience quality. Along the same lines, Oh, Fiore, and Jeoung (2007) cite the work of MacCannell (1989) and the concept of 'the tourist experience' as an example for tourists to be able to have authentic experiences. This is an interesting reflection that relates the variable 'experience quality' with the variable 'authenticity'. Despite these interesting reflections, there is limited research contrasting the possible positive influence of authenticity on the quality of the experience. Shen and Wen (2016) identified that authenticity considered as a one-dimensional construct exerts a positive influence on the quality of experience. As we have stated previously, we believe that the double dimension of authenticity is much more enriching and we believe it reasonable to think that tourists who enjoy architecture, historical buildings, materials, the landscape, the events, the related histories, the atmosphere of peace and calm in the town ... all these factors can make the tourist enjoy the culture and history of the city, can make the tourist feel relaxed and connected to the customs and daily life of the city, and can definitely help the tourist achieve a higher level of quality of experience. In order to analyse further the relationship that may exist between the two dimensions of the variable authenticity and the variable experience quality, the testing of the following hypotheses is proposed:

H4: The higher the object authenticity that the heritage tourists perceive, the higher the level of quality experience they have.

H5: The higher the existential authenticity that the heritage tourists perceive, the higher the level of quality experience they have.

Authenticity and emotions

Emotions have been widely studied in the field of tourism in general, (Bigné, Andreu, & Gnoth, 2005; Duman & Mattila, 2005; Del Bosque and San Martín, 2008; Hosany, 2012; Han & Jeong, 2013; Kim & Fesenmaier, 2015) and in cultural tourism in particular (De Rojas and Camarero, 2008; Prayag et al., 2013; Palau-Saumell, Forgas-Coll, Sánchez-García and Prats-Planaguma, 2013). According to Del Bosque and San Martín (2008), in general, the emotional component is an important factor in any consumer experience, although its protagonism may be more relevant when the experiential component is important (Dubé-Riboux, 1990), or when there is a certain ambiguity and uncertainty around the consumer experience (Jayanti & Ghosh, 1996). The three characteristics mentioned – experience, ambiguity and uncertainty – can be considered as three fundamental characteristics of tourism products and services. In this sense, Bigné et al. (2005) state that emotions are particularly relevant in the field of tourism, since the enjoyment of individuals is based on their own experience and participation. Kim and Fesenmaier (2015) argued that tourism experiences are fundamentally shaped by emotions. Emotions contribute to experiences processing onsite and affect the creation of long-lasting memories, thus influencing future behaviour and travel choices (Volo, 2017).

According to academic literature, emotions are specific forms of affect that can be primarily characterised by three aspects: (1) short duration, usually minutes or hours; (2) high intensity; and (3) tendency to have a trigger or stimulus that occurs at an immediately preceding point in time, that is, emotions are a consequence or response to a specific event (Bagozzi, Gopinath, & Nyer, 1999). Holbrook (1995) states that the consumer experience has mutually interdependent emotional elements: physiological responses, cognitive interpretations, feelings, and expressions of behaviour.

In relation to the components that can be distinguished within the emotional process, the majority of authors defend the existence of several components (Holbrook, 1995). The work of Russell (1980) considers two dimensions: pleasure and arousal. The dimension of pleasure-displeasure varies between liking and disliking, while the arousal dimension varies between activation and no activation. The mixture or intersection of these two dimensions leads to a variety of emotional situations. This second model by Russell (1980) is the most commonly followed in the marketing literature to model the emotional state of individuals in a consumption experience and, in our specific case, for tourists.

It is apparent that there are no studies in the academic literature that analyse the influence of the authenticity on emotions variables. Due to the dual cognitive–affective nature of authenticity, this relationship may constitute an important precedent in the formation of the satisfaction of cultural-heritage tourists. To further explore this gap in the academic literature on the subject, and considering the authenticity variable in its double dimension, we propose the testing of the following hypotheses:

> H6: The higher the Object authenticity that the heritage tourists perceive, the higher the level of emotions they experience.

> H7: The higher the existential authenticity that the heritage tourists perceive, the higher the level of emotions they have.

Experience quality and satisfaction

Traditionally, the academic literature used the service quality as an explanatory variable of the satisfaction of the tourists. Chen and Chen (2010) proposed the quality of experience in its objective to explain the satisfaction and loyalty of tourists. They consider the quality of service a well-studied variable in the academic literature, but not experience quality, which they consider to be a variable still little explored, especially at the empirical level. Following the recommendations of Otto and Richie (1996), they substitute quality of service for experience quality, considering it a much more suitable variable to explain satisfaction and loyalty in the context of cultural-heritage tourism. The possible influence of the experience quality on satisfaction has been studied in previous works from a cultural-heritage tourism context (Chen & Chen, 2010; Altunel & Erkut, 2015; Shen and Wen; 2016). These studies show that those tourists who reach higher levels of experience quality, also reach high levels of satisfaction. In order to analyse further this relationship, we address the testing of hypothesis number eight:

> H8: The higher the experience quality that the heritage tourists perceive, the higher the level of satisfaction they have.

Experience quality, emotions and satisfaction

Zins (2002) discusses the role of emotions and experience quality in the formation of satisfaction. For Zins (2002), the cognitive assessment of service cannot be independent of its emotional or affective assessment. This leads him to analyse how the different components and aspects of experience quality can influence the perception of emotions, with inconclusive results. The data support the hypothesis that there is a positive association between a number of the components of the experience quality and emotions, but fails to support this hypothesis for other components. This hypothesis is therefore only partially accepted.

As far as we know, there are no works analysing the relationship of these two variables in the field of tourism. We believe that there is a gap in academic literature regarding the subject and propose to deepen the knowledge of this relationship by contrasting the following hypothesis:

> H9: The higher the experience quality that the heritage tourists perceive, the higher the level of emotions they experience.

The work of Cohen and Areni (1991) established that the emotions triggered during the consumption experience cause memory traces that are subsequently recovered by the individual for the evocation and construction of satisfaction. In addition to this work, other studies carried out in a general tourism context found that the emotions variable exerts a positive or direct influence on the satisfaction of tourists (Del Bosque and San Martín, 2008; Prayag et al., 2013, Ali, Amin, & Ryu, 2016). The works by De Rojas and Camarero (2008) and Palau-Saumell, Forgas-Coll, Sánchez-García, and Prats-Planagumà (2013) were carried out in a context of cultural-heritage tourism. Thus, we believe that the relationship between emotions and satisfaction has still been little studied especially in a context of cultural-heritage tourism destination and we propose to deepen the study of the relationship between these two variables. All these arguments lead us to specify the following hypothesis:

> H10: The higher the emotions that the heritage tourists perceive, the higher the level of satisfaction they experience.

Methodology

Sampling and data collection

In this work, the population that forms the object of this study is made up of tourists over 18 years old who visit the city of Seville as a cultural destination. Although the survey was conducted at different cultural sites, 80% of tourists have as the main purpose of their visit 'cultural tourism'. For the other 20% of tourists cultural attractions appeared to be a secondary activity.

The information for this study was collected in March 2014, since this is one of the months when there is a greater flow of tourists in Seville. According to the data of the Town Hall Tourism Office of Seville (Consorcio de Turismo del Ayto. de Sevilla, 2014), in December 2013, the city broke its record by having 144,000 visitors. Based on a structured questionnaire, data were collected face-to-face with visitors by the authors in the historical quarter: the Cathedral-Giralda, the Reales Alcázares, and the Flamenco Museum where 229 completed questionnaires were obtained. After excluding 19 cases due to excessive missing data, and when a response pattern was observed (Hair, Hult, Ringle, Sarstedt, & Thiele, 2017), 210 questionnaires (91.70%) were retained as valid for the empirical analysis. Table 1 shows the profile of the respondents.

Measures

The questionnaires design-base is a literature review of cultural tourism. The questionnaire was translated into Spanish, English, French, German and Mandarin according to Seville Tourism

Table 1. Respondent demographics.

	Percentage
Gender	
Male	37.1
Female	62.9
Age	
18–24	24.7
25–34	26.4
35–44	16.5
45–54	19.8
55–64	6.6
Over 65	6.0
Level of studies	
Primary	0.00
Secondary	14.42
A-levels/Professional training	32.69
University studies	52.88
Origin	
Spain	11.54
European Union (except Spain)	45.19
Rest of the world	43.27
Main aim of the visit	
Visit friends or family	2.86
Cultural tourism	80.00
Congress/Business	0.48
Studies	1.43
Shopping	0.00
Other	15.24

Consortium in order to access tourists of different nationalities who visit the city. The measurement scales for the constructs are taken from scales validated in the literature and refined by experienced experts from the Seville Tourism Consortium. The questionnaires design also included a pre-test whereby interviewing 50 tourists of different nationalities were interviewed in order to detect and smooth out any problems in the various translations of the items. The items on the measurement scales were on a seven-point Likert Scale. The questionnaire items are listed in Table 2.

The measurement of the authenticity variable in its double perspective (objective authenticity and existential authenticity) – has been based on the work of Kolar and Zabkar (2010, p. 657). An item regarding the perception of the restoration of the historic heritage has been added to the 10-item scale proposed by Kolar and Zabkar (2010) in the objective authenticity construct. In the end, objective authenticity has 6 items and existential authenticity 5.

Otto and Ritchie (1996) empirically developed the construct quality of experience and their scale was composed of four dimensions (hedonic, peace of mind, involvement, and recognition). The construct quality of experience used in our work is adapted from the study by Otto and Ritchie (1996) with tourists from a cultural background.

To measure emotions we opted for a bipolar scale in which the intensity of emotions was measured, whereby 1 represents the experimentation with a high intensity of negative emotion and 7 represents the experimentation with a high intensity of positive emotion. The emotions construct which is presented in the work is an adaptation of that proposed by Russell and Pratt (1980).

We adopt Del Bosque and San Martín's (2008) definition of satisfaction, according to which, satisfaction is a cognitive judgment derived from the tourists' experience after their stay in the destination visited. In our work, the measurement of the satisfaction variable is an adaption of the multidimensional scale by Oliver (1997). We have included two items which refer to the affective and cognitive evaluation of satisfaction, and a third item for a global evaluation of satisfaction.

Table 2. Measurement model for Mode A composites: loadings, construct reliability and convergent validity.

	Weights	Loadings	Composite reliability	Ave	VIF
Objective authenticity					
Aut1: The overall architecture and impression of the buildings inspired	0.272***(t = 19.865)	0.785	0.878	0.592	
Aut2: Restoration of historic buildings respects the same style (architecture, furniture, utensils, etc ...)	0.256***(t = 17.194)	0.796			
Aut3: I liked the peculiarities about the interior design and furnishings	0.267***(t = 16.868)	0.779			
Aut4: I liked the way the site blends with the attractive landscape, scenery, historical ensemble, the town	0.268***(t = 19.821)	0.795			
Aut5: I liked the information about the site and I found it interesting	0.236***(t = 15.040)	0.685			
Existential authenticity			0.871	0.53	
Aut6: I liked special arrangements, events, concerts, celebrations connected to the site	0.211***(t = 16.247)	0.673			
Aut7: The visit provided a thorough insight into different historical periods of the city	0.223***(t = 16.549)	0.73			
Aut8: During the visit I sensed the related history, legends and historical personalities	0.217***(t = 18.587)	0.75			
Aut9: I enjoyed a unique experience that allowed me to be in contact with the local people, their traditions and customs	0.203***(t = 19.865)	0.731			
Aut10: I liked the calm and peaceful atmosphere during the visit	0.253***(t = 15.935)	0.725			
Aut11: I felt connected with human history and civilization	0.265***(t = 17.199)	0.759			
Experience quality			0.838	0.509	
Exp1: I've had fun	0.276***(t = 10.092)	0.775			
Exp2: I've felt at ease and relaxed during the visit	0.282***(t = 9.536)	0.725			
Exp3: I believe that visiting a cultural heritage site has been a good learning experience and instructive	0.311***(t = 11.698)	0.744			
Exp 4: I have actively participated in the experience of the visit (Past View, interaction with the guides, local people, etc.)	0.273***(t = 9.960)	0.504			
Exp 5: I have escaped from the daily routine and done something really new in my visit	0.273***(t = 9.960)	0.658			
Exp 6: I believe that my belongings and myself have been safe during the visit	0.261***(t = 8.650)	0.658			
Satisfaction			0.893	0.677	
Sat1: This is one of the best destinations I could have visited	0.295***(t = 18.593)	0.817			
Sat2: Overall, I am pleased with my decision to visit the cultural heritage in Seville/York	0.321***(t = 20.761)	0.852			
Sat 3: My overall satisfaction towards visiting York's/Seville's cultural heritage	0.267***(t = 14.473)	0.867			

Note: *$p < .05$; **$p < .01$; ***$p < .001$.

Data analysis

The research model displayed in Figure 1 has been tested using Partial Least Squares (PLS), which is a variance-based structural-equation modelling technique. (i) The presence of composites either in Mode A or B suggests the use of PLS (Sarstedt, Hair, Ringle, Thiele and Gudergan, 2016). (ii) The complexity of the research model and the different effects established between the variables (direct and mediating relations). (iii) The non-normality of the variables of the research model. In our model all the skewness values of indicators are not over −1.3 and which reveals that the degree of skewness is not severe showing PLS-SEM is suitable for estimating the model. (iv) The number of cases is under 250 observations, thus, according to Reinartz, Haenlein, and Henseler (2009), PLS is advisable regarding covariance-based SEM.

Results

A PLS model must be analysed and interpreted in two stages (Hair, Hult, Ringle, and Sarsted, 2017). First, the measurement model is evaluated (outer model). The measurement model allows us to

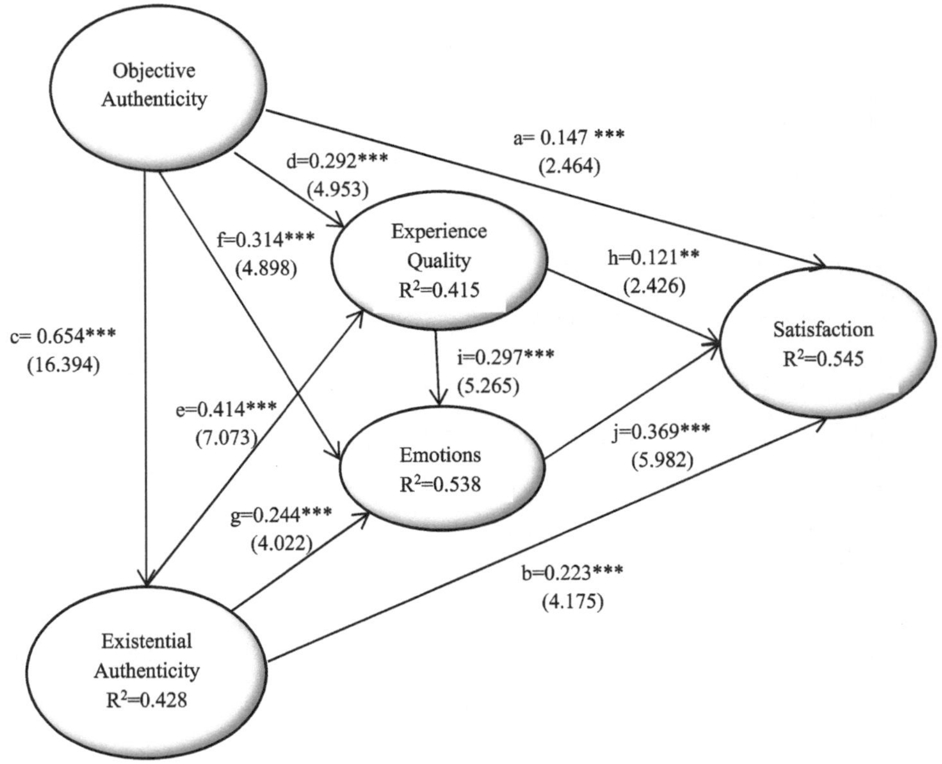

Figure 1. Estimated model.

Notes: BC, Bias, Corrected 5000 bootstrap samples. *$p<.05$;**$p<.01$, ***$p<.001$ (based on $t(4999)$, one-tailed test).

evaluate if the theoretical concepts or constructs are measured correctly through the items observed. The evaluation is different depending on whether the construct is formative or composite Mode A. Second, the structural model is evaluated (inner model). The magnitude and significance of the causal relations between the different variables is assessed from this model.

Measurement model

In the research model, all the constructs except the emotions variable are considered to be composite measurements with a reflective design approximation (Mode A), where all indicators and dimensions represent different facets, although correlations do exist among them (Becker, Rai, & Rigdon, 2013). The emotions variable is modelled as Mode B (formative design) due to the nature of the theoretical construct. According to our results, the measurement model is completely satisfactory, both for Mode A and Mode B composites.

First, in the case of the composite Mode A constructs, item 4 of the Experience Quality variable has a factorial loading of less than 0.5. After removing this item, we again carried out the estimation of the model and subsequently evaluated the measurement model for the Mode A composite (Table 2). With respect to the individual reliability of the items, all the loadings are over 0.707, except for two items belonging to the construct experience quality and two items belonging to the constructs objective and existential authenticity, respectively. Nevertheless, we kept these items given that, in addition to their loadings being close to 0.707, their contents are also important in the definition of each of the constructs. The item's individual reliability is appropriate (Falk & Miller, 1992). With respect to the internal consistency of the measurement scales, it is noted that the composite reliabilities of the constructs are over 0.7. We can state that the items or manifest variables are really measuring each of the latent variables (Gefen, Straub, & Boudreau, 2000; Nunnally & Bernstein, 1994). The AVE coefficient (Average Variance Extracted) represents the proportion of variance of the construct that can be explained by its indicators. It is verified that this coefficient is over 0.5 for all of the constructs. This means that we can state that there is convergent validity for each of the latent variables (Fornell & Larcker, 1981).

Table 3 shows the analysis of discriminant validity between the constructs via the calculation of the HTMT coefficients (Henseler, Ringle, & Sarstedt, 2015) and using the Fornell–Lacker criterion (Fornell and Lacker, 1981). Table 3 shows that all constructs attain discriminant validity following the Forner-lacker and the strictest HTMT85 criterion (Hair, Hult, Ringle, & Sarstedt, 2017). Thus, all constructs are measuring different aspects.

Second, the emotions variable is the only construct estimated in Mode B, and for this reason to evaluate the measurement scale at the indicator level, it is necessary to ascertain whether there is any multicollinearity between the items. To this end, the Variance Inflation Factor (VIF) is calculated (Table 4). It is noted that the VIFs are all less than 3.3, which indicates that the items have no problems of multicollinearity (Diamantopoulos & Siguaw, 2006).

Structural model

First, we evaluate the possibility of there being multicollinearity between the constructs (Hair et al., 2017). In each of the partial multiple regressions, the VIF index for each of the exogenous constructs is less than 5. We can therefore state that there are no problems of multicollinearity between the exogenous constructs of each endogenous variable. We then analyse the structural model's direct relations (Baseline model). Figure 1 displays the details concerning the path coefficients, and Table 5 shows the path coefficients (direct effects). To evaluate the significance of the path coefficients, we use a bootstrapping procedure with 5,000 subsamples to generate t-statistics and confidence intervals (Henseler, Ringle, & Sinkovics, 2009). The results from Table 5 support the ten hypotheses related to the main effects (or direct effects). Both the objective and existential authenticity has a significant and positive effect on satisfaction ($a = 0.147$, $t = 2.464$; $b = 0.223$, $t = 4.175$), thus supporting hypotheses H1 and H2. Likewise, the objective authenticity has a significant and

Table 3. Measurement model for Mode A composites. Discriminant validity.

	Fornell–Larcker criterion						Heterotrait–Monotrait ratio (HTMT)				
	EA	OA	EQ	Satisf	Emot		EA	OA	EQ	Satisf	Emot
EA	**0.728**					*EA*					
OA	0.654	**0.769**				*OA*	0.795				
EQ	0.605	0.563	**0.713**			*EQ*	0.731	0.712			
Satisf	0.628	0.640	0.621	**0.822**		*Satisf*	0.711	0.715	0.702		
Emot	0.623	0.596	0.567	0.621	**NA**	*Emot*	NA	NA	NA	NA	

Notes: EA: Existential Authenticity; OA: Objective Authenticity; EQ: Experience Quality; Satisf: Satisfaction; Emot: Emotions. Fornell-Larcker Criterion: Diagonal elements (bold) are the square root of the variance shared between the constructs and their measures (AVE: averange variance extracted). Off-diagonal are the correlations among constructs. For the discriminant validity, diagonal elements should be larger than off-diagonal elements.

Table 4. Measurement model for Mode B composite. Outer weight and VIF.

		Bootstrapping 95% Confidence intervals BC		
Emotions	Weights	Lower	Upper	VIF
Emo1: Pleased/Displeased	0.480 (7.473)*	0.338	0.589	1.880
Emo2: Enchanted/Angry	0.136 (2.264)*	0.026	0.260	1.848
Emo3: Impressed/Bored	0.439 (7.760)*	0.313	0.537	1.796
Emo4: Surprised/Disappointed	0.135 (2.394)*	0.034	0.258	1.655

Notes: BC: Bias Corrected. 5000 bootstrap samples; *$p < .05$ (two-tailed *t*-distribution).

Table 5. Hypotheses testing, path and confidence interval.

	Direct effect estimate	Boostrapping 90% confidence interval BC	
		Lower	Upper
H1: Obj. Aut. – >Satisfac = a	0.147** (2.464)	0.046	0.242
H2: Exist. Aut. ->Satisfac = b	0.223*** (4.175)	0.128	0.304
H3: Obj. Aut. -> Exist. Aut.=c	0.654*** (16.394)	0.585	0.717
H4: Obj. Aut. -> Qua. Exp.=d	0.292*** (4.953)	0.203	0.397
H5: Exist. Aut. -> Qua. Exp.= e	0.414*** (7.073)	0.316	0.510
H6: Obj. Aut. -> Emotions = f	0.314*** (4.898)	0.199	0.407
H7: Exist. Aut. -> Emotions = g	0.244*** (4.022)	0.144	0.340
H8: Qua. Exp. ->Satisfac = h	0.121** (2.426)	0.043	0.207
H9: Qua. Exp -> Emotions = i	0.297*** (5.265)	0.220	0.403
H10: Emotions ->Satisfac = j	0.369*** (5.982)	0.271	0.473

Notes: BC, Bias, Corrected 5000 bootstrap samples. *$p < .05$;**$p < .01$, ***$p < .001$ (based on $t(4999)$, one-tailed test).

positive influence on existential authenticity ($c = 0.654$, $t = 16.394$), which in turn supports hypothesis H3. The objective authenticity has a significant and positive influence on both experience quality and emotions ($d = 0.292$, $t = 4.953$; $f = 0.314$; $t = 4.898$). Thus, the hypotheses H4 and H6 are supported. The hypotheses H5 and H7 are also supported according to the significant and positive effects obtained from the influence of the existential authenticity on both experience quality and emotions ($e = 0.414$, $t = 7.073$; $g = 0.244$, $t = 4.022$). The experience quality, as hypothesised, has a significant positive effect on emotions ($i = 0.297$, $t = 5.265$) as well as on satisfaction ($h = 0.121$, $t =$ 2.426), thus supporting H8 and H9. Finally, the emotions the heritage tourist perceives has a significantly positive effect on satisfaction ($j = 0.369$, $t = 5.982$), thereby supporting H10.

Table 6 shows the coefficient of determination (R^2), which indicates the proportion of variance of the endogenous construct that is explained by the regressors. Table 6 provides the cross-validated redundancy measure (Q^2), which is particularly recommended to examine the predictive relevance of the research model (Hair, Sarstedt, Ringle, & Mena, 2012). All the Q^2 values are positive, thereby indicating predictive relevance for the endogenous constructs of the research model: existential authenticity, experience quality, and satisfaction. Table 6 also reports the f^2-effect size to evaluate whether the omitted construct has a substantive impact on the endogenous construct (Hair et al., 2017). As observed, the objective authenticity has a major effect on the existential authenticity, and existential authenticity has a major effect on experience quality. The other effects are considered to present medium effects on those respective endogenous variables that are higher than 0.15 and lower than 0.35.

Table 6. Coefficient of determination, cross-validated redundancy measures, f^2-effect size and Q^2-effect size.

Constructs	R^2	Explained variance (%)	f^2	Q^2
Existential Authenticity	0.428			0.220
Objective Authenticity		42.8	0.654	
Quality Experience	0.415			0.205
Objective Authenticity		16.44	0.292	
Existential Authenticity		24.92	0.414	
Emotions	0.538			0.332
Objective Authenticity		20.10	0.314	
Existential Authenticity		15.32	0.244	
Quality Experience		18.44	0.297	
Satisfaction	0.545			0.361
Objective Authenticity		8.76	0.157	
Existential Authenticity		13.89	0.223	
Quality Experience		6.86	0.151	
Emotions		25.02	0.369	

The standardised root mean square residual (SRMR) is considered to be a *goodness of fit* measure for PLS-SEM in the detection of model misspecification (Henseler et al., 2015). A threshold of 0.10, or, more conservatively, of 0.08 (Hu and Bentler, 1999), is considered a good fit. For our model, the SRMR is 0.054, showing that the model specification is within the thresholds that are considered satisfactory.

Discussion and conclusions

The present study tests a structural model integrating constructs of perceived authenticity, quality of experience, emotions and satisfaction to consume cultural attractions. Some of the results obtained in this work confirm results obtained in previous works. (i) Focussing on the research model relationships that reflect the influence of objective and existential authenticity on satisfaction was also found to be significant. Findings suggest that tourists with positively perceived authenticity are better satisfied with the cultural site. The findings achieved are partially in accordance with recent work, such as that by Lee et al. (2016), where the direct influence of objective authenticity on satisfaction is obtained, but not in the same way as existential authenticity. (ii) From the research model and based on the cognitive–affective causal sequence, objective authenticity can be considered a determinant of existential authenticity, as has also been observed in Kolar and Zabkar (2010) and Shen et al. (2012). These results mean that the perceived object-based authenticity induces the tourist to experience subjective perceptions attached to the objects' authenticity. (iii) The study also shows the significant influence of the experience quality on satisfaction; this is consistent with other studies in the literature (Altunel & Erkut, 2015; Chen & Chen, 2010). (iv) This paper also shows that the relationship reflecting the positive influence of emotions on satisfaction is also significant. This coincides with the results obtained in previous studies (De Rojas & Camarero, 2008; Zins, 2002; and Del Bosque & San Martín, 2008; Ali et al., 2016; Palau-Saumell et al., 2013; Prayag et al., 2013).

The model shows interesting relationships that have not been studied in previous tourism literature and therefore constitutes a contribution to finding factors leading to cultural consumption: (i) This work confirms the direct and positive influence of the two dimensions of authenticity (objective and existential) on experience quality. While it is true that Shen and Wen (2016) confirmed the positive and direct influence of authenticity, defined as a one-dimensional construct, on the quality of experience, no previous studies have analysed this relationship considering each of the two dimensions of authenticity. We conclude that tourists who provide positive ratings on aspects such as architecture, historical buildings, materials, landscape, events, related histories, the atmosphere of peace and calm in the town also reach higher levels of experience quality. (ii) This work confirms the direct and positive influence of the two dimensions of authenticity (objective and existential) on emotions. We conclude that tourists who leave positive ratings on objective and existential authenticity also reach higher levels of positive emotions on their visit. Taking into account this result and that emotions exert a direct and positive influence on satisfaction, we could also affirm that emotions are a mediating variable in the relationship of each of the dimensions of authenticity with satisfaction. (iii) On the other hand, our work makes a third contribution, the confirmation of the direct and positive influence of experience quality on emotions. Higher levels in the evaluation of aspects of the visit such as having fun, feeling relaxed, and perceiving the visit as an instructive and enriching experience, disconnecting from the routine and feeling safe lead the tourist to experience higher levels of positive emotions. We could therefore conclude that emotions are also a mediating variable in the relationship that unites the quality of experience with satisfaction.

This study was motivated by the need to strengthen the understanding of the role of cognitive–affective variables, such as those of objective authenticity, existential authenticity, experience quality, and emotions, on satisfaction. Testing these relationships leads to a better understanding of how these variables interact in a cultural-heritage tourist destination. To the best of our knowledge, this study is a pioneer in jointly analysing the influence of authenticity, experience quality, and emotions on satisfaction in a cultural-heritage context. The results confirm the importance of concepts such as authenticity, quality of experience and emotions during the visit in cultural tourism consumption.

Cultural tourism attractions in a destination should be offered to provide visitors with an authentic, positive and high-quality experience which in turn should favour the satisfaction of the tourist.

Regarding the notion of authenticity, the findings of this study reveal that cultural offerings were perceived not only as tangible tourism attractions but also as existential experiences derived from the different feeling attached to the tourism products (sense of enjoyment and escape). Results clearly show that visitors interpret authenticity in its double dimension (object-based and existential authenticity) and that the concept of authenticity may have different meanings depending on the destination characteristics. The consideration of authenticity constitutes a key element in the present study since not many studies in the generic and cultural-heritage tourism literature have paid attention to the influence of perceived authenticity on either satisfaction or behavioural intentions (Ramkissoon & Uysal, 2011; Sedmak & Mihalič, 2008). The findings are in line with Kolar and Zabkar (2010) and Ramkissoon and Uysal (2011) who also noted that perceived authenticity in its double perspective influences successful consumption of cultural attractions. The theoretical contribution of this research aims at enriching the understanding of the complexity of the authenticity concept as a multi-dimensional construct and to provide relevant information for tourism marketers, planners and policy-makers to offer authentic experience at the heritage sites.

Another theoretical implication derived from the research model is the significant influence of perceived authenticity on quality of experience and emotions experienced by tourists during the cultural visit. Cultural offerings seek to provide visitors with an authentic experience, influencing the quality of the tourists' experience during the visit while generating positive emotions. Thus, the present study also contributes to the generic and cultural-heritage literature by examining those relations which have not been analysed so far.

A distinctive remark derived from the research model is that emotions appear to be a main driver in influencing satisfaction unlike other studies in tourism literature where emotions appear as a moderating variable (De Rojas & Camarero, 2008).

According to the relationships found in the research model, tourism marketers, planners and policy-makers have to pay attention to the cognitive and affective dimension of authenticity to improve the quality of the tourists' experience. Objective and existential dimensions must be considered as key factors in achieving differentiation and the competitive positioning of a destination in relation to other cultural-heritage destinations.

In order to provide a positive cultural experience, it is necessary to meet the expectations of visitors with regard to architecture, faithful restoration of buildings, harmony of the buildings with the scenery of the city, and provide attractive and complete heritage information which enhance the perceived information quality. However, the cultural experience improves if heritage managers design strategies to meet expectations regarding the components of peace of mind, cultural experience, and involvement in the traditions and customs with the local population. In this sense, it is crucial that cultural tourism authorities present the cultural heritage within a setting that allows tourists to immerse themselves in different historical periods of the city with accurate and detailed information, while at the same time allowing them to enjoy cultural and gastronomic events so that visitors can interact with the local people and their traditions and customs, improving in turn the quality of the experience and allowing them to experience positive emotions during their visit.

Limitations and future research

This study suffers from certain limitations that may be overcome in future research. First, no minimum period of stay by the respondent has been stipulated. If the length of stay were longer, it would also be possible to include another affective variable in the model, such as that of mood. Certain studies in the academic literature recognise the moderating role of this variable in the relations that bind to other variables, such as authenticity, experience quality, and satisfaction (De Rojas & Camarero, 2008; Sirakaya, Petrick, & Choi, 2004). In future research, we would like to investigate further into these moderating relations.

The analysis of causal relationships has hitherto been restricted to the city of Seville and therefore limits generalisation of the study's finding. It would therefore be interesting to contrast the relations explored in the research model with those of another cultural destination. Furthermore, sample size is another limitation that should be acknowledged in future works. Although the sample size used meets the sample size requirements for Partial Least estimation, the fairly small sample size limits the degree of generalisation and validation of the model.

Disclosure statement

No potential conflict of interest was reported by the authors.

ORCID

Ana M. Domínguez-Quintero http://orcid.org/0000-0001-5066-0216
M. Rosario González-Rodríguez http://orcid.org/0000-0002-6484-4128
José Luis Roldán http://orcid.org/0000-0003-4053-7526

References

Ali, F., Amin, M., & Ryu, K. (2016). The role of physical environment, price perceptions, and consumption emotions in developing customer satisfaction in Chinese resort hotels. *Journal of Quality Assurance in Hospitality & Tourism*, *17*(1), 45–70.

Altunel, M. C., & Erkut, B. (2015). Cultural tourism in Istambul: The mediation effect of tourist experience and satisfaction on the relationship between involvement and recommendation intention. *Journal of Destination Marketing and Management*, *4*, 213–221.

Bagozzi, R., Gopinath, M., & Nyer, P. (1999). The role of emotions in Marketing. *Journal of the Academy of Marketing Science*, *27*(2), 184–206.

Becker, J.-M., Rai, A., & Rigdon, E. (2013). Predictive validity and formative measurement in structural equation modelling: Embracing practical relevance. *Thirty Fourth International Conference on Information Systems*, 1–19. Milan.

Bigné, J. E., Andreu, L., & Gnoth, J. (2005). The Theme Park experience: An analysis of pleasure, arousal and satisfaction. *Tourism Management*, *26*(6), 834–844.

Castéran, H., & Roederer, C. (2013). Does authenticity really affect behaviour? The case of the Strasbourg Christmas market. *Tourism Management*, *36*, 153–163.

Chen, C.-F., & Chen, F.-S. (2010). Experience quality, perceived value, satisfaction and behavioral intentions for heritage tourists. *Tourism Management*, *31*, 29–35.

Cohen, J. B., & Areni, C. S. (1991). Affect and consumer behaviour. In T. S. Robertson & H. H. Kassarjian (Eds.), *Handbook of consumer behaviour* (Vol. 2, pp. 188–240). Englewood Cliffs, NJ: Prentice Hall.

Consorcio de Turismo del Ayuntamiento de Sevilla. (2014). *Annual Report*. From http://www.visitasevilla.es/es/informes-observatorio-turistico-sevilla

De Rojas, C., & Camarero, C. (2008). Visitors' experience, mood and satisfaction in an heritage context: Evidence from an interpretation center. *Tourism Management*, *29*, 525–537.

Del Bosque, I. R., & San Martín, H. (2008). Tourist satisfaction: A cognitive-affective model. *Annals of Tourist Research*, *35*(2), 551–573.

Diamantopoulos, A., & Siguaw, J. A. (2006). Formative versus reflective indicators in Organizational measure development: A Comparison and empirical Illustration. *British Journal of Management*, *17*(4), 263–282.

Dubé-Riboux, L. (1990). The power of affective reports in predicting satisfaction judgments. *Advances in Consumer Research*, *17*, 571–576.

Duman, T., & Mattila, A. S. (2005). The role of affective factor on perceived cruise vacation value. *Tourism Management*, *26*(3), 311–323.

Falk, R. F., & Miller, N. B. (1992). *A primer for soft modelling*. Akron, OH: University of Akron Press.

Fornell, C. G., & Larcker, D. F. (1981). Evaluating structural equation models with unobservable variables and measurement error. *Journal of Marketing Research*, *18*(1), 39–50.

Gefen, D., Straub, D., & Boudreau, M. C. (2000). Structural equation modelling and regression: Guidelines for research practice. *Communications of the Association for Information Systems*, *4*(1), 7.

Girish, V. G., & Chen, C.-F. (2017). Authenticity, experience, and loyalty in the festival context: Evidence from the San Fermin Festival, Spain. *Current Issues in Tourism*, *20*(15), 1551–1556.

Hair, J. F., Hult, G. T. M., Ringle, C. M., Sarstedt, M., & Thiele, K. O. (2017). Mirror, mirror on the wall: A comparative evaluation of composite-based structural equation modelling methods. *Journal of the Academy of Marketing Science*, *45*(5), 616–632.

Hair, J. F., Sarstedt, M., Ringle, C. M., & Mena, J. A. (2012). An assessment of the use of partial least squares structural equation modeling in marketing research. *Journal of the Academy of Marketing Science*, *40*(3), 414–433.

Hair, J. F. J., Hult, G. T. M., Ringle, C. M., & Sarstedt, M. (2017). *A primer on partial least squares structural equation modeling (PLS-SEM)* (2nd ed.). Thousand Oaks, CA: SAGE.

Han, H., & Jeong, C. (2013). Multi-dimensions of patrons' emotional experiences in upscale restaurants and their role in loyalty formation: Emotion scale improvement. *International Journal of Hospitality Management*, *32*, 59–70.

Henseler, J., Ringle, C. M., & Sarstedt, M. (2015). A new criterion for assessing discriminant validity in variance-based structural equation modeling. *Journal of the Academy of Marketing Science*, *43*(1), 115–135.

Henseler, J., Ringle, C. M., & Sinkovics, R. R. (2009). The use of partial least squares path modeling in international marketing. *Advances in International Marketing*, *20*(1), 277–319.

Holbrook, M. B. (1995). *Consumer research. Introspective essays on the study of consumption*. California: Sage.

Hosany, S. (2012). Appraisal determinats of tourist emotional responses. *Journal of Travel Research*, *51*(3), 303–314.

Hu, L. T., & Bentler, P. M. (1999). Cutoff criteria for fit indexes in covariance structure analysis: Conventional criteria versus new alternatives. *Structural Equation Modeling: A Multidisciplinary Journal*, *6*(1), 1–55.

Jayanti, R. K., & Ghosh, A. K. (1996). Service value determination: An integrative perspective. *Journal of Hospitality and Leisure Marketing*, *34*(4), 5–25.

Kim, J., & Fesenmaier, D. R. (2015). Measuring emotions in real time: Implications for tourism experience design. *Journal of Travel Research*, *54*(4), 419–429.

Kolar, T., & Zabkar, V. (2010). A consumer-based model of authenticity: An oxymoron or the foundation of cultural heritage marketing? *Tourism Management*, *31*, 652–664.

Lee, S., Phau, I., Hughes, M., Li, Y. L., & Quintal, V. (2016). Heritage tourism in Singapore Chinatown: A perceived value approach to authenticity and satisfaction. *Journal of Travel and Tourism Marketing*, *33*(7), 981–998.

MacCanell, D. (1989). *The tourist: A new theory of the leisure class*. New York: Schocken.

Nguyen, T. H. H., & Cheung, C. (2016). Chinese heritage tourists to heritage sites: What are the effects of heritage motivation and perceived authenticity on satisfaction? *Asia Pacific Journal of Tourism Research, 21*(11), 1155–1168.

Novello, S., & Fernandez, P. M. (2016). The influence of event authenticity and quality attributes on behavioral intentions. *Journal of Hospitality and Tourism Research, 40*(6), 685–714.

Nunnally, J. C., & Bernstein, I. H. (1994). The assessment of reliability. *Psychometric Theory, 3*(1), 248–292.

Oh, H., Fiore, A. M., & Jeoung, M. (2007). Measuring experience economy concepts: Tourist Applications. *Journal of Travel Research, 46*, 119–132.

Oliver, R. L. (1997). *Satisfaction: A behavioral perspective on the consumer*. New York: The McGraw-Hill Companies, Inc.

Otto, J. E., & Ritchie, J. R. (1995). Exploring the quality of the service experience: A theoretical and empirical analysis. *Advances in Services Marketing and Management, 4*, 37–61.

Otto, J. E., & Ritchie, J. R. (1996). The service experience in tourism. *Tourism Management, 17*(3), 165–174.

Palau-Saumell, R., Forgas-Coll, S., Sánchez-García, J., & Prats-Planagumà, L. (2013). Tourist behavior intentions and the moderator effect of knowledge of UNESCO world heritage sites: The case of La Sagrada Família. *Journal of Travel Research, 52*(3), 364–376.

Prayag, G., Hosany, S., & Odeh, K. (2013). The role of tourists' emotional experiences and satisfaction in understanding behavioral intentions. *Journal of Destination Marketing and Management, 2*, 118–127.

Ramkissoon, H., & Uysal, M. S. (2011). The effects of perceived authenticity, information search behaviour, motivation and destination imagery on cultural behavioural intentions of tourists. *Current Issues in Tourism, 14*(6), 537–562.

Reinartz, W., Haenlein, M., & Henseler, J. (2009). An empirical comparison of the efficacy of covariance-based and variance-based SEM. *International Journal of Research in Marketing, 26*(4), 332–344.

Reisinger, Y., & Steiner, C. J. (2005). Reconceptualizing object authenticity. *Annals of Tourism Research, 33*(1), 65–86.

Romero, C. (2001). Ciudad, cultura y turismo: calidad y autenticidad. *Boletín del Instituto Andaluz de Patrimonio Histórico, 36*, 100–109.

Russell, J. A. (1980). A circumplex model of affect. *Journal of Personality and Social Psychology, 39*(6), 1161–1178.

Russell, J. A., & Pratt, G. A. (1980). A description of affective quality attributed to environments. *Journal of Personality and Social Psychology, 38*(2), 311–322.

Sedmak, G., & Mihalič, T. (2008). Authenticity in mature seaside resorts. *Annals of Tourism Research, 35*(4), 1007–1031.

Sarstedt, M., Hair, J. F., Ringle, C. M., Thiele, K. O., & Gudergan, S. P. (2016). Estimation issues with PLS and CBSEM: Where the bias lies!. *Journal of Business Research, 69*(10), 3998–4010.

Shen, S., Guo, J., & Wu, Y. (2012). Investigating the structural relationships among authenticity, loyalty, involvement, and Attitude toward world cultural heritage sites: An empirical study of Nanjing Xiaoling Tomb, China. *Asia Pacific Journal of Tourism Research, 19*(1), 10–121.

Shen, X. L. H., & Wen, W. (2016). A study on tourists perceived authenticity towards experience quality and behavior intention of cultural heritage in Macao. *International Journal of Marketing Studies, 8*(4), 117–123.

Sirakaya, E., Petrick, J., & Choi, H.-S. (2004). The role of mood on tourism product evaluations. *Annals of Tourism Research, 31*(3), 517–539.

Volo, S. (2017). Emotions in tourism: From exploration to design. In D. R. Fesenmaaier & Z. Xiang (Eds.), *Design science in tourism. Foundations of destination management* (pp. 31–40). Cham: Springer International.

Wang, N. (1999). Rethinking authenticity in tourism experience. *Annals of Tourism Research, 26*(2), 349–370.

Zins, A. H. (2002). Consumption emotions, experience quality and satisfaction: A structural analysis for complainers versus no complainers. *Journal of Travel and Tourism Marketing, 12*(2–3), 3–18.

Authenticity and nostalgia – subjective well-being of Chinese rural-urban migrants

Zhenhao (Mark) Meng, Liping A. Cai, Jonathan Day, Chun-Hung (Hugo) Tang, Ying (Tracy) Lu and Hongmei Zhang

ABSTRACT

This study investigates the subjective well-being of Chinese rural-urban migrants by examining the effects of nostalgia and perceived authenticity in the context of rural tourism. Founded on the concepts of tourist motivation and nostalgia and drawn on selected Chinese philosophical values, this study identifies the unique Chinese philosophical value of 'old home' as the key factor of motivation for migrants returning to rural destinations. Rural-urban migrants deem rural regions, as well as, mentalities, cultures, and environments in general, as their cultural and spiritual hometowns. The study also reveals that migrants pursue authentic rural destinations, which would have an emotional and memorable appeal, because it stimulates their nostalgic feelings. The study proposes the necessity of investigating Chinese issues through the lens of Chinese philosophical values and invokes an age-old value to understand their perception process of authenticity: 'one can't have fish and bear at the same time.' Returning to rural destinations improves these tourists' subjective well-being because they achieve an important lifetime goal based on their traditional Chinese philosophical value of 'searching for ancestral roots.' The study suggests that preserving rural authenticity can improve the social and cultural welfare of hosting communities and the subjective well-being of tourists.

Introduction

As a result of the rapid economic, social, and urban development in the past 30 years, the issue of urban immigration became a phenomenon in China. This population spent their childhood in rural regions but moved to cities in adulthood. Their lifelong experiences changed significantly. Many people migrated from their rural hometowns, where they had been living for many years, to big cities in other distant regions in China. This prominent phenomenon has also generated numerous issues, such as family separation, homesickness, and high stress (Du, Park, & Wang, 2005; Zhang & Song, 2003; Zhao, 1999).

Most of these young migrants mature and become elders; their lifelong experiences are significantly changed. However, their memories from childhood and adolescence are deeply imprinted in their minds and hearts, which they begin to cherish, especially as they enter the latter part of their lives. Many of them are even actively looking for those memories by returning to rural regions and by participating in various types of rural tourism activities. This type of tourism motivation is often termed 'nostalgia.' A few researchers in the past have studied rural tourism in China and concluded that people visit rural regions because they consider these areas to be healthy, wholesome, authentic, and nostalgic (Chio, 2014; Oakes, 2005; Park, 2014; Su, 2011; Zhou & Huang, 2004). However, the rapid development and reconstruction did not only occur in urban China; it also occurred to a commensurable degree in rural regions at the same time. Therefore, whether these migrants can still perceive the authentic experiences they once had decades ago and whether their feelings and perceptions during current rural tourism activities can fulfill their nostalgia becomes an issue.

Although the influence of nostalgia on consumer behavior has been widely studied in psychology and sociology, this influence has not received sufficient attention in rural tourism settings, especially considering rural-urban migrant tourists in China (Davis, 1979; Havlena & Holak, 1991; Holbrook & Schindler, 1991). Few studies have been conducted to explore this particular group of tourists concerning their experiences while returning to rural destinations after living in urban regions for decades. Moreover, many past scholars utilized Western theories and models to study their subjects, which did not fully explore the uniqueness of China and Chinese tourists. The current research aims to study how the search for nostalgia and perceived authenticity influences the subjective well-being of rural-urban migrants while returning to rural destinations. In addition, the current research attempts to develop a new theory to explain such a reverse influx of rural-urban migration in modern China.

Understanding nostalgia is very important for the promotion of rural destinations; the understanding of such influence can be used by destination marketers to target tourists who are motivated by nostalgia in rural tourism destinations, as well as to design images, slogans, music, products, and activities that can evoke nostalgia. Moreover, the connection between nostalgia and tourists' subjective well-being remains unclear. The current research aims to understand the extent of the influence of returning to rural regions on those rural-urban migrant tourists' subjective well-being and how perceived authenticity in particular affects their nostalgic feelings in rural destinations. In addition, the study plans to discover and create a list of items that can generate and influence migrants' nostalgic feelings. The outcomes of the conceptual model can be used by rural destination marketers to target rural-urban migrant tourists who are motivated or partially motivated by nostalgia, and to eventually improve their subjective well-being during and after their rural visits.

This study also investigates the subjective well-being of Chinese rural-urban migrants in the context of rural tourism by examining the effects of nostalgia, perceived authenticity, and relationships. Founded on the concepts of tourist motivation and nostalgia and drawn on selected Chinese philosophical values, this study aims to construct a conceptual model of rural tourism motivation for rural-urban migrants that can be used by tourism businesses and rural communities to evaluate their market segments and improve tourists' subjective well-being and community welfare. The current study examines the following research questions:

(1) What are push and pull motivations of rural-urban migrant tourists?
(2) How can their nostalgic feelings be explained by push and pull motivations?
(3) How do rural-urban migrant tourists perceive and evaluate authenticity of destinations when returning to rural regions?
(4) How does their perceived authenticity affect their nostalgic feelings?
(5) How does nostalgia affect their subjective well-being during and after the rural visit, and why?
(6) How do Chinese culture and traditions affect their desire of returning to rural regions, as well as their subjective well-being in rural destinations?

Literature review

Many western countries have adopted tourism as an important development strategy for the social and economic regeneration because there is considerable rural industrialization, economic decline, out-migration of higher-educated young people, and reorganization of the agricultural industry

(Alonso, O'Neill, & Kim, 2010; Dernoi, 1991; Hannigan, 1994). Briedenhann and Wickens (2004) stated that rural tourism is increasingly recognized as a crucial tool to increase the economic viability of remote areas, to help social regeneration, and to improve the standard of living in rural communities. They also believed that developing countries with rural poverty could have huge potential to attract tourists who search for authentic and unique experiences in areas of unexploited cultural and natural riches.

Tourist motivation

Most of the conceptual foundation of this research derives from the push and pull theory. The psychologist, Allport (1937), first proposed the push and pull theory in motivation. Allport (1937) divided motivation into two stages: infancy and maturity. Push factors are non-purposive in the earlier stage, while pull factors are purposive in the later stage. Dann (1977, 1981) was one of the earliest scholars who discussed push and pull in the tourism context and specified detailed examples for these concepts, both of which have been generally accepted and applied by scholars in the area of tourism. Push factors can be understood as some reasons that stem from tourists themselves, such as experiencing a different life, meeting with friends, and relaxing physically and/or mentally. Pull factors are usually motives created by destinations, such as the beautiful architecture in a city and the traditional local culture in a small town.

Nostalgia

In terms of push and pull theory, nostalgia can be considered a push factor. From this perspective, nostalgia is regarded as an intrinsic motivation, which drives tourists to seek a past experience, search for their ancestral roots and heritage, and bring back memories (Hsu, Cai, & Wong, 2007; Leong, Yeh, Hsiao, & Huan, 2015). Nostalgia can also arouse the desires of people to escape from their daily routines (Osbaldiston, 2012). Rural-urban migrants who are dissatisfied with their present situations are more likely to pursue nostalgic feelings, in which nostalgia serves as a push factor. Tourists with nostalgic motivation tend to go to places that can aid them in recalling feelings about the past. Thus, the destinations specifically associated with nostalgic attributes can be attractive to people, in which tangible things (i.e. rivers and farmlands) could allow people to associate themselves with memories and good feelings. Many features can attract tourists who pursue nostalgia, such as rural destinations (Gannon, 1994; Knudsen & Greer, 2011), wilderness destinations (Acharya, Paudel, & Hatch, 2009), historical ruins (Leong et al., 2015), and heritage destinations (Chhabra, Healy, & Sills, 2003; Korstanje, 2012; Nyaupane, White, & Budruk, 2006).

As a psychological requirement, things that arouse nostalgic feelings in people are not limited to what happened in their past, but they can also be things that trigger their memories (Chen, Yeh, & Huan, 2014). For example, a rural destination may arouse nostalgic feelings in people about their hometowns, even if the destination is not actually where they grew up. Nostalgia implies a comparison between the past and present: the past is usually viewed as beautiful and memorable; on the contrary, the present is regarded as full of pressure, ugliness, and less-satisfying experiences (Davis, 1979). In general, nostalgia implies an aspiration for the joyful past lives and experiences, and it can help people evoke positive and idealized memories. Caton and Santos (2007) also found that what inspires people to pursue nostalgic feelings is their dissatisfaction about present situations.

Perceived authenticity

Nostalgia, or the willingness to go back to a former place, can also cause tourists to evaluate perceived authenticity and compare situations to their past experiences (Budruk, White, Wodrich, & Van Riper, 2008; Yeoman, Brass, & McMahon-Beattie, 2007). Some tourists choose to go to certain destinations in order to experience their past and learn their heritage (Lev Ari & Mittelberg, 2008). Rural destinations have become a place not only for people to have fun, relax, escape, or taste healthy food, but also a place for tourists to relive experiences of their good old days (Yeoman et al., 2007). For example, Bessiere (1998) stated that authentic rural homemade products (i.e. food and artefacts) could create nostalgic feelings for the nostalgia seeker in rural destinations (Timothy & Ron, 2013). Therefore, the perceived authentic level of product, architecture, and activity can influence the degree of nostalgic feeling found in a rural destination. Hence, it is arguable that perceived authenticity is a key factor in determining whether tourism products, activities, local people, or scenery can arouse the nostalgic feelings of tourists in a rural destination.

Authenticity is a term that has become ambiguous due to varied usages and contexts (Golomb, 1995). One of its original usages was in a museum setting where experts in such matters tested to see whether objects of art were what they appeared to be or were claimed to be, and hence, worth the price they are tagged or the price they already paid for, and worth the admiration they were given (Trilling, 2009). This term was also borrowed to refer to human existence and the peculiar nature of our fallen condition, of our anxiety over the credibility of existence and of individual existence (McCartney & Osti, 2007; Trilling, 2009). However, it is mainly its museum-linked usage that has been extended to tourism (Chhabra, 2007; MacCannell, 1973).

An important concept of tourism authenticity is constructive authenticity (Condevaux, 2009). Cohen's (1988) 'emergent authenticity' and Wang's (1999) description of 'constructive authenticity' belong to the constructive aspect of authenticity. The focus of the constructive way of defining authenticity shows that the understanding of the concept varies. Authenticity is a constructed and negotiable concept that develops over time, and the interpretation depends on the meaning of different scenarios (Cohen, 1988). Wang (1999, p. 352) claimed that constructive authenticity 'refers to the authenticity projected onto toured objects by visitors or tourism producers in terms of their imagery, expectations, preferences, beliefs, powers, etc.' Besides the constructive authenticity, there are two other categories of authenticity in terms of tourists' perception: objective authenticity and existential authenticity.

Both objective authenticity and constructive authenticity are object related, whereas existential authenticity is activity related (Chhabra, Lee, Zhao, & Scott, 2013; Kelner & Phil, 2001; Uriely, 2005; Yang & Wall, 2009). According to Wang (1999), existential authenticity is not object related; rather, it involves tourists' personal experiences throughout tourism activities. Carrying out some unique activities, meeting with certain people, and attending some special events can generate such experiences and feelings. Existential authenticity is fulfilled through tourists' self-expression, not the authenticity of the object (Kim & Jamal, 2007). Objective authenticity means the authentic experience is based on the authenticity of originals (Wang, 1999). It also implies that the authenticity of an object is independent of the tourists' own perceptions (MacCannell, 1973). For example, a reconstructed historical town is not regarded as authentic from the view of objective authenticity. In sum, object-related authenticity (objective and constructive) is perceived through tangible elements during travel, such as tourism products, architecture, food, and so forth. On the contrary, existential authenticity does not necessarily have a connection with an object; it is an authentic experience stimulated by visitor activities and experiences. For example, if one perceived a once-in-a-lifetime experience during travel, it can help to form existential authenticity.

Subjective well-being

Previous studies demonstrated that tourism and recreational activities could improve tourists' subjective well-being (Diener, 2000; Gilbert & Abdullah, 2004; Sirgy, 2010). Ashley (2000) and Sharpley and Jepson (2011) mentioned that tourists embark on trips to rural destinations not only on the physical level, but also on a deeper and more spiritual level. Rural tourism destinations provide tourists opportunities to enjoy the natural world and wildlife; throughout this process, tourists can enjoy their surroundings spiritually (Curtin, 2009). Voase (1995) mentioned that staying in a farmhouse bed-and-breakfast with family style hospitality is a form of a rural tourism experience, which creates psychological differences as compared to time spent in cities. As previously stated, rural destinations are regarded as some of the wealthiest, healthiest, and best-educated places to improve the well-being of people because most rural destinations are located in places that are far away from noisy cities and surrounded by beautiful scenery (Reeder & Brown, 2005). Figure 1 presents the diagram of the conceptual framework of this study.

There are many different ways to measure subjective happiness and satisfaction in life. Tourist happiness was understood as a status of subjective well-being, which means it is a positive experience gained by people during travel phases (Filep, 2014). There is a link between tourism participation and well-being. Holidays can contribute to the quality of life because they can help people release the pressures from life or work, thereby increasing their subjective well-being (McCabe, Joldersma, & Li, 2010). Quality of life (QOL) is a concept that has been used to measure subjective well-being in tourism research. QOL can be defined in terms of life satisfaction or an important part of life satisfaction (Dolnicar, Yanamandram, & Cliff, 2012); for example, vacation activities can contribute to QOL (Dolnicar et al., 2012). Sirgy (2010) claimed that QOL is an important concept in tourism, and it depends on tourists' travel goals. Once the travel goals are achieved, it is very likely that tourists will experience a higher QOL and in turn have a higher subjective well-being. It has also been demonstrated that positive travel experiences can produce positive moods in tourists, which eventually increases their sense of well-being (Gilbert & Abdullah, 2004). Therefore, subjective well-being was also used to assess the outcome of a project or activity in tourism (McCabe & Johnson, 2013).

Some levels of human desire in Maslow's hierarchy are related to subjective well-being. Tourist motivation has been an important topic of study for many years. There are several key theories related to tourist motivation. Maslow (1943) proposed one of the most classic theories about motivation in his paper, 'A Theory of Human Motivation.' Maslow (1943)'s Hierarchy of Needs explained the structure of motivation and illustrated this in the shape of a pyramid, with the most fundamental levels of need, including physiological needs, placed at the bottom, followed by safety, belonging and love, esteem, and self-actualization.

The structure of Maslow's theory can be summarized as a pyramid shape with five levels of needs, where the bottom is humans' physiological and biological needs, followed by safety needs, social needs, esteem needs (such as achievement and prestige), and self-actualization needs at the top (such as morality and lack of prejudice; Pearce & Caltabiano, 1983). In terms of Maslow's theory, nostalgia can be considered the needs of belonging and self-actualization, which are located at a higher level of the hierarchy. Yeoman et al. (2007) concluded that consumers pursuing nostalgia are in search of their personal heritage and ancestral roots. The tourists motivated by nostalgia cherish their good old days and want to return to that special time. Chhabra et al. (2003) stated that for people who are seeking their good old days, tourism could be used to arouse their nostalgic feelings. Many rural tourism destinations offer resources and environments that can be satisfying to nostalgia seekers.

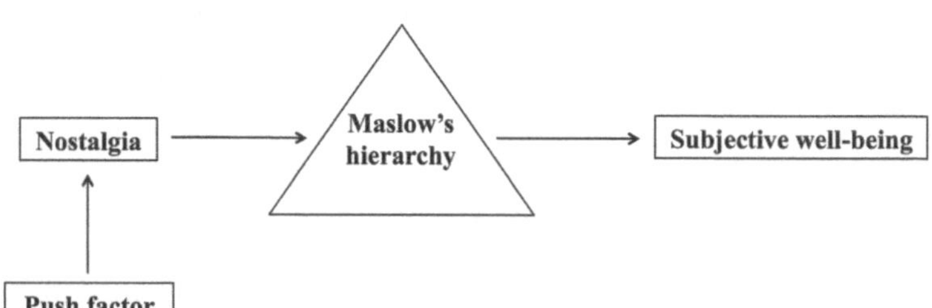

Figure 1. Conceptual framework.

Methodology

The primary research employed in this study was gathered by integrating sources from qualitative research with a phenomenological approach to build knowledge from the research results, largely because the topics, the interrelationships among them, and the subjects examined in this study received little attention previously. Scholars who have used the qualitative research methodology often suggest beneficial methods from previous experiences (Legard, Keegan, & Ward, 2003; Liamputtong & Ezzy, 1999; Mathison, 1988). The process of the methodology involves both the actual composition of research and the study of previous works; therefore, besides literature reviews, authors used the qualitative methodology in the current study, which enabled flexibility to understand inner ideas of interviewees and interpret the meaning behind the information they provided (Legard et al., 2003). Semi-structured in-depth interviews were used in this study; as one qualitative research method, the in-depth interview is a very effective way of collecting information, especially when scholars want to understand the perceptions and attitudes of participants (DiCicco-Bloom & Crabtree, 2006).

Beijing is one of the biggest metropolitan areas in China, as well as a major rural-urban migration destination; massive populations come to this city to look for new opportunities. Moreover, Beijing is a major city surrounded by multiple developed rural tourism destinations within three hours' driving distance. Data was collected in the winter of 2015 from several popular rural tourism destinations surrounding Beijing, including Yanqing County and Miyun County, as these counties are the most popular rural tourism destinations. During the past decade in China, experiencing rural life, eating rural food, staying in farmhouses, and engaging in some farm work have become very popular to urban residents as a means of relaxation and escaping from pressures in cities.

Targeted interviewees were those who were born in rural China and who grew up in their hometowns. Scientists studying early childhood memory, infantile amnesia, and children's long-term memory suggested that even though solid memory can be formed by 2- and 3-year-olds in some cases, children older than 5–8 years old can recall most (57–75%) of their major autobiographical events (Peterson, 1999, 2002; Rubin, 2000; Usher & Neisser, 1993; Van Abbema & Bauer, 2005; Wang, 2003). Therefore, in order to collect rich data for this study, people who left their rural hometown when they were about 10 years old or older were selected for this study, which means that they spent their first decade or more in rural regions and have reliable memories from their rural living experiences (Burger, 2011; Peterson, Warren, & Short, 2011).

To approach the targeted interviewees, the following locations were chosen: entrances and exits of parks, public rest areas, teahouses, restaurants, farmlands, and farmhouses. First, tourists who appeared to be midle-age or older were selected because they are more likely to have past rural living experiences than younger people are. Second, after introducing the research purpose to them, they were asked if they had any previous long-term rural region living experiences; if not, the next potential candidate was interviewed. After obtaining permission from the tourists, nearby quiet areas were chosen for the one-on-one interviews. Fifteen qualified tourists were interviewed. All interviews were audio recorded with participants' permission. Notes on important points were also taken. Before the audio recording, interviewees were informed of the purpose of the recording device: all information would be confidential and used for academic purposes only. On average, each interview lasted for about 40–90 minutes.

With the help of qualitative research software, NVivo, the data analysis process of the interview was subjected to the three-stage method proposed by Huberman and Miles (1994): data reduction, data display, and conclusion drawing. In the stage of data reduction, interview transcripts were thoroughly screened and coded according to relevant interview questions. Coded information was then organized into key themes during the data display stage. Finally, answers of different questions were categorized into several streams. The entire transcripts were checked several times for accuracy. Codes were checked for consistency while coding for all results (Leydon et al., 2000; Merriam, 1998). During the later interpretation stage, the generated findings were brought back to previous parts of the study, such as the theory, purpose, and research questions, in order to immediately rectify the mistakes. To further ensure the reliability and validity of the data, apart from the interviews, extra time was spent with interviewees in the field for better and deeper understanding of the participants (Taylor & Trujillo, 2001). Figure 2 illustrates the most frequently used words mentioned by all interviewees.

It is hard to come to a conclusion about a universal rule or formula of determining the exact number of interviewees needed (Eysenbach & Kohler, 2002); however, thick and rich data was attained in the current study. Of all rural tourists who matched with characteristics of the targeted segment described in an earlier section, 15 were chosen for the final in-depth interviews. The interviewee pool represents a wide range of ages, a balanced gender representation, various education levels, different occupations, diverse cultural backgrounds, and disparate geographic representations (i.e. northern China and southern China due to the huge historical and traditional differences between the two). In many cases, studies focusing on exploring general trends may choose to use a larger number of samples, whereas studies exploring meaning, depth, and ethnomethodology may choose to use a smaller number of informants (Liamputtong & Ezzy, 1999). After all, the key to determining the appropriate number of interviewees is largely evaluated by whether the research questions were sufficiently answered and whether the textual interview data gave sufficient reasons for the answers provided by the interviewees. The interviewee pool in this study is also sufficient to make meaningful comparisons.

Findings

In this section, a thorough summary is provided, which includes all key findings and discusses them according to the research questions. Each key construct was further explained and discussed. Nostalgia in the context of rural-urban migrants' motivation was illustrated first, followed by the discussions of their perceived authenticity, subjective well-being, unique life experiences, cultural backgrounds, and the impacts of these on the migrants. The results and findings were synthesized and formed in the proposed conceptual model of rural tourism motivation for rural-urban migrants.

Motivations

Interviewees' key pull motivations include beautiful natural landscapes, authentic rural architecture, village layout, clean air, clear water, fresh rural food ingredients and materials, working farm available for tourism purposes, local people, and customs and lifestyles. All interviewees expressed that

Figure 2. Word frequency of all interviewees.

they looked for different rural elements and objects, which can help them arouse nostalgic feelings. Therefore, certain objects, activities, or environmental elements in rural destinations serve as pull factors, and they are critical to evoke rural-urban migrants' nostalgic feelings. Figure 3 presents key pull motivations.

In order to further comprehend why rural destinations are such prominent places in terms of their nostalgic motivations, the findings suggested taking the Chinese philosophical value of 'old home (老家)' into consideration. Many interviewees mentioned this concept and discussed their feelings about it. 'Old home (老家)' in their philosophical value does not merely mean their previous homesite where they once lived. Rather, it represents where they came from and who they are; more specifically, rural regions are their 'old home (老家),' making them rural people deeply in their hearts. To them, returning to rural regions means they are returning to their pasts, their roots, and their homes, but it does not necessarily need to be their original hometowns or villages per se. Figure 4 presents key push motivations.

During the past two decades in China, there have been more and more urban visitors to the countryside year-round, and the number of visitors, including rural-urban migrants, is still on the rise. Those migrant tourists come back to rural regions for similar reasons; for example, relaxation, family and friend gathering, seeking healthy foods and lifestyles, and enjoying beautiful natural landscapes. The length of time spent at their destinations varies, but it's mainly short-term; some of them stay in the countryside for a day or two while others stay for about a week. Rural communities surrounding cities have become the main destinations for those urban residents who want to enjoy a short trip, and Beijing has been an strong example among many Chinese cities. This is because the number of such visitors has been growing dramatically during the past decade, and Beijing has also been known as a major migration city. Clearly, nostalgia is a key motivation of migrant tourists, which will be thoroughly discussed in a later session.

Nostalgia

Due to their unique backgrounds and life experiences in the context of social reshaping, nostalgia is indeed the most important push motivation that migrants pursue in rural destinations. Many

Figure 3. Key pull motivations.

Figure 4. Key push motivations.

scholars have studied push motivations such as nostalgia; however, few have focused on nostalgia as a key push motivation for this particular group of rural tourists. In addition, the results showed that traditional Chinese philosophical values also play a key role in why nostalgia is such an important push motivation for this group. Therefore, among different motivations, nostalgia is clearly the key push factor, leading rural-urban migrant tourists to go back to rural regions. Figure 5 presents specific things and objects associated with their nostalgic feelings.

'Fallen leaves return to the roots (落叶归根)' is another key philosophical value in Chinese migrants' minds, driving them to search for nostalgic feelings and to return to rural regions. This literally means that the nutrients and essence of fallen leaves will return to the soil and eventually be absorbed by tree roots. In this case, it suggests that migrants have intrinsic desires to return to

Figure 5. Key memories.

their cultural and spiritual hometowns even after having moved into cities. Chinese people use this ancient idiom to suggest that people are like leaves on a giant tree: when the leaves fall in the autumn, they drop to the ground close to the tree itself and eventually return the nutrients back to the tree through its roots. Some interviewees describe such a process as 'reincarnation (轮回),' which is one of the creeds and foundations of Chinese Buddhism – the dominant religion in China for thousands of years. With such a metaphor, one can better understand why nostalgia is so important for those migrants and see that their 'roots' are actually their 'old home (老家)' – rural regions instead of urban regions.

Perceived authenticity

Overwhelmingly, interviewees affirmed that their nostalgic feelings depend heavily on whether they can find authentic aspects of rural destinations, no matter how they perceive authenticity itself. Quite often, they talked about nostalgia with perceived authenticity or the other way around, and they inevitably would like to compare their current experiences with their past memories. This is largely due to the fact that they had lived in rural regions for a very long time, and nostalgia is one of the fundamental reasons why they went back. They expressed that they would hardly have any nostalgic feelings when there was no object considered authentic to them. Therefore, a higher level of authenticity perceived by rural-urban migrant tourists can increase their nostalgic feelings.

Some interviewees stated that they were looking for pure forms of the rural communities, such as original buildings that have been well protected since the old days. Some interviewees voiced that reconstructed objects would still be considered authentic as long as they kept certain traditions and characteristics. Landscape, architecture, local people, and food are the most tangible aspects of rural communities. Many interviewees described communicating and interacting with local residents as authentic rural experiences. Further, many interviewees noted that they could learn typical northern rural culture through chatting with local people, visiting their homes, and experiencing their lifestyles, which can also help them recall their past memories in their rural hometowns.

To many interviewees, rural tourism has already become an alternative way to relieve stress and arouse nostalgic feelings. Some interviewees emphasized that tourism businesses should understand such unique motivations; those tourists have a great desire to know about authentic local lifestyles, cultures, and customs, and they often compare to with their own. Many of them primarily see rural regions as cultural environments with great differences from urban regions. Therefore, they believe that business operators and rural administrations should carefully maintain such environments and their uniqueness without damaging them during the processes of development and reconstruction. Figure 6 shows key things and objects contributing to their overall perceived authenticity.

Many migrants believe in the philosophical value of 'one can't have fish and bear at the same time (鱼和熊掌不可兼得),' and they utilize its meaning in many different ways. Literally speaking, one should accept the fact that two good things (fish meat and bear meat) cannot be acquired at the same time. This basically means that one can hardly obtain all benefits or achieve all desires without sacrifice, especially when there are contradictions among them. It not only teaches people to be less greedy, but also to act rationally and think from different aspects, taking all kinds of possibilities into consideration. With such a traditional philosophical value in their mindset, in addition to their previous impoverished life experiences in rural regions in general, they evaluate authenticity with mixed feelings and criteria, which cannot be explained perfectly with theories proposed by previous scholars. Figure 7 shows key things and objects at rural regions damaging their overall perceived authenticity.

Rural-urban migrants' subjective well-being

Migrant tourists are motivated by the key push factor of nostalgia. They return to rural regions particularly searching for nostalgic feelings. Through such rural tourism activities, they recall their good

Figure 6. Perceived positive authenticity factors.

old days and beautiful past memories. Moreover, they return to the natural and cultural environments with which they were once very familiar; therefore, they want to experience rural life again and search for their self-identity. Such special tourism experiences and activities eventually contribute to migrant tourists' subjective well-being because their emotional and spiritual needs are satisfied.

To study how rural tourism affects migrants' subjective well-being, it is important to put it in the Chinese context with the understanding of traditional beliefs and philosophical values. Due to traditional Chinese philosophical values, such as 'fallen leaves return to the roots (落叶归根)' and 'searching for ancestral roots/heritage (寻根),' their behavior of returning to rural regions was considered an important life goal and purpose; it means so much to them and their families, which is a crucial construct of Chinese culture. This research argues the connection between self-actualization and subjective well-being. Migrants' subjective well-being is improved by seeking nostalgia: they look

Figure 7. Perceived negative authenticity factors.

for the most spiritually important things in their lives, including restoring their personal heritage and recalling their family stories, and passing them both on to their descendants, which are their higher level of human needs, according to Maslow's theory of self-actualization. Figure 8 presents key words of migrants' answers regarding subjective well-being.

In terms of Maslow's hierarchy theory, the findings suggest that such desire of root searching is clearly beyond those lower levels of human demands (e.g. physiological demand and safety). Such a mentality is closely related to the desire to feel senses of belonging (e.g. cultural identity and social status), self-esteem (e.g. they are happy to see the improvement taking place in rural regions, find connections with rural communities during travel, and enjoy the compliments received from rural residents about their achievements through hard work in urban regions), and self-actualization (e.g. searching for and returning to their ancestral roots/heritage and reminding themselves who they are and where they came from are core spiritual desires and lifelong goals). Many people value their personal and family heritage very much and would not forget about their past regardless of how long they have left their hometowns. By returning to rural destinations and mixing with rural communities again, it helps them to find their past, recall good memories, and actualize their life goals. Therefore, the higher the degree of rural-urban migrant tourists' nostalgic feelings fulfilled, the higher the level of subjective well-being of those tourists achieved.

Discussions and conclusion

This research proposes the necessity of investigating Chinese issues through the lens of Chinese philosophical values. With proper knowledge of the Chinese philosophical values of 'old home (老家)' and 'searching for ancestral roots (寻根),' people can fully understand why rural-urban migrants deem rural communities their cultural and spiritual hometowns. Such philosophical values carry their perceptions of affiliation and belonging, even though these are not exactly the villages in which they once lived. Rural-urban migrants consider rural regions, as well as, mentalities, cultures, and environments in general, as their hometowns, rather than their actual towns or villages when they think about 'old home (老家).' For those rural-urban migrants, nostalgia is clearly the key push factor that motivates them to return to rural destinations. An authentic rural destination that can help them arouse nostalgic feelings will be more attractive to those tourists; therefore, rural authenticity serves as a key pull factor.

Figure 8. Subjective well-being.

Rural-urban migrants' personal heritage

Because of their unique backgrounds, those migrants have a great desire to return to rural regions in search of their past memories, ancestral roots/heritage, and the taste of their 'old homes.' This study proposes to take traditional Chinese philosophical values into consideration when examining rural-urban migrants' motivations of rural tourism. To those migrants, the Chinese philosophical value of 'old home (老家)' means more than any particular rural destination: it represents their entire personal and family heritage, as well as their true identity. Therefore, a visit to rural destinations is not merely a tourism activity to them; it is a particular way to find their inner peace and value, thus fulfilling their needs for self-actualization. In this sense, nostalgia serves as a push factor, making those people nostalgic tourists. To them, nostalgia largely contains a positive meaning, reminding them of past good memories and stories. They defined nostalgia as the willingness to go back to their places of origin and search for their personal heritage and ancestral roots, which is the need for belonging and self-actualization. Figure 9 presents key words of their answers regarding Chinese philosophical values.

To comprehend a migrant tourist's perception of authenticity, it is also important to know what factors may influence their perceptions. For this group of tourists, authenticity can be represented by traditional custom, rural history, dialect, architecture, cuisine, and the sense of rural residents' genuineness. These aspects are the key criteria for migrant tourists to arouse nostalgic feelings. Their perception of authenticity is significantly associated with their past and current life experiences. Conclusively, three aspects dictate authenticity perceived by migrant tourists: physical objects and environments, activities, and interactions with local people. Additionally, experience, age, and place of residence influence those people's nostalgic feelings and the ways they perceive authenticity.

Moreover, this study reveals that in order to explain migrants' complicated motivations of visiting rural destinations, additional Chinese philosophical values should be introduced: 'fallen leaves return to the roots (落叶归根).' In particular, this research revealed that the concept of 'root' in Chinese is related to both 'searching for ancestral roots and heritage (寻根)' and 'nostalgia,' and rural-urban migrants connect roots to nostalgia. Such ancient philosophical values can help people explore their inherent desires to return to rural regions, which helps one to understand why those migrants are so eager to revisit rural destinations in general in order to trace their past memories and ancestral roots. Even more importantly, they want to pass that personal heritage and those traditions on to their children and grandchildren. Therefore, it is a higher level of psychological need, according

Figure 9. Chinese philosophical values.

to Maslow's hierarchy theory, which can affect their subjective well-being. Figure 10 presents the conceptual model of this study.

During the past several decades, rural-urban migrants' lifetime experiences have shifted dramatically; they moved from their hometowns to other completely different places; however, their memories about their childhood and adolescence are deeply imprinted in their minds, and they begin to treat this part of their memories as precious personal heritage while advancing in age. In addition to escaping from urban pressures and stressful environments, many of them are actively looking for past memories by returning to rural regions and participating in various types of rural tourism activities. This type of tourism motivation can be considered nostalgia with the consideration of their unique backgrounds and Chinese philosophical values.

Theoretical implications and contributions

Building on the theory of push–pull rather than retesting the theory, this research investigates a particular push factor: nostalgia. Moreover, this research examines how migrants' key push factor (nostalgia) affects their perception and evaluation of other pull factors in terms of authenticity (e.g. culture, food, and architecture). The research findings contribute to the academic advancement of rural tourism research. This research merits attention by shedding light on rural-urban migrants when returning to rural regions, which, in contrast to other thoroughly researched rural tourist studies, is still in its infancy. In particular, this study contributes to the literature of rural-urban migrants by investigating key elements that can generate and affect nostalgic feelings, as well as their impact on subjective well-being both during and after traveling.

Additionally, the incorporation of authenticity promises new insights into nostalgia. This study focuses on the currently under-researched relationship between perceived authenticity and nostalgia. Although previous scholars have acknowledged the connection between perceived authenticity and nostalgia, how these two concepts interact with each other was not given much attention by scholars. The current study integrated the impacts of perceived authenticity into nostalgia fulfillment with the unique understanding of Chinese philosophical values. Additionally, due to the combination of past memories from rural regions and current life experiences in urban regions, those migrants perceive authenticity in rural destinations in different ways, including existential, objective, constructive, and mixed models; how different types of authenticity perceptions influence migrants' nostalgia fulfillment were also examined.

The current research confirmed and further extended the model proposed by Sznajder, Przezbórska, and Scrimgeour (2009), in which they investigated urban population and rural population

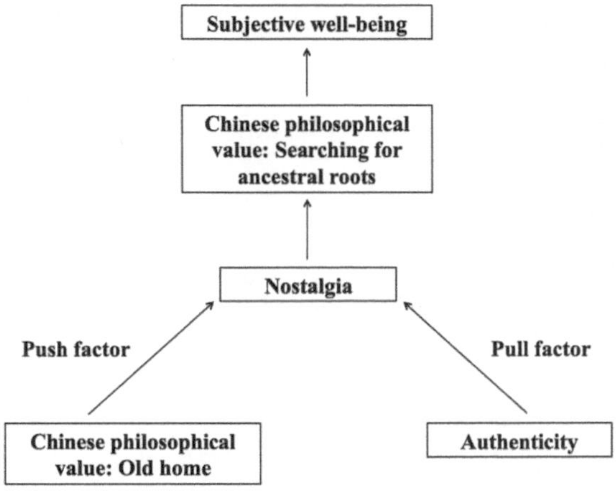

Figure 10. A conceptual model of rural tourism motivation for rural-urban migrants.

in terms of behavior and movement. The current research revealed that part of the rural population migrated to urban regions and eventually became part of the urban population throughout the process of China's industrialization. However, due to these migrants' desires to evoke nostalgic feelings and search for ancestral roots, as well as their unsatisfied life experiences in modern cities, they are seeking opportunities to return to rural China as rural tourists. This makes them a unique sector of the modern rural tourism field in China in terms of their travel motivation, desired activities and objects, authenticity perceptions, and overall subjective well-being as a result of such visits. As opposed to other tourists, they are not merely short-term rural tourists; instead, they consider themselves to be returning to their rural 'old home (老家).' Deep in their hearts, they still believe that they are inseparable from their rural ancestral roots, carrying the good, rustic, and unsophisticated rural characteristics that make them instinctively recall their past and memories by returning to rural China. In addition, many of them would like to bring their descendants with them in order to pass on that tradition and personal heritage. Figure 11 presents the context of those rural-urban migrant tourists.

Practical implications and contributions

The rich culture and history in rural China, as well as its natural resources, provide tourists with great opportunities for rural tourism. Nowadays, rural tourism has become very important to China's tourism market. Although rural tourism has developed very quickly in China, many rural tourism destinations are facing a common problem: most rural tourism businesses are operated with a family based model, and operators are local farmers who do not necessarily have comprehensive knowledge of marketing, customer research, and business operations. Therefore, many rural tourism businesses lack sufficient management skills and thus cannot provide the desired products to the corresponding tourist group.

The findings of this research demonstrate that consuming local food and cuisine, visiting historical architectures, learning local history and customs, sightseeing natural landscapes, communicating with rural people, and participating in agricultural works contribute the most to migrant tourists'

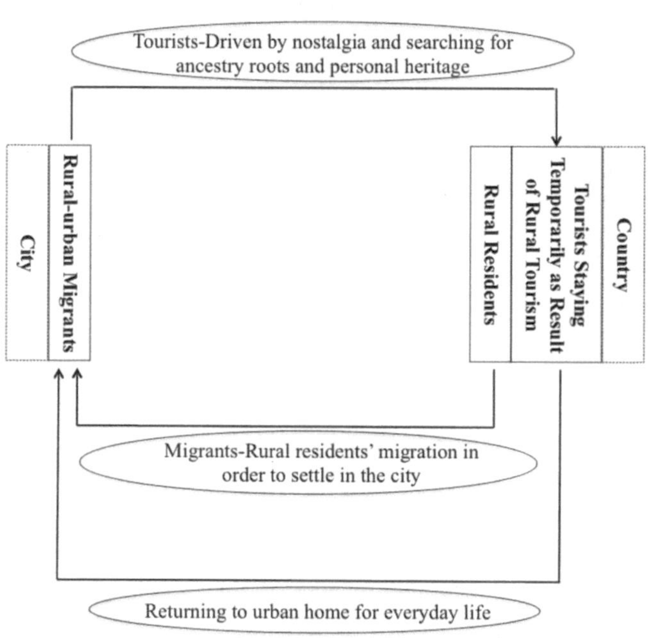

Figure 11. The context of rural-urban migrant tourists.

perceptions of authenticity, which in turn allow them to arouse their nostalgic feelings and memories about their past experiences. After decades of rapid processes of urbanization and rural development, many rural regions in China have been reconstructed or reshaped, especially those surrounding big cities; there are some modern-looking buildings and amenities, which of course facilitate rural people's lives and their standards of living. However, based on the above findings, the traditional architecture and rural housing contribute significantly to migrant tourists' perceived authenticity. Therefore, preserving the original buildings is crucial for this purpose.

Because of migrants' unique and shifted lifelong experiences, pursuing nostalgia is a key motivation for migrant tourists, especially when they are advancing in age. This can improve their subjective well-being both during and after their rural stays because they have achieved an important lifetime goal based on one of their traditional Chinese philosophical values: searching for ancestral roots. Most migrant tourists are also short-term rural visitors who want to emotionally relax in a peaceful environment, and they very often do so with their friends and families. Because of their understanding of 'one can't have fish and bear at the same time (鱼和熊掌不可兼得),' it is likely that they really enjoy the modern developments, which provide great convenience for their daily activities. However, they have defined rural regions as unique places to seek memories of 'good old times'; therefore, the reconstruction of some historical districts, restaurants, and lodging facilities should not destroy rural traditions and cultures. Accordingly, stores and activities that combine cultures and creative ideas can be promoted. Such strategies can also be used to resolve the conflict between the preservation of traditions and modern development in general.

Limitations and future research

Several limitations should be noted. First, the current study only investigated tourists in rural destinations surrounding Beijing. Results may not be generalizable to the tourists of other rural destinations in China (especially in southern China, which has a very different level of development, history, and culture from northern China) or worldwide. Further quantitative studies will be adopted to test and examine constructs and their interrelationships in other regions of China with different histories, cultures, and levels of development. Second, although the interview plan was designed with the goal of providing reliable estimates of the population, the results are only representative of the visitors during periods of the winter season, whereas tourists traveling to rural destinations during the summer season may have different motivations; thus, the results may not apply to tourists who visit during other times of the year. Third, no interview was conducted during the evening; therefore, the data from this population may not be sufficient to show all the characteristics of rural-urban migrant tourists and the full spectrum of their activities, as there are plenty of meaningful events and celebrations in rural villages at night.

Although significant valuable information was found about rural-urban migrant tourists' perceptions of authenticity, motivation, and subjective well-being, the differences among other types of tourists remain unclear. Therefore, further research is needed, particularly quantitative research, to determine how specific factors may affect their attitudes and perceptions, such as length of time living in rural regions before migrating, age, gender, occupation, education, and so forth. At that point, the reasons for certain groups of people's perceptions of subjective well-being and authenticity can be further explored. Future research can focus on similar populations in southern parts of China to explore their motivations and perceptions of authenticity and compare cultural and regional differences.

Disclosure statement

No potential conflict of interest was reported by the authors.

References

Acharya, R. N., Paudel, K. P., & Hatch, L. U. (2009). Impact of nostalgia and past experience on recreational demand for wilderness. *Applied Economics Letters, 16*(5), 449–453.

Allport, G. W. (1937). *Personality: A psychological interpretation.* Oxford, UK: Holt.

Alonso, A. D., O'Neill, M. A., & Kim, K. (2010). In search of authenticity: A case examination of the transformation of Alabama's Langdale Cotton Mill into an industrial heritage tourism attraction. *Journal of Heritage Tourism, 5*(1), 33–48.

Ashley, C. (2000). *The impacts of tourism on rural livelihoods: Namibia's experience.* London, UK: Overseas Development Institute.

Bessiere, J. (1998). Local development and heritage: Traditional food and cuisine as tourist attractions in rural areas. *Sociologia Ruralis, 38*(1), 21–34.

Briedenhann, J., & Wickens, E. (2004). Tourism routes as a tool for the economic development of rural areas—Vibrant hope or impossible dream? *Tourism Management, 25*(1), 71–79.

Budruk, M., White, D. D., Wodrich, J. A., & Van Riper, C. J. (2008). Connecting visitors to people and place: Visitors' perceptions of authenticity at Canyon de Chelly National Monument, Arizona. *Journal of Heritage Tourism, 3*(3), 185–202.

Burger, J. M. (2011). *Returning home: Reconnecting with our childhoods.* Lanham, MD: Rowman & Littlefield.

Caton, K., & Santos, C. A. (2007). Heritage tourism on Route 66: Deconstructing nostalgia. *Journal of Travel Research, 45*(4), 371–386.

Chen, H. B., Yeh, S. S., & Huan, T. C. (2014). Nostalgic emotion, experiential value, brand image, and consumption intentions of customers of nostalgic-themed restaurants. *Journal of Business Research*, *67*(3), 354–360.
Chhabra, D. (2007). Exploring market influences on curator perceptions of authenticity. *Journal of Heritage Tourism*, *2* (2), 110–119.
Chhabra, D., Healy, R., & Sills, E. (2003). Staged authenticity and heritage tourism. *Annals of Tourism Research*, *30*(3), 702–719.
Chhabra, D., Lee, W., Zhao, S., & Scott, K. (2013). Marketing of ethnic food experiences: Authentication analysis of Indian cuisine abroad. *Journal of Heritage Tourism*, *8*(2–3), 145–157.
Chio, J. T. (2014). *A landscape of travel: The work of tourism in rural ethnic China*. Seattle, WA: University of Washington Press.
Cohen, E. (1988). Authenticity and commoditization in tourism. *Annals of Tourism Research*, *15*(3), 371–386.
Condevaux, A. (2009). Māori culture on stage: Authenticity and identity in tourist interactions. *Anthropological Forum*, *19*(2), 143–161.
Curtin, S. (2009). Wildlife tourism: The intangible, psychological benefits of human-wildlife encounters. *Current Issues in Tourism*, *12*(5-6), 451–474.
Dann, G. (1977). Anomie, ego-enhancement and tourism. *Annals of Tourism Research*, *4*(4), 184–194.
Dann, G. (1981). Tourist motivation an appraisal. *Annals of Tourism Research*, *8*(2), 187–219.
Davis, F. (1979). *Yearning for yesterday: A sociology of nostalgia*. New York, NY: Free Press.
Dernoi, L. (1991). Prospects of rural tourism: Needs and opportunities. *Tourism Recreation Research*, *16*(1), 89–94.
DiCicco-Bloom, B., & Crabtree, B. F. (2006). The qualitative research interview. *Medical Education*, *40*(4), 314–321.
Diener, E. (2000). Subjective well-being: The science of happiness and a proposal for a national index. *American Psychologist*, *55*(1), 34–43.
Dolnicar, S., Yanamandram, V., & Cliff, K. (2012). The contribution of vacations to quality of life. *Annals of Tourism Research*, *39*(1), 59–83.
Du, Y., Park, A., & Wang, S. (2005). Migration and rural poverty in China. *Journal of Comparative Economics*, *33*(4), 688–709.
Eysenbach, G., & Köhler, C. (2002). How do consumers search for and appraise health information on the world wide web? Qualitative study using focus groups, usability tests, and in-depth interviews. *BMJ*, *324*(7337), 573–577.
Filep, S. (2014). Moving beyond subjective well-being: A tourism critique. *Journal of Hospitality & Tourism Research*, *38*(2), 266–274.
Gannon, A. (1994). Rural tourism as a factor in rural community economic development for economies in transition. *Journal of Sustainable Tourism*, *2*(1–2), 51–60.
Gilbert, D., & Abdullah, J. (2004). Holiday taking and the sense of well-being. *Annals of Tourism Research*, *31*(1), 103–121.
Golomb, E. (1995). Oracles in Ladakh: A personal experience. In L. L. Adler & B. R. Mukherji (Eds.), *Spirit versus scalpel: Traditional healing and modern psychotherapy* (pp. 59–75). Westport, CT: Bergin & Garvey.
Hannigan, K. (1994). A regional analysis of tourism growth in Ireland. *Regional Studies*, *28*(2), 208–214.
Havlena, W. J., & Holak, S. L. (1991). "The good old days": Observations on nostalgia and its role in consumer behavior. *Advances in Consumer Research*, *18*(1), 323–329.
Holbrook, M. B., & Schindler, R. M. (1991). Echoes of the dear departed past: Some work in progress on nostalgia. *Advances in Consumer Research*, *18*(1), 330–333.
Hsu, C. H., Cai, L. A., & Wong, K. K. (2007). A model of senior tourism motivations—Anecdotes from Beijing and Shanghai. *Tourism Management*, *28*(5), 1262–1273.
Huberman, A. M., & Miles, M. B. (1994). Data management and analysis methods. In N. K. Denzin & Y. S. Lincoln (Eds.), *Handbook of qualitative research* (pp. 428–444). Thousand Oaks, CA: Sage Publications, Inc.
Kelner, S., & Phil, M. (2001). *Narrative construction of authenticity in pilgrimage touring*. Paper presented at the 96th Annual Meeting of the American Sociological Association, Anaheim, CA.
Kim, H., & Jamal, T. (2007). Touristic quest for existential authenticity. *Annals of Tourism Research*, *34*(1), 181–201.
Knudsen, D., & Greer, C. (2011). Tourism and nostalgia for the pastoral on the island of Fyn, Denmark. *Journal of Heritage Tourism*, *6*(2), 87–98.
Korstanje, M. (2012). Reconsidering cultural tourism: An anthropologist's perspective. *Journal of Heritage Tourism*, *7* (2), 179–184.
Legard, R., Keegan, J., & Ward, K. (2003). In-depth interviews. In J. Ritchie & J. Lewis (Eds.), *Qualitative research practice: A guide for social science students and researchers* (pp. 138–169). London, UK: Sage.
Leong, A. M. W., Yeh, S. S., Hsiao, Y. C., & Huan, T. C. T. (2015). Nostalgia as travel motivation and its impact on tourists' loyalty. *Journal of Business Research*, *68*(1), 81–86.
Lev Ari, L., & Mittelberg, D. (2008). Between authenticity and ethnicity: Heritage tourism and re-ethnification among diaspora Jewish youth. *Journal of Heritage Tourism*, *3*(2), 79–103.
Leydon, G. M., Boulton, M., Moynihan, C., Jones, A., Mossman, J., Boudioni, M., & McPherson, K. (2000). Cancer patients' information needs and information seeking behavior: In depth interview study. *BMJ*, *320*(7239), 909–913.
Liamputtong, P., & Ezzy, D. (1999). *Qualitative research methods*. Melbourne: Oxford University Press.

MacCannell, D. (1973). Staged authenticity: Arrangements of social space in tourist settings. *American Journal of Sociology*, *79*(3), 589–603.
Maslow, A. H. (1943). A theory of human motivation. *Psychological Review*, *50*(4), 370–396.
Mathison, S. (1988). Why triangulate? *Educational Researcher*, *17*(2), 13–17.
McCabe, S., & Johnson, S. (2013). The happiness factor in tourism: Subjective well-being and social tourism. *Annals of Tourism Research*, *41*, 42–65.
McCabe, S., Joldersma, T., & Li, C. (2010). Understanding the benefits of social tourism: Linking participation to subjective well-being and quality of life. *International Journal of Tourism Research*, *12*(6), 761–773.
McCartney, G., & Osti, L. (2007). From cultural events to sport events: A case study of cultural authenticity in the dragon boat races. *Journal of Sport & Tourism*, *12*(1), 25–40.
Merriam, S. B. (1998). *Qualitative research and case study applications in education. Revised and expanded from "case study research in education"*. San Francisco, CA: Jossey-Bass.
Nyaupane, G. P., White, D. D., & Budruk, M. (2006). Motive-based tourist market segmentation: An application to native American cultural heritage sites in Arizona, USA. *Journal of Heritage Tourism*, *1*(2), 81–99.
Oakes, T. (2005). *Tourism and modernity in China*. London, UK: Routledge.
Osbaldiston, N. (2012). *Seeking authenticity in place, culture, and the self: The great urban escape*. New York, NY: Palgrave Macmillan.
Park, C. H. (2014). Nongjiale tourism and contested space in rural China. *Modern China*, *40*(5), 519–548.
Pearce, P. L., & Caltabiano, M. L. (1983). Inferring travel motivation from travelers' experiences. *Journal of Travel Research*, *22*(2), 16–20.
Peterson, C. (1999). Children's memory for medical emergencies: 2 years later.. *Developmental Psychology*, *35*(6), 1493–1506.
Peterson, C. (2002). Children's long-term memory for autobiographical events. *Developmental Review*, *22*(3), 370–402.
Peterson, C., Warren, K. L., & Short, M. M. (2011). Infantile amnesia across the years: A 2-year follow-up of children's earliest memories. *Child Development*, *82*(4), 1092–1105.
Reeder, R. J., & Brown, D. M. (2005). *Recreation, tourism, and rural well-being*. Washington, DC: US Department of Agriculture, Economic Research Service.
Rubin, D. C. (2000). The distribution of early childhood memories. *Memory*, *8*(4), 265–269.
Sharpley, R., & Jepson, D. (2011). Rural tourism: A spiritual experience? *Annals of Tourism Research*, *38*(1), 52–71.
Sirgy, M. (2010). Toward a quality-of-life theory of leisure travel satisfaction. *Journal of Travel Research*, *49*(2), 246–260.
Su, B. (2011). Rural tourism in China. *Tourism Management*, *32*(6), 1438–1441.
Sznajder, M., Przezbórska, L., & Scrimgeour, F. (2009). *Agritourism pillars*. Wallingford: CABI.
Taylor, B. C., & Trujillo, N. (2001). Qualitative research methods. In F. M. Jablin & L. L. Putnam (Eds.), *The new handbook of organizational communication: Advances in theory, research, and methods* (pp. 161–194). Thousand Oaks, CA: SAGE.
Timothy, D. J., & Ron, A. S. (2013). Understanding heritage cuisines and tourism: Identity, image, authenticity, and change. *Journal of Heritage Tourism*, *8*(2-3), 99–104.
Trilling, L. (2009). *Sincerity and authenticity*. Cambridge, MA: Harvard University Press.
Uriely, N. (2005). The tourist experience: Conceptual developments. *Annals of Tourism Research*, *32*(1), 199–216.
Usher, J. A., & Neisser, U. (1993). Childhood amnesia and the beginnings of memory for four early life events. *Journal of Experimental Psychology: General*, *122*(2), 155–165.
Van Abbema, D. L., & Bauer, P. J. (2005). Autobiographical memory in middle childhood: Recollections of the recent and distant past. *Memory*, *13*(8), 829–845.
Voase, R. (1995). *Tourism: The human perspective*. London, UK: Hodder & Stoughton.
Wang, N. (1999). Rethinking authenticity in tourism experience. *Annals of Tourism Research*, *26*(2), 349–370.
Wang, Q. (2003). Infantile amnesia reconsidered: A cross-cultural analysis. *Memory*, *11*(1), 65–80.
Yang, L., & Wall, G. (2009). Authenticity in ethnic tourism: Domestic tourists' perspectives. *Current Issues in Tourism*, *12*(3), 235–254.
Yeoman, I., Brass, D., & McMahon-Beattie, U. (2007). Current issue in tourism: The authentic tourist. *Tourism Management*, *28*(4), 1128–1138.
Zhang, K. H., & Song, S. (2003). Rural–urban migration and urbanization in China: Evidence from time-series and cross-section analyses. *China Economic Review*, *14*(4), 386–400.
Zhao, Y. (1999). Leaving the countryside: Rural-to-urban migration decisions in China. *American Economic Review*, *89* (2), 281–286.
Zhou, L. Q., & Huang, Z. H. (2004). Sustainable development of rural tourism in China: Challenges and policies. *Economic Geography*, *4*, 572–576.

Conclusion: well-being and moral orientations of existentialist authenticity

The pandemic (covid-19) has altered the face of heritage tourism. The notion of authenticity, today, has become more relevant today in times of de-escalated mobility, as the world copes with the harsh reality of covid-19. The continued expansion of its conceptualizations has resulted in multiple perspectives as several authors have pointed out in their chapters. Few authors have acknowledged that the different authenticities go through different authentication processes; And that these processes are shaped and legitimized by power relations. External authentication processes of heritage resources can be molded by supply or demand dynamics or both simultaneously and mutual authentication lends support to strategies coping with equity and social inclusion issues. However, the internal (self) authentication process follows a different path. A perusal of recent scholarship reveals increasing attention towards existentialist authenticity and although, still sparsely covered, I will like to discuss this notion in the context of well-being and morality. The prevailing pandemic is exposing the interdependence between health, authenticity, and moral behavior. In this chapter, I extend the dialogue on existentialist authenticity from these standpoints. I will conclude with insights on how existentialist authenticity or its negotiated version and its self authentication can comply with the ethical aspects of hedonic and eudaimonic pursuits to promote overall well-being of the self and the host societies.

The existential view is a deep concept. In fact, it is a philosophy (Kirillova 2019). Its roots can be traced to the times when the 'pre-given' traditional society structures became fractured. A sense of disenchantment was noted during the industrial revolution times. As the new awareness of self versus the society influenced transformed lifestyles in urban settings, individualistic behavior became the new norm. According to Kirillova, this change from traditional notions to "absolute, with built-in value and meaning in life" generated a sense of fear of being tossed "into this world with no pre-defined direction or meaning" (2019, p. 430). The human beings become cognizant of their mortality at the early phase of their life and seek to rationalize the existence of their 'Being.' From an existentialist standpoint, a person's existence goes beyond the gratification of basic needs and desires; it is about deliberations on the value of the superficial/extrinsic needs and the presence of self in life (Kirilloava 2019). The existence ordeal dominates humans throughout their life span and can be characterized by four key phases: meaning(lessness) of life, inevitability of death, pervasive alienation, and boundarylessness of freedom (Yalom 1980). One key element of existentialism philosophy is existential authenticity. It is a state of existence which holds mirror to values meaningful to one's inner being (Wang 1999). The human existence is deemed to be authentic, if one's personal image is modeled based on the self. On the contrary, if the image or existence is molded by extrinsic factors such as life's events, moral, economic, social or political systems, a human being can be labeled as inauthentic. In other words, the existentialist authenticity refers to the establishing of a relationship with the 'life givens' or the external environment in a way that the intrinsic self is not compromised in terms of values, passions, and beliefs it holds (Kirillova 2019, p. 431). It implies transcendence guided by a sense of activity or disposition that can go beyond the actuality of an external influence or situation (Sartre 1996). It is postulated that a person should hold a candle to one's true inner value systems and not be swayed by situational factors.

Several scholars have contended that feelings of anxiety triggers desire for existential authenticity, particularly, when human beings cope with the fluid reality of life and the inevitable nature of mortality. A person is pushed into a web of arduous choices, thereby facilitating a departure from the intrinsic self. Cohen initiated the effort to fertilize the field of tourism with the existential theory and suggested an existential way of experiencing, where the tourists seek a preferred spiritual ground beyond their home and society, in a tourist place. Cohen's ideas of a spiritual center and alienation echo the fundamental tenets of existential authenticity and anxiety noted in the works of existential philosophers and they offer "the first glimpse of a unique experience of the human condition in tourism" (Kirillova 2019, p. 430). Wang (1999) forwarded this initiative with notable articulation of existential authenticity in the context of other perspectives and presented its interpersonal (with the self) and intrapersonal (with others) delineations. Authenticity manifests in various forms and shapes. Although essentialist (object-based) authenticity continues to be the reference point in heritage tourism, two other dimensions of authenticity: existentialist and theoplacity continue to be recognized for their significance in terms of their value for optimizing the self. Existentialist authenticity aims to bring harmonious balance through exhilarated and truth of the moment experiences and theoplacity enables connection with the inner self in an essentialist setting; both prominently contribute towards individual well-being. In the recent decades, these existentialist concerns are recognized by the suppliers of heritage tourism; they understand that "in addition to positive emotions, sensations of pleasure and comfort that modern tourists encounter, quest is also for products and experiences that assist to address the existentialist aspects of life such as discomfort and fear of a tragedy or death" (Kirillova 2019, p. 432).

A plethora of studies in tourism have examined existentialist authenticity in the context of other authenticity dimensions and from visitor behavior and experience standpoints. For instance, Stepchenkova and Belyseva (2020) examine the association between a person's inclination towards essentialist authenticity and existentialist authenticity experienced by tourists and their subsequent intention towards post visitation behavior. Two settings are used: a museum which aims at essentialist authenticity and a museum that embraces the constructivist version of authenticity, that is, it recreates, reconstructs, and interprets authenticity to please audience. The authors report that the nature of the setting influences the type of authenticity experienced by the visitors. Audience is delineated into two types of patrons: realists and postmodernists. It is argued that the postmodernists pursue existentialist authenticity while the realists seek the essentialist version. A key finding is "intended behavior does not depend on authenticity orientation when the impact of existential authenticity is controlled" (Stepchenkova & Belyseva 2020, p. 1). Not everyone seeks existentialist or essentialist authenticity is the takeaway point and these authenticities are mostly desired by niche target markets.

The theoplacity position of authenticity gives a location/place context to existentialist authenticity, particularly in heritage tourism. As acknowledged by Yu et al., "although there is an evident distinction between object-oriented and existential authenticities in ontology and epistemology" (2020, p. 145), they seem to be existing simultaneously and are related, particularly in heritage settings, where people are motivated by both, essentialist and existential authenticities (Chhabra 2010; Kolar & Zabkar 2010). Positive relationships have been noted between objective authenticity and existential authenticity (Fu 2019; Lin, Jin & Luo 2020). Fu (2019) examines existential authenticity and destination loyalty for a world heritage site. The author reports that existential authenticity is a significant predictor of loyalty and serves as a conduit for richer experiential encounters with the self. Existential authenticity is about self-discovery because "tourists in such spaces may find new interests and unique experiences, including moments of spiritual awareness and feelings of connection with the past" (Fu 2019, p. 85). Additionally, it also about seeking disorientation to lose oneself and reduction of alienation from the inner child (self) so that id, ego, and super ego are aligned with each other.

More and more tourism organizations specializing in immersive and transformative experiences/products, seek to offer solutions to mitigate anxiety and offer opportunities for self-discovery and to experience existential authenticity. Non-formulized authentic experiences, particularly those that harmonize the self at home or in visited 'othered' (essentialist) settings, can contribute towards well-being. To date, existentialist authenticity and well-being have been mostly examined as two separate trajectories of inquiry (Yu et al. 2019). Pursuits related to the optimization of the self, by immersing oneself in niche subsets of heritage tourism (such as spiritual tourism, ecocultural tourism, and volunteer tourism), offer pathways to build healthy body-mind systems (Olsen & Timothy 2006). Well-being is often used as a proxy to explain psychological and physiological health, quality of life, life satisfaction, happiness, and overall well-being (Hudson, Cárdenas & Meng 2017; Karn, Amarkantak & Swain 2017; Smith & Diekmann 2017). The concept of well-being revolves predominantly around two philosophies: the hedonic and the eudaimonic schools of thought (Smith & Diekmann 2017). Smith and Diekmann posit that "many people travel in search of self and anonymity, to lose themselves first and then to find themselves again" (2017, p. 6). The state of forgetting of oneself echoes Tiberghien, Bremmer And Milne's (2020) state of disorientation. The authors posit that disorientation can generate a sense of feeling lost in othered settings and this state contributes to an optimal existentially authentic experience. Therapeutic state of 'being' conforms to the fundamental tenets of an eudaimonic experience. Disoriented or novel landscapes are often sought where the natural and built environment, social conditions, and human interactions offer an atmosphere conducive to mental sanitizing and spiritual healing.

A surge in recent studies on existentialist authenticity has long term implications in the field of scholarship and in terms of practical application. The entire purpose of seeking authenticity in heritage tourism is hedonistic or eudaimonic. While the former appears in the form of satisfaction, enhancement of quality of life, entertainment and enjoyment, the latter is fleetingly mentioned in the context of health-based tourism such as spa or yoga tourism. Both existentialist state of mind and essentialist settings hold potential to promote feelings of relaxation and relief from stress which can translate to happiness and well-being. Although numerous studies have scrutinized the hedonic benefits of existential authenticity especially in the context of enjoyment and satisfaction, few have taken the eudaimonic path (Yu, Li & Xiao 2020).

During the last few decades, the increasing popularity of oriental and indigenous South Asian alternate healing and hedonic and eudaimonic pursuits (such as yoga, tai chi, meditation) have become recognizable paths to enhance psychological and physiological health and overall well-being of the self and the society. It has been increasingly reported that ancient indigenous and natural remedies and activities nurture and harmonize mind, body and spirit and boost health, spirituality, and overall well-being (Ali-Knight 2017; Bowers & Cheer 2008; Olsen &

Timothy 2006). They are recognized as transcendental and 'body-self transforming' practices (Brown & Leledaki 2010, p. 125). Yoga retreats are actively known for transcendental or spiritual experiences (Smith and Sziva 2018) and "part of the therapeutic potential of the retreat focus on transporting the body away from the 'day-to-day' events, paying attention to the body, and foregrounding its connection to the universe (Lea 2008). Such practices optimize theoplacity and existentially authentic experiences and offer "a panacea for the ailments of modern society— tech overload, disconnection and alienation, insomnia, stress and anxiety" (Gregorie 2013, p. 5).

Recent studies are focusing on well-being and are drawing attention to personification and ways in which bodies can feel, encounter, influence, and interact with the therapeutic environments in which they are located (Little 2012). Several theories and transformational frameworks have been suggested to examine the health outcomes of healing experiences (Little 2012; Smith & Szvia 2016) such as serious leisure (Patterson, Getz & Gubb 2016; Stebbins 1992), positive psychology (Coghlan 2015; Keyes 2007), and flourishing (Keyes 2007; Slade 2010). Serious leisure is a systematic search for "an amateur, hobbyist, or volunteer core activity that is highly substantial, interesting, and fulfilling and where, in the typical case, find a career in acquiring and expressing a combination of its special skills, knowledge, and experience" (Stebbins 1992). It is founded on six distinct traits: desire to sustain interest in the selected activity or pursuit; seeking opportunities to pursue a leisure career ladder; dedicated efforts to gather proficiency and understanding; recognition of unique values of the embraced pursuit; promotion of a special attitude and shared environment with like-minded individuals; and promoting a desirable individual and communal sense of existence and personality (Stebbins 2001).

Positive psychology is premised on the hedonistic (happiness) concept and uses a psychological perspective to pursue research and mediation practices to understand the optimistic, acclimatizing, innovative and emotionally rewarding facets of human behavior (Seligman 1998). The concept of flourishing, on the other hand, is a general assessment of well-being and refers to selected goals that need to be achieved to feel good about self and perform efficiently. Examples include experiencing positive emotions, high level of interest and engagement, and a sense of purpose and meaning to accomplish an optimistic disposition, self-respect, resilience, liveliness, self-determination, and positive bonding (Coghlan 2015). According to Keyes (2007), indigenous therapeutic programs such as yoga and meditation offer immersive or favorably disoriented experiences in 'other' cultures and generate positive feelings and flourishing in people who are alienated/unhappy with their day-to-day existence. Key message drawn from the aforementioned is that the positive inter-connections unfolding between the searching self and therapeutic programs and health enhance the optimal state of mind or existential authenticity and well-being.

Few studies can be identified that examine existentialist authenticity in the context of disorientation, happiness, and well-being. It is postulated that tourists seek disorientation in othered settings to free themselves of daily stress and these dislocated experiences hold potential to optimize the benefits they receive, both from happiness and well-being standpoints. Disorientation refers to emotional feelings of 'foreignness' when an optimal flow is experienced when people are challenged and feel a loss of consciousness of self and sense of time. Disorientation in time and space is an important parameter of peak-flow for tourists seeking optimum emotional levels through an authentic experience (Mannell & Iso Ahola 1987). Discovery of the unknown and the othered settings stimulate intellectual enhancement and self- fulfillment through deeply engaging and profound experiences (Tiberghien et al. 2020). Tiberghien et al. write that "visitor's perceptions enter into a liminal state and produce a sense of self-awareness, resulting in an experience that is existentially authentic. This serendipitous moment, when a tourist ceases to be a tourist is thought to be automatically authentic (2020, p. 3). In other words, unfamiliar settings hold potential to disorient the visitors and distance them from their comfort zones and stimulate high level of authenticity perceptions. The authors offer deliberations on the numerous authenticity and disorientation views of stakeholders' and the manner in which they offer disorienting experiences in eco-cultural engagements. In this regard, the authors stress on balanced perceptions of cultural authenticity that takes in account both supply and demand perspectives and both personal as well as institutional agenda.

The authors further report that key stakeholders perceptions can differ and complicate consensus on how local culture can be staged or unstaged to increase disorienting experiences of visitors. These issues are often more complicated by power dynamics and needs/traits of different target markets. For instance, "the perception of nomadic lifestyle by some visitors from both tours created a culture shock while travelling in the country for which they had to adjust. Interestingly, some visitors suggested that enduring involvement in villages during their stay would not only greatly influence the perception of authenticity of their experience, but also reduce their culture shock and the disorientation resulting from it" (Tiberghien et al. 2020, p. 7). Mixed emotions of visitors are noted in their journey of disoriented settings. Positive emotions include gratification/contentment, astonishment, and interest where as negative emotions portray confusion. These are influenced by their cultural traits, motivations to experience the level of otherness, and perceptions and expectations of the gypsy type of culture. Particularly, homestays have potential to offer immersive othered experiences which depart from the preconceptions and information gathered by visitors before arrival. It is the unpredictable natural events and opportunities beyond their comfort thresholds which generate optimal authenticity moments and enrich their journey. However, the disorientation levels triggered by the staging of some events by the hosts are contested by certain agencies on the grounds that these events do not conform to local culture and traditions. Nevertheless, these othered disoriented experiences serve their purpose in that they promote existentialist authenticity. The enshrined process through which visitors authenticate their inner selves for an existential experience can be referred as the self-authentication process.

Extending Sartre's view of self-authenticity, Daigle explains that: self-authenticity must constantly be reclaimed as one continues in this life. To be authentic, one must hold oneself thoughtfully to embrace one's world and one's relationships with the others. In fact, such relations become crucial to the process of 'distantiation' - the key of authentic becoming; The self makes itself and is always evolving. One must actively engage in the formation of the self. Humans, being worldly beings, are subject to power relations and the subject of their own relations to themselves. To become active subjects of our own lives requires us to acknowledge that we will always unwrap historically and through our relationships and experiences. In other words, "our existence will always precede and supersede essence" (2017, p. 57–65).

Self authentication can be facilitated by the self even without traveling (such as in the backyard or in the comfort of home) or by the self in a favorable essentialist tourist setting. Aligned with the later view, Hopper, Costley and Friend (2015) opine that visitors experience existentialist authenticity only in the presence of others. That is, others or social settings perform an important role in the self authentication process. Along similar lines, Golomb (1995) argues that a person's sense of personal or self authenticity cannot be distanced from the broader context of existence in the world. In the examining the heritage value of a poetic expression (rock concert), it is noted that the crowd, the setting, the music, and the self mutually facilitate the self-authentication process; for instance, "the touch dominates the senses. People authenticate themselves through physical contact with others and by merely being there with others, feeling their presence, their energy, chanting, making eye contact and smiling" (Hopper et al. 2015, p. 322). Optimal flow results in transcendence and it transforms into an intangible deep experience of the present moment through a feeling of 'being there'. Hopper et al. show how "patrons experience utopia, tunnel vision, feeling out of their bodies and are transported to a different place. They shed the skin of inauthentic self and cleansed away their false selves and groomed their existential authenticity" (2015, p. 322–323). According to Schouten et al. (2007), this transformation is the outcome of a transcendental or self authentication process which invigorates the sense of self and stimulate the overall well-being.

Goffman (2012) argues that the social moral order of daily life compels people to spontaneously disguise their identity and this process corrupts the authentic self (Foucault 1995) and the outcome is inauthenticity of the self. Some events, tangible or intangible can free an individual from the everyday moral order (Riches 2011). In other words, inauthenticity gives a feeling of mortality or the end and transformation is needed to recover the real self and regain one's existential authenticity. The authors argue that the body is essential to self-authentication and a person can become closer to the self and feel rejuvenated through symbolic realization. That is, one becomes competent in being closer to the self through embodied knowing. In other words, it is claimed that experiencing the self in an authentic setting can stimulate existentially authentic experiences. That is, optimization of the self can happen by experiencing theoplacity (existential authenticity in settings that conform to essentialist authenticity to, at least, some extent).

Hopper et al. (2015), by using the example of poetic depictions, illustrate a tangible and metaphysical path to experiencing existential authenticity. Being refers to the notion of 'I myself am;' in other words, 'I exist' and 'I am myself' (Heidegger 1962). Hopper et al. argue that "when an individual orients towards their unique essential state of 'Being,' they experience existential authenticity, but when they orient towards the standards and expectations of society, they live an inauthentic existence; My being authentic is a state when, 'I' am in my authentic existence and the whole sense of 'Being' or my presence" (2015, p. 323). Transcendental experiences and encounters, with the self and between the self and the other, contribute to both hedonic and eudaimonic well-being and existentially authentic feelings are aligned with one's true self (Waterman 1993).

Clearly authenticity is important for the health of the mind and body and in fact, the overall well-being. One of its primary orientations, existential authenticity, can result in enjoyment as well as eudaimonic well-being (Chhabra 2010; Kolar and Zabkar 2010; Yu, Li & Xiao 2019). Cultural and heritage settings offer opportunities to optimize a sense of happiness and well-being. Alienation and disorientation impact existentially authentic experiences. Yu et al. 2020 write: tourists feel themselves to be more authentic when they stay or experience otherness, different from their daily life, and it can be assumed that the cultural distance is positively associated with feelings of authenticity. The authors examine the impact of cultural distance on hedonic and eudaimonic aspects of well-being. They also make an effort to determine if hedonic and eudaimoic experiences make authentic tourists are happier. To address their research questions, they scrutinize relationship between perceived cultural distance, existentialist authenticity, and hedonic/eudaimonic well-being. The authors report that existential authenticity facilitates eudaimonic well-being.

Aligned with this view, Mkono (2020) writes that existential authenticity, if unchecked, runs the risk of compromising moral values and can promote self-centeredness – 'all about myself' attitude. It is suggested that existential authenticity should be morally rooted in flourishing and ethical consumption approaches. Moving beyond the personal gains to moral values, Mkono argues that the well-being of the self should be connected to the well-being of host societies. In other words, visitors should be guided by moral or ethical dispositions when they seek self-rejuvenating and immersive experiences; Extended well-being should be the ultimate goal of existential authenticity. Huppert and So frame human flourishing as "feeling good and functioning effectively" (2013, p. 838). It encompasses "pleasure, well-being, welfare, affluence, and virtue, as well as those denoting various excellences and accomplishments" (Pogge 1999, p. 333). According to Pollock (2019), global tourism has surpassed planetary boundaries and compromised social and ecological resources. She proposes a reformative growth paradigm predominantly rooted in three conceptual pillars: (1) human being are a part of nature and apart from it; (2) human beings are equivalent to other living beings; (3) all living beings are inter-dependent and inter-related. The aspiration is to leave the earth in a condition that brings harmony between economic, social and environmental benefits and externalities. Cheer suggests praxis-based approaches that "link human flourishing and tourism largely espouse decoupling of growth-oriented policies, with myriad prescriptions from de-growth, enhancement of community engagement and agency, preservation of sense of place, elevation of the worth of the nature and the wider non-human world, acknowledgement of spirituality and conscious consumption and production" (2020, p. 519).

Mkono (2020) argues that issues associated with sustainable travel and ethical consumption can be addressed by examining the existential notions of autonomy and accountability. He poses several inquiries associated with: the potential of responsible tourism to promote individual freedom, the potential of tapping into existential concerns of tourists in the context of autonomy, mortality, meaning, and estrangement to encourage responsible behavior, the manner tourists internalize/experience outside of home, and impact of freedom restrictions on travel experiences. Next, with regard to power relations between tourists and non-tourist players, existential freedom can offer insights on the manner in which host communities compromise their freedom thresholds in their encounters with tourists and present tourism using existential standpoints.

It is purported that the modernist approach is more slanted towards in examining the manner in which alienation and anxiety exacerbate already existing issues: "First, this means that existential analyses should not be limited to the traveling individual but must pay attention to persons hosting (formally or informally), serving and entertaining the guests. Second, this position suggests that, regardless of the fact that the latest trends may change human behavior, human nature will remain; people will always be concerned about the meaning of life and death, limits of their freedom and alienation. In this way, existential philosophy in the theoretical platform to understand more fundamental behavior in tourism that is not volatile with respect to modern fashion and tendencies" (Kirillova 2019, p. 438). Kirillova (2019) also posits that it is important to conduct a comparative study to enable treatment of key existential issues across different demographic and socio-economic cohorts. Kirillova, Leho and Cai (2017) report that women and less education people are more likely to benefit from existential authenticity leading to a more optimal travel experience, as compared to men and higher educated groups.

The pandemic era is a unique time of de-globalization which has de-compressed or reversed time and space although innovative digital communications continues to interlink people and news between across the world. Nation states are focusing more inwardly as the global markets have not been able to dissolve the crisis triggered by the pandemic (Flew & Kirkwood 2020). International tourism was one of the most popular expressions of successful globalization spanning international boundaries and air spaces. However, distances between home and away have taken a reverse turn and continue to shrink to the point that people are looking inwardly and seeking proximate travel activities (Niewiadomski 2020). Niewiadomski says that "the world had to stop in order not to fall" is fully relevant to the tourism situation today" (2020, p. 634).

The congruency between one's everyday behavior and one's 'real' self forms the basis for evaluating the existential authenticity we seek in our lives (Rinder & Campbell 1952). The sustainable outcome of pursuing existentialist authenticity at heritage sites has received meager attention. Existentialist authenticity can become inauthentic if the 'truth of the moment' experience does not align with the moral image one showcases outwardly. The consequences of inauthenticity can include a sense of alienation (departure from one's intrinsic self), triggering a sense of purposelessness. Mkono writes that the pre-pandemic and the intra-pandemic times are "particularly antithetical to the retention of authenticity—with a large proportion of our existence … spent and shared in the digital world, where the boundaries between real and fake, personal and social, private and public, have become more blurry than ever. An eco-conscious tourist must deal with all of these pressures and realities" (2020, p. 3).

Truth of the moment experiences and immersions are using digital platforms (such as virtual reality). Social media and video conferencing platforms have emerged as key bonding tools as social distancing and virtual engagements in the safety of home continue to be an important part of the new norm. As an instance, Agostino, Arnaboldi and Lampis write: "museums unable to open their doors to a visiting public have had to take the only option of spreading culture and knowledge through online means. Lockdown has caused social media to take over from the museum's own websites and become the tool for spreading information, proposing live streaming, interviews and sharing artwork created through online means as well as setting quizzes and running treasure hunts. This change in time has paved the way for reflections on whether it will be possible to use our visiting time differently when we museums reopen" (2020, p. 362, 370).

To what extent these digital immersions (such as digital surrogates) can guide sustainable use of heritage resources, when people step out to recreate, while offering the much needed therapeutic benefits is a question that requires probing by tourism scholars. Moral selving can tone down quest for self-centered hedonic experiences and open the path for responsible existentialist immersions. Rising global consciousness for a sustainable planet is likely to strengthen a sense of moralness which, in turn, can then shape existential quest in a manner that the freedom pursued is not antithetical to the viability of visitation settings. Mkono (2020) writes about the inauthenticity dilemma in the context of ecotourism scenarios where tourists advocate themselves as environmentally accountable but fly to a pristine fragile area, intrude, and return. And ecotourism experiences have a strong heritage element in them. For instance, backpackers use homestays and immerse themselves in the culture of host communities. Aligned with an environmentally conscious tourist, a self- authentic or existentially authentic tourist claims to be genuine and seeks optimal state of exhilaration and oneness within a heritage setting or with a heritage object. Existentialist authenticity, in a way promotes, self-gratification at the cost of objective authenticity although one might argue that a self-authentic tourist in a heritage setting is likely to generate less negative impacts than tourists who are soaking in the heritage ambience of the setting instead of seeking their inner self. Morally driven existentialism or theoplacity can alter self-gratification behavior and re-configure moral consciousness in tourists.

Existentialist authenticity can be re-configured to prompt deeper inquiry into the ethical way of enjoying 'truth of the moment' experiences. Theories associated with flourishing and ethical consumption processes support the potential of authenticity to align with the sustainable transformation of one's optimized state of relaxation, one which is channeled by responsible behavior. In other words, ethical consumption can both guide and lay the foundation of the moral selving process, thereby mitigating the sense of inauthenticity. Some studies have reported a close synergy between slow heritage tourism (particularly through its unique subsets such as yoga tourism, volunteer tourism, spiritual tourism, or ecotourism) and authenticity. Slow heritage tourism can offer opportunities to enhance eudaimonic well-being. Shang, Qiao and Chen (2019) write that the people are revisiting the concept of time as distances continue to grow, both physically and psychologically. The pandemic era has realized dreams of diversion from fast-paced work and life and the new norm has slowed all movement stimulating slow living and self-reflection. In fact, patterns of demand for these can be evidenced in the new normal as slow tourism settings hold promise for the optimization of self authenticity and moral selving.

Certain kind of heritage places, cultural experiences, and indigenous programs can facilitate slow heritage tourism experiences (Everingham & Chassagne 2020). For instance, "slow cities support local small scale producers, craftsmen, farmers and family-run retailers, and aim to make their own town distinctive by highlighting its natural environment, traditional characteristics, uniqueness, and authenticity. Changing lifestyle to a slower state means embracing and accurately representing their true self. Thus, exploring the perception of authenticity in slow tourism will provide new insights into the phenomenon. In addition, there are also strong linkages with the slow tourism and place attachment" (Shang et al. 2019, p. 171). It can be argued that in slow travel, visitors seek more authentic experiences which a have a degree of moral consciousness of the negative impact subjected to a destination. In the new normal, attention is shifting towards the quest for engaging in time and space in a way that facilitates a sense of place, personal satisfaction, and well-being of the self and the visited community (Chhabra 2020).

An existential authenticity perspective can serve as a vantage point to meaningfully gather insights on slow tourism experience in heritage site encounters. Staging and unstaging of heritage by hosts are evolving processes. Very few studies have focused on the "existentialist side of other stakeholders such as local residents, and tourism providers such as travel agents, hotel housekeeper etc... although equal in humanness to tourists, these individuals may attend to their existential issues in unique ways" (Kirillova 2015, p. 430). A mutually beneficial slow tourism can enhance the self authenticity of both the guests and the hosts. As an example, in her slow tourism model, Chhabra offers a holistic route to scrutinize the factors that influence the behavior of slow spiritual tourists in a yoga retreat in a developing country. According to Little (2012), yoga is the core element of spiritual tourism because its key purpose is to harmonize the self, the world, and the visited people and their environment (Little 2012). The full transformative power of yoga tourism is a promising area of study in heritage tourism as it has strong indigenous underpinnings, either in the context of physical, social and/or psychological benefits for the self (Luskin 2004) and the host community. Smith and Szvia posit that, "yoga starts with the self but can lead to greater benefits for communities and society" (2017, p. 179) especially if a healthy body-mind systems path for visitors is designed by developing indigenous healing programs in therapeutic settings. The therapeutic value of indigenous culture in the context of existentialist authenticity, both for the guests and the hosts remains a sparse field of research.

In summary, spontaneous moments of existence and exhilaration occur, both, in staged or unstaged (objectively authentic) disoriented settings or in cognizance of one's domestic environment (Heidegger 1962). Self authentication at home or away from home can be groomed to diminish alienated feelings and harmoniously inculcate moral dispositions to transform and transcend the self in a holistic sense of being. Future research should scrutinize the eudaimonic healing power of moral existential authenticity for the self and the society. I close the chapter with an optimist note stressing on the tremendous and untapped welfare potential of existentialist and theoplacity authenticities and the self authentication encounters facilitated by them or vice versa, particularly to counter the challenges of the pandemic times. I call for formal efforts and innovative pathways to further dialectical introspection of these trajectories from health, economic and sustainability standpoints as the world searches for remedies and experiments with medical and non-medical therapeutic interventions to find a cure for covid-19. For a more nuanced appreciation of well-being and moral orientations of existential authenticity, it would be of practical as well as academic significance to study how self authentication and its moralizing and existentially authentic encounters with traditionally cultural, indigenous aspirations of wellness/immersive heritage programs offer eudaimonic and therapeutic benefits.

References

Ali-Knight, J. & Ensor, J. (2017). Salute to the sun: an exploration of UK Yoga tourist profiles. *Tourism Recreation Research, 42*, 484–497.

Bowers, H., & Cheer, J. M. (2017). Yoga tourism: commodification and western embracement of eastern spiritual practice. *Tourism Management Perspectives, 24*, 208–216.

Brown, D., & Leledaki, A. (2010). Eastern movement forms as body-self transforming cultural practices in the West: towards a sociological perspective. *Cultural Sociology, 4*(1), 123–154.

Cheer, J. (2020). Human flourishing, tourism transformation and COVDID-19: a conceptual touchstone. *Tourism Geography, 22*(3), 514–524.

Chhabra, D. (2010). Back to the past: generation Y's perceptions of authenticity. *Journal of Sustainable Tourism, 18*(6), 793–809.

Chhabra, D. (2020). A conceptual paradigm to determine behavior of slow spiritual tourists. *HTHIC* (Heritage, Tourism and Hospitality, International Conference). Published in the Preceedings, p. 115: Mendrisio (Ticino), Switzerland.

Coghlan, A. (2015). Tourism and health: using positive psychology principles to maximise participants' well-being outcomes–a design concept for charity challenge tourism. *Journal of Sustainable Tourism, 23*(3), 382–400.

Cohen, E. (1979). Phenomenology of tourism experience. *Sociology, 13*, 179–201.

Daigle, C. (2017). *Authenticity and distantiation from oneself: an ethico-political problem. Substance, 46*(1), 55–68.

Flew, T. & Kirkwood, K. (2020). The impact of COVID-19 on cultural tourism: art, culture and communication in four regional sites of Queensland, Australia. *Media International Australia*, 1329878X20952529.

Foucault, M. (1995). *Discipline and punishthe birth of the prison* (No. 365.9 F6).

Fu, X. (2019). Existential authenticity and destination loyalty: evidence from heritage tourists. *Journal of Destination Marketing & Management, 12*, 84–94.

Goffman, E. (2012). *Imagining Each Other: Blacks and Jews in Contemporary American Literature*. SUNY Press: University of New York.

Golomb, J. (1995). *In Search of Authenticity*, Routledge: London.

Gregorie, C. (2013, 16 December). *How Yoga became a $27 Billion Industry and Reinvented American Spirituality*. Huffington Post.

Heidegger, M. (1962). *Being and Time*. SCM Press: London.

Hudson, S., Thal, K., Cárdenas, D., & Meng, F. (2017). Wellness tourism: stress alleviation or indulging healthful habits? *International Journal of Culture, Tourism and Hospitality Research, 11*(1), 35–52.

Hopper, D., Costley, C. L., & Friend, L. A. (2015). Embodied self-authentication. *Australasian Marketing Journal (AMJ), 23*(4), 319–324.

Jin, L., Xiao, H. & Shen, H. (2020). Experiential authenticity in heritage museums. *Journal of Destination Marketing & Management, 18*, 100493.

Karn, S., Amarkantak, A. M., & Swain, S. K. (2017). Health consciousness through wellness tourism: a new dimension to new age travelers.' *African Journal of Hospitality, Tourism and Leisure*, *6*(3), p. 1–9.

Keyes, C. (2007). Promoting and protecting mental health as flourishing in life. A complementary strategy for improving national mental health. *American Psychologist*, *62*(2), 1112–1125.

Kirillova, K. (2019). Existentialism and tourism: new research avenues. *International Journal of Tourism Cities*, *5*(3), 429–442. https://doi.org/10.1108/IJTC-02-2019-0033.

Kirillova, K., Lehto, X. & Cai, L. (2017). Existential authenticity and anxiety as outcomes: the tourist in the experience economy. *International Journal of Tourism Research, 19*(1), 13–26.

Kolar, T. & Zabkar, V. (2010). A consumer-based model of authenticity: an oxymoron or the foundation of cultural heritage marketing? *Tourism Management*, *31*(5), 652–664.

Little, J. 2012. Transformational tourism, nature and well-being: New perspectives on fitness and the body. *Sociologia Ruralis, 52*, 257–271.

Lea, J. (2008). Retreating to Nature: Rethinking 'Therapeutic Landscapes.' *Area, 40*(1), p. 90–98.

Mannell, R. & Iso Ahola, S. (1987). Psychological nature of leisure and tourism experience. *Annals of Tourism Research, 14*(3), 314–331.

Mkono, M. (2020). Eco-hypocrisy and inauthenticity: criticisms and confessions of the eco-conscious tourist/traveller. *Annals of Tourism Research, 84*, 102967.

Niewiadomski, P. (2020). COVID-19: from temporary de-globalisation to a re-discovery of tourism?. *Tourism Geographies, 22*(3), 651–656.

Olsen, D. & Timothy, D. (2006) Tourism and religious journeys. In D. J. Timothy and D. H. Olsen (eds) *Tourism, Religion and Spiritual Journeys*, pp. 1–21. Routledge: London.

Park, E., Choi, B. K. & Lee, T. J. (2019). The role and dimensions of authenticity in heritage tourism. *Tourism Management, 74*, 99–109.

Patterson, I., D. Getz, & K. Gubb. 2016. The social world and event travel career of the serious yoga devotee. *Leisure Studies, 35*, 296–313

Pogge, T. W. (1999). Human flourishing and universal justice. *Social Responsibility and Policy, 16*(1), 333-361.

Pollock, A. (2019). Flourishing beyond sustainability the promise of regenerative tourism. Presentation to ETC Workshop in Krakow, February 6

Poulston, J. & Pernecky, T. 2017. Accommodating new age: understanding the needs of a growing segment. *Hospitality and Society, 7*, 245–262.

Rinder, I. & Campbell, D. (1952). Varieties of inauthenticity. *Phylon (1940–1956), 13*(4), 270–275.

Sartre, J. (1966). *Being and Nothingness*. Washington Square Press: New York, NY.

Shang, W., Qiao, G., & Chen, N. (2020). Tourist experience of slow tourism: from authenticity to place attachment–a mixed-method study based on the case of slow city in China. *Asia Pacific Journal of Tourism Research, 25*(2), 170–188.

Shehade, M., & Stylianou-Lambert, T. (2020). Revisiting authenticity in the age of the digital transformation of cultural tourism. In V. Katsoni and T. Spyriadis, (eds) *Cultural and Tourism Innovation in the Digital Era*, pp. 3–16. Springer: Cham.

Slade, M. (2010). Mental illness and wellbeing: the central importance of positive psychology and recovery approaches. *British Medical Council Health Services Research, 10*, 26–40.

Smith, M. K., & Diekmann, A. (2017). Tourism and well-being. *Annals of Tourism Research, 66*, 1–13.

Smith, M. & Sziva. I. (2017). Yoga, transformation, and tourism. In M. K. Smith and L. Puczko, (eds) *The Routledge Handbook of Health Tourism*, pp. 168–180. Routledge: New York, NY.

Stebbins, R. (1992). *Amateurs, Professionals and Serious Leisure*. McGill-Queen's University Press: Montreal.

Stebbins, R. (2001). Serious Leisure. *Society, 38*, 53–57.

Stepchenkova, S. & Belyaeva, V. (2020). The effect of authenticity orientation on existential authenticity and postvisitation intended behavior. *Journal of Travel Research*, 0047287519899989.

Tiberghien, G. (2019). Managing the planning and development of authentic eco-cultural tourism in Kazakhstan. *Tourism Planning & Development, 16*(5), 494–513.

van de Port, M., & Meyer, B. (2018). Introduction: Heritage dynamics politics of authentication, aesthetics of persuasion and the cultural production of the real. In *Sense and Essence. Heritage and the Cultural Production of the Real*, pp. 1–39. Berghahn.

Wang, N (1999). Rethinking authenticity in tourism experience. *Annals of Tourism Research*, *65*, 97–107.

Waterman, A. S. (1993). Two conceptions of happiness: contrasts of personal expressiveness (eudaimonia) and hedonic enjoyment. *Journal of personality and social psychology*, *64*(4), 678.

Yalom, I. (1980). *Existential Psychotherapy*. Basic Books: New York, NY.

Yu, J., Li, H., & Xiao, H. (2020). Are authentic tourists happier? Examining structural relationships amongst perceived cultural distance, existential authenticity, and well-being. *International Journal of Tourism Research*, *22*(1), 144–154.

Index